Tomorrow's Lawyers

Edited by
Philip A. Thomas

D1473850

Blackwell Publishers

Copyright © Basil Blackwell Ltd.

ISBN 0-631-18267-5

First published 1992

Published simultaneously as Vol. 19, No. 1
of Journal of Law and Society ISSN 0263-323X

Blackwell Publishers
108 Cowley Road, Oxford, OX4 1JF, UK.

3 Cambridge Center,
Cambridge, MA. 01242, USA.

British Library Cataloguing in Publication Data
Tomorrow's Lawyers. – (Journal of Law &
Society Series)
I. Thomas, Philip A.   II. Series 344.207

ISBN 0-631-18267-5

Library of Congress Cataloging in Publication Data applied for.

Printed on recycled paper

Typeset by Megaron, Cardiff, Wales.
Printed in Great Britain by Whitstable Litho, Kent.

11. 95

Contents

Thatcher's Will

PHILIP A. THOMAS*

The effects of the Thatcher decade have been profound. As pundits evaluate her legacy, a matter that looms large is the impact of Thatcherite changes on the social structure of the United Kingdom along with the effect on access to justice and the legal profession. In essence, the provision of legal services at the top end of the socio-economic scale changed and improved while the polar effects were equally dramatic in the failure to respond to growing need. This chapter, which examines the years between 1979 and 1990, offers an explanation of these polarized changes in terms of the tension between the ideology of the legal profession and the ideology of the enterprise culture.

THE SOCIAL LEGACY

Margaret Thatcher's policies made the rich much richer. It is estimated that the United Kingdom has over 20,000 sterling millionaires. The *Sunday Times* stated that the 200 richest people were collectively worth an estimated £38 billion. That is equivalent to 8 per cent of the country's gross domestic product.[1] More recent figures indicate that the top 25 per cent of individuals owned 71 per cent of the marketable wealth in 1976 which increased to 75 per cent in 1989.[2] Following the 1988 budget, Thatcher claimed that 'everyone in the nation has benefited from the increased prosperity – everyone'.[3] Despite the government's questionable and, indeed, questioned attempts to produce supporting figures,[4] recent evidence refutes this claim. Between 1979 and 1989 the poorest 20 per cent lost £160 a year in real disposable income, while the richest 20 per cent gained £7,986, or more than a third. The respective 'shares' of the poorest and the next poorest fifths of the population had declined by 1987 by between 10 and 20 per cent. At the same time the richest fifth experienced a gain of about 15 per cent. In the latter year their incomes 'swallowed' the incomes of the poorest two-fifths twice over.[5] Latest

* *Cardiff Law School, University of Wales, PO Box 427, Museum Avenue, Cardiff CF1 1XD, Wales*

This paper was prepared when I was a visiting professor at the Law Department, Polytechnic of Hong Kong in 1991. I thank Ruth Costigan and staff members there for their help and support. The paper was delivered at the Law School, University of Windsor, Ontario, Canada and an earlier version was published in the (1991) 10 *Windsor Yearbook: Access to Justice* 521.

information confirms this trend. The share of total income going to the richest fifth of households has grown since 1979 'at each stage of the tax benefit system'.[6]

In 1989 the former Social Services Secretary, John Moore, claimed that the 'nanny state created a sullen apathy of dependence'[7] and that Britain's economic success under Thatcher had put an end to absolute poverty. To reinforce this position, the word 'poverty' was dropped from government documents and replaced by 'low income'. Evidence shows this claim to be entirely misleading. Inequalities within the working population have spread to their widest point since records began in 1886. The proportion living in poverty, defined as 50 per cent of average income, doubled from five to ten million in the 1980s. In percentage terms, this means that in 1979 some 9 per cent of the population and 12 per cent of children were in the poverty trap. By 1987 the corresponding figures were 19 per cent and 26 per cent.[8] Children have borne the brunt of the rise in poverty with a quarter of all children being born into families living solely on social security.[9] Poverty increased faster in the United Kingdom between 1975 and 1985 than in any other European Community state.[10] Professor Townsend has concluded that 'the divergence of incomes (confirmed also in the trends in personal wealth) has been rapid during the last decade – and has contributed to forms of multiple deprivation which harmed many parts of national life'.[11]

ENTERPRISE CULTURE

Margaret Thatcher's keynote address to the Conservative Party conference in 1979 included this statement: 'If you ask whether the next Conservative government will cut controls and regulations and keep interference in people's lives to a minimum, my answer is 'Yes, that is exactly what we shall do'.'[12] In fact, that proved not to be the case. More choice by freeing up the market did not occur as state regulation was used to make an artificial space for the market to operate. The New Right thinkers believe that only through a strong state can there be a free economy. The period of the Thatcherite governments assumed the popular title of the 'enterprise culture' time. This redefinition of the relationship of the state and the economy aimed to produce a free market through the development of a strong state. Thus, welfarism, which involved central commitment of massive financial resources, was to be dramatically pruned and replaced by regulation and spending to ensure an infrastructure conducive to market expansion. Paradoxically, and in contrast to her conference statement in 1979, market freedom requires major legal regulation and, as a consequence, more regulatory lawyers. The replacement of political decision-makers by producers and consumers underpins planning and, in turn, provides the rationale for the introduction of the enterprise culture into the provision of legal services.[13] As a consequence of this economic rationale, private, fee-paying clients would be well served by those elements of the legal profession anxious to be part of and benefit from the enterprise culture.

2

Yet, to see the progress of the enterprise culture as a steady, uneventful programme is, according to Gamble, incorrect.[14] Perhaps the steadiest plank of this eclectic programme was the privatization policy originally suggested by Nicholas Ridley in 1978.[15] The movement of nationalized industries and public assets, such as steel, water, electricity, gas, telephones, and public housing, into private hands became a feature of the political programme. These transitions also prepared the ideological ground for similar discussions and action concerning the police, prisons, bail hostels, and prisoners' transport to courts.[16] Contracting out services provided within the state welfare system has become commonplace. Garbage collection within the local authority structure and cleaning functions within the national health services are but two examples. What is more problematic is contracting out the commitments of state security, public safety, and issues of access to justice. Yet these have occurred, as illustrated by certain security services at government buildings and Ministry of Defence establishments.[17] New procedures are being considered, introduced, and evaluated for the franchising of legal services to poor people.[18] Services may be contracted out to lay personnel with Citizens' Advice Bureaux being a likely provider of new services.[19] Lord Mackay, the Lord Chancellor, stated that 'It is an opportunity to produce new and imaginative ways of getting good quality advice from those best equiped to give it to those who need it.'[20] However, despite this statement, this is believed to be motivated not by the principle of deprofessionalization of dispute resolution but simply by the matter of economics. The Civil Justice Review's terms of reference included the need to 'reduce delay, cost and complexity'.[21] This financial concern was supported by Lord Mackay in a public lecture: 'Justice is priceless, but it must not be too pricey if it is to be accessible. To be accessible it must be affordable to the individual both as tax payer and litigant.'[22] For example, it is cheaper for the state to employ or allow the appearance of a lay adviser in court than to retain a solicitor through legal aid.[23] This economic fact has received statutory recognition through section 11 of the Courts and Legal Services Act 1990. As the state was purportedly rolled back, so the commitment to state supported professional legal services was diminished. In such a political climate there emerges a tension between the concept of justice and the demands of the market which look first at cost effectiveness. Demand-led provision for indigents, paid for out of public funds, had no place in the Thatcherite programme.

THE LEGAL PROFESSION

Professions were not comfortably placed within the ethos of the enterprise culture. The restrictive practices enjoyed by their members run contrary to the expectations of the market. As a consequence, under Thatcher, their privileges were scrutinized and their dominant positions challenged through dereg-ulation. For example, opticians have lost their exclusive right to prescribe

3

glasses, and other professional groups such as estate agents have been subjected to scrutiny and change.

Lawyers were not immune from review by the Treasury and the government appointed businessmen anxious to establish that the dominant principle of value for public money was being honoured.[24] In addition, there remained the paradox of the profession's exercise of independence whilst simultaneously enjoying substantial financial state support through legal aid. The profession survived the enquiry of the Royal Commission on Legal Services under Sir Henry Benson[25] and managed to convince the commission to frame its findings in the rhetoric of the profession's own ideology. Regulation was to be left to the profession, as the report stated: 'The profession should have a period of orderly development free, so far as possible, from external interventions'.[26]

The commission also accepted the definition of a profession as laid down by those sociologists offering a 'trait' model of professionalism. The classification of attributes associated with a professional body represent the common core of professional occupations. The work of A.R. Carr-Saunders and P. A. Wilson[27] was presented by the Law Society as the preferred model:

> The attitude of the professional man to his client . . . is one of pride in service given rather than of interest in opportunity for personal pride. The professional man who gave a lower standard of service in necessitous cases, where his remuneration was little or nothing, would be regarded as an unworthy colleague by his professional bretheren.[28]

Although agreement on these traits amongst sociologists of the professions is difficult to find, there are a number commonly accepted as essential. These are: skill based on theoretical knowledge; the provision of training and education; testing the competence of members; organization; adherence to a professional code of conduct; altruistic service.

This approach to understanding the legal profession ensured that, among other things, self-regulation would continue and that the 'altruistic' nature of the the lawyer/client relationship would preclude the introduction of the market. The client would continue to be grateful to the lawyer for a service based on trust, confidentiality, and independence rather than upon competition and economic choice. The term 'money' was not to be discussed with or by the client, as the crucial terms were 'service' and 'justice' – and on justice no price can be placed. The individualistic nature of the service, usually arrived at through personal and discreet recommendation, contrasted sharply with the growing importance of the image maker and the corporate advertiser. Keeping the lawyer/client relationship out of the market helped maintain the special privileges enjoyed by these professionals. The exclusive right to convey interests in real property for a fee, conveyancing, represented a significant element of their work,[29] and, whilst the fixed scale was dropped and the Administration of Justice Act 1985 permitted licensed conveyancers to compete with solicitors, there was no serious threat to the continuation of this lucrative work. A later enquiry, the Marre Committee,[30] followed a similar path and again concluded that legal services were safe in the hands of the profession. Consequently, any change that was necessary should occur through and with the support of the professional bodies. 'Any changes which weaken the ability of the Law Society and the General Council of the Bar to regulate the conduct and competence of their members are unlikely to be in the public interest.'[31] The ideology of legal professionalism, articulated through the trait theory, was embedded in both the profession and also in the recommendations and legacy of the Benson and Marre Reports. But under Thatcherism this was to change.

THE GREEN PAPERS

Three Green Papers, government discussion documents on the legal profession and legal services, were published on 25 January 1989.[32] In the stark reality of the wording of their proposals, they appeared to represent a major challenge to the legal profession.

The documents were worded in the language of the market. Consumerism, choice, and value for money replaced the notions of altruism and self-regulation which for so long had justified the protected status of the legal profession. The ideas are believed to have emerged from a committee in the Lord Chancellor's Department in which officials from the Treasury and the Department of Trade and Industry played a particularly significant role.[33]

Lord Mackay laid out the government's stall in simple market terms in the Green Paper on the legal profession when he wrote:

> The government believes that free competition between the providers of legal services will, through the discipline of the market, ensure that the public is provided with the most effective network of legal services at the most economic price.[34]

The reaction of the profession and its allies was both immediate and hostile. Evaluating professional activities by consumerist principles failed to recognise the inappropriate nature of such a test. The Bar stated: 'We preface our comments on advocacy by noting that in this field great care must be exercised in the application of simple principles of competition.'[35] The Bar took the extra precaution of raising a fighting fund of one million pounds and retaining the services of Saatchi and Saatchi, the corporate image makers. The chairman of the Bar Council further argued that 'justice cannot be measured in terms of competition and consumerism; justice is not a consumer durable; it is the hallmark of a civilised and democratic society.'[36]

It was the judiciary that created perhaps the greatest furore in responding to these proposals. For example, Lord Hailsham, a former conservative Lord Chancellor, stated that the papers 'are not particularly well timed, not particularly well thought out, and some aspects, particularly the suggested compromise with contingency fees, are definitely sinister.'[37] Later he went on to say, in his inimitable style:

> The one thing that has worried me about the whole exercise is that one does not know whether the government is sitting on its head or its bottom. Its trouble is, it is thinking with its bottom and sitting on its head.[38]

The sitting judges were equally uncompromising in their criticism of change motivated by market forces. 'We preface our comments on advocacy by noting that in this field great care must be exercised in the application of simple principles of competition.'[39] They even discussed effecting a one-day strike as a sign of their opposition. The Lord Chief Justice described the Paper as 'one of the most sinister documents ever to emanate from Government'[40] while Lord Ackner declared that 'threatening and deeply depressing stormclouds are hanging over the entire legal profession and the judiciary.'[41] Lord Hailsham, in the debate in the House of Lords, in an indirect reference to Margaret Thatcher's family background, stated that the legal profession could not be regulated like a grocer's shop in Grantham.

Whilst these concerns were real, what underpinned them was the changed ideology which created the new and radical suggestions found in the Green Papers. Markets and consumers are terms alien to the functional sociologists of the professions and, more importantly, were also alien to the profession itself. Mere tinkering with the profession was not the suggestion. Instead there was to be the removal of ancient privileges which supported lucrative restricted practices. There was to be the deconstruction of working relationships between the two branches of the profession which threatened the viability of the common-law barrister through enhanced rights of audience for solicitors. Clearly, the efforts of the legal profession during the decade of the 80s to put their house in order had been deemed insufficient. Now, it was feared, the government threatened to pull it down and build a new one, designed by architects of the New Right.

COURTS AND LEGAL SERVICES ACT: ACCESS TO JUSTICE

The strident tone of the Green Papers was muted when the government's White Paper was published. The potential damage that could be inflicted by traditional conservative supporters, the judges and legal practitioners, was enough to alert even the toughest ideologues in the Conservative party. The references were now to 'access to justice' and 'legal services to meet clients' needs'.[42]

In November 1990, the Courts and Legal Services Act was passed. What does it mean in terms of access to justice? Have the statements about market forces and consumer rights produced legislation committed to a radically revised legal-services programme? Changes have occurred and frameworks established which promise further change. The Act put in place an advisory committee of judges concerning rights of audience. Solicitors may apply for extended rights of audience into courts which were formerly the exclusive preserve of barristers. How generous these judges, themselves former barristers, will be in extending rights of audience is a moot point. Whilst the right to convey property has been opened up, the Law Society has been able to restrict financial institutions, in particular building societies and banks, from swamping the private solicitors. No cross-subsidies are allowed which would make one-stop house buying/selling through these financial institutions attractive. In addition, conveyancers may not provide services for both parties of a transaction, nor to a buyer where the instition is providing estate agency services for the seller. It is possible that the conveyancing work will be contracted out to private practitioners or in-house solicitors will be employed.

Paradoxically, the Courts and Legal Services Act, to a large extent, merely endorses changes within the practice of law which have taken place during the past decade. For example, there has been a major restructuring of solicitors' practices. Dramatic mergers of solicitors' practices have occurred throughout England and Wales to the point that the sole practitioner is an increasing rarity. The Law Society has established that 62 per cent of solicitors work in firms of five partners or more and 22 per cent of the 978 solicitors who were interviewed stated they were actively considering mergers with other firms.[43] Within the City of London, the growth rate has been dramatic. The largest firm has doubled the number of its partners to over 150 in under ten years. More generally, the number of lawyers in the fifteen largest firms was virtually the same in 1960 as it had been twenty years earlier (195); but it increased 50 per cent by 1970 to 313 people, then more than doubled by 1983 to 667, and nearly doubled again five years later to 1,102. The number of assistant solicitors in the twenty largest firms more than doubled in the three years 1985–88, from 1,229 to 2,581. In 1988, the twenty largest firms contained at least one out of every nine private practitioner in England and Wales.[44] The demand by City firms for clerks was so rapacious that they were capable of offering articles to every student from university law schools in England and Wales who graduated with a 'good honours degree'.[45] When articled clerks, aged 22, could start in the City at a salary of £16,000, as compared with non-City salaries of less than half, it is scarcely surprising that the bright lights of London proved so attractive to under-graduates.[46]

However, the change was not simply quantitative. The qualitative change was equally dramatic and showed obvious signs of market influence. The internationalization of these large firms with branch offices throughout the world, coupled with a clear commitment to the European Community, meant that the client-driven practice was developed even further to ensure that a total service was provided. Increased specialization within the practice, which offered service packages to clients at times convenient to the client, bore the hallmarks of market forces rather than the ideology of altruism which for so long had underpinned lawyer/client relationships. 'Billable hours' replaced 'friendly chats', and accountants, computer consultants, and time-and-motion experts were found analysing City practices. Image making and promotion of the firm demanded large budgets, as firms competed with each other in terms which bear a striking similarity to those found in the market.

7

Firms increasingly identified themselves as 'collective entrepreneurs' in the business of making money by providing a service. What changed is that both the private and public image of lawyers became 'modern', which meant market-driven. The commercial reality of large firms was that they increasingly saw and promoted themselves as competitive, efficient, business enterprises geared to providing a service for the client. Consumerism, for those who could afford to pay the bill privately, was already entrenched. At the level of the City and metropolitan commercial firms, the transition from the old to new ideology had already taken place. In this sense, the Courts and Legal Services Act merely acknowledged an accomplished fact at a certain practice level rather than radically restructured legal services.

At the other end of the social spectrum, consumerism was far less successful. It has been subjected to a shift from demand- to supply-led economics of legal aid. The presentation of welfare support as that associated with 'state scroungers' has done nothing to lift the professional standing of those lawyers who operate in this area.[47]

The initial response of the chair of the Bar Council, Desmond Fennell QC, was that 'the key to increased access is to halt the decline in the availability of legal aid. Nothing in the proposals will assist those who need advice or representation before courts or tribunals.'[48] John Aucott, chair of the remuneration and practice development committee at the Law Society, viewed the future of legal aid with gloom:

> I can only think that the government's intention is deliberately to allow the service to decline. In the context of legal aid, the Lord Chancellor sees himself as a purchaser of legal services . . . We are selling ourselves short, selling our professionalism. The government is not in the business of looking for the best quote. It looks for the cheapest.[49]

Whilst the Lord Chancellor is being accused of commercialism, the echoes of the old ideology continue to be voiced by practitioners:

> The image of the solicitor as businessman, the member of the board, maker of decisions for the client, is alien to the legal aid practitioner . . . . I therefore conclude, gloomily, that the next four to five years will see a serious thinning in the ranks of young solicitors doing legal aid work.[50]

This could well be true, for the work, income, and status of the legal aid practitioner does not match that of the City commercial practitioner. The enterprise culture, as it penentrates the culture and ideology of practitioners, encourages this thinking and promotes an expectational drive that will produce the very effect that the legal aid practitioner seeks to avoid. A visible wedge between the corporate and general practitioners becomes apparent. This was summed up by the president of the Plymouth Law Society who stated:

> The law is no longer a profession but has become almost a retail trade. That feeling makes for a distance between solicitors because we feel we must constantly be competing with each other. The politics of the last decade have destroyed the comradeship which used to exist in practising law.[51]

Whilst the Courts and Legal Services Act is repeatedly singled out by presidents of local law societies as representing the depths of the decline into the rough and tumble world of grafting competition, they fail to recognize that the legislation is essentially of an enabling rather than an engineering character. It reflects and endorses the operational commercial practice rather than sets out to restructure legal services and the legal profession.

Inflation and overheads grew faster than legal fees increased.[52] Lawyers are already voting with their feet when it comes to offering a legal aid service. For example, Roberta Trish, former chair of the Legal Aid Practitioners' Group, stopped legal aid work in 1989 but two years later was still owed some £30,000 by the Lord Chancellor's Department for work completed.[53] A Law Society survey showed that 40 per cent of legal aid solicitors had given up offering criminal legal aid and 27 per cent said the same thing about matrimonial legal aid.[54] Only 9 per cent of solicitors' firms now handle any legal aid work and in some rural areas there is no legal practitioner willing to undertake this work.[55] Touche Ross, independent management consultants, were commissioned jointly by the Law Society and the Lord Chancellor's department to survey the overheads of firms undertaking criminal work. The results show that, on average, solicitors in London make a 40 per cent loss on criminal legal aid work and those outside make a loss of 33 per cent. Only firms with a high volume of work can do the work profitably.[56] Solicitors felt obliged to threaten a strike in order to obtain a 6 per cent increase in legal aid payments.[57] Allen Knight, president of the Corwall Law Society, made the argument in the very same terms as those used by the government:

> If the only argument that the Lord Chancellor's Department understands is 'market forces', it is time that we as a profession show some muscle and threaten to withdraw from the market.[58]

Civil legal aid has fared badly. In the decade since 1979, eligibility almost halved, falling to include only about 40 per cent of the population and taking more than fourteen million out of eligibility. Between 1987 and 1989, two million people fell through the legal aid net. The result was that access to justice, even second class justice, has been denied to an extra five and a half million households since 1979.[59] The divisive two-nation strategy for which Margaret Thatcher[60] is responsible is well illustrated by the growing inability of the socially deprived to gain access to justice.

CONCLUSION

The decade of Thatcherism leaves a tangible legacy in the United Kingdom.[61] As the rich became richer and the poor were sidelined by the state, so the legal profession moved to accommodate these new interests. The result was major demographic shifts, restructuring and amalgamations of firms, as well as reordering of work patterns. These changes were not simply structural. They were also ideological. We have experienced the removal of the old and the introduction of new ideologies. 'Justice' has been replaced by 'market' and the practices and expectations of many practitioners formally and publicly reflect the new ways.

9

The enterprise culture, which underpins the Conservative government's plans and actions for legal services, has impacted upon the professional body; its members who operate different and 'packaged' services; law students who clamour for the bright lights of City firms and for training and educational courses attractive to these firms; the large firms that invested heavily in law schools by offering cash inducements,[62] and last, and sometimes least, the consumer. For the consumer, particularly commercial clients, with private financial resources, the Thatcher decade produced an uplift in legal services but for the remainder, it proved to be a bleak period. Her legacy for the profession is that of turmoil, change, uncertainty, and opportunity. Practitioners and academics in the 1990s are faced with dramatic challenges which, in turn, are addressed by my co-authors in the following pages.

NOTES AND REFERENCES

1 *Sunday Times*, 2 April 1989.
2 *Economic Trends, No. 457* (1992).
3 *Labour Research*, May 1989, 8.
4 Widespread public concern about the government's willingness to 'manipulate' official statistics resulted in the Royal Statistical Society setting up a working party on 'Official Statistics in the UK'. Its recommendations, as yet ignored, included, among other things, the establishment of an advisory National Statistical Commission and an Official Statistics Act to safeguard the autonomy of the service. Royal Statistical Society, *Official Statistics: Counting with Confidence* (1991). See, also, M. Phillips, 'Private Lies and Public Servants' *Guardian*, 9 January 1991.
5 P. Townsend, *The Poor are Poorer: A Statistical Report on Changes in the Living Standards of Rich and Poor in the United Kingdom* (1991) 47.
6 *Social Trends 22* (1992).
7 *Guardian*, 14 November 1990, 21.
8 C. Oppenheim, *Poverty: The Facts* (1990).
9 *Guardian*, 24 December 1991.
10 See, also, A. Walker and C. Walker, *The Growing Divide: A Social Audit, 1979–87* (1987).
11 Townsend, op. cit., n. 5, p. 48.
12 Reported in F. O'Gorman, *British Conservatism* (1989) at 221.
13 D.C. Mueller, *Public Choice* (1979). See, also, the interesting article by C. Stanley, 'Enterprising Lawyers: Changes in the Market for Legal Services' (1991) 25 *Law Teacher* 44.
14 A.Gamble and C.Wells, *Thatcher's Law* (1989) introduction.
15 *Economist*, 27 May 1978.
16 Cost-effectiveness is now a term widely used is assessing court efficiency. There is at least one court which is self-financing. The Court of Protection is financed by those who use it. In 1990–91 it generated a fee income of £7,750,423. In April 1991 the total number of patients whose affairs were administered by the court was 30,842. The Adam Smith Institute has suggested that Chief Constables should have the power to hire private security on contract to support their officers working in inner city areas and high-crime estates. In addition, other services including police driving training, registration of aliens, surveillance of motorway traffic should be contracted out. (T. Evans, *An Arresting Idea* (1991).) Wolds prison, Humberside, was contracted out to Group 4 in June 1991 and private bids for the management of Blakenhurst Hereford, and Worcester prisons were requested by the Home Office in December 1991. The Port of London police is being privatized as part of the port authority's scheme for the docks sale. A High Court application by the Port of London Police

Federation for judicial review of the government's decision was refused (*Financial Times*, 18 January 1992).

17 There was serious criticism of the 'contracted out' perimeter security services at the Marine Barracks at Deal, Kent, when it was bombed by the IRA in September 1989.

18 In some cases legal services are being withdrawn as illustrated by the Home Secretary's decision, announced on 2 July 1991, to withdraw civil legal aid from immigrants.

19 See the Legal Aid Act 1988 which established the Legal Aid Board.

20 Lord Mackay L.C., 491 *H.L. Debs*. col. 613 (15 December 1987).

21 (1988; Cm. 394) para. 1.

22 'Litigation in the 1990s' (1991) 54 *Modern Law Rev*. 176.

23 See P.A. Thomas, 'The Case of the Poll Tax: *R*. v. *Leicester City Justices Ex parte M. and C. Barrow*' (forthcoming 1992).

24 For example, the chair of the Legal Aid Board is John Pitts. He is a former chair and chief executive of Dioxide Group plc, and prior to that was a divisional director of ICI plc.

25 P.A. Thomas, 'Royal Commission on Legal Services In England and Wales' (1981) 1 *Windsor Yearbook: Access to Justice* 179. See, also, P.A. Thomas (ed), *Law in the Balance: Legal Services in the Eighties* (1982).

26 *Report of the Royal Commission on Legal Services in England and Wales* (1979; Cmnd. 7648; chair, Sir Henry Benson) recommendation 3.2.

27 A.R. Carr-Saunders and P.A. Wilson, *The Professions* (1933).

28 id., p. 471.

29 Conveyancing income was just under 30 per cent of solicitors' gross income in 1984–85.

30 General Council of the Bar/Council of the Law Society, *A Time for Change: Report of the Committee on the Future of the Legal Profession* (1988).

31 id., para. 4.23.

32 *The Work and Organisation of the Legal Profession* (1989; Cm. 570); *Conveyancing by Authorised Practitioners* (1989; Cm. 572); and *Contingency Fees* (1989; Cm. 571). A good summary of the background, on which I have drawn, is found in F. Cownie, 'The Reform of the Legal Profession' in *The Changing Law*, eds. F. Patfield and R. White (1990).

33 M. Zander, 'The Notorious Green Papers' in *The Future of Legal Education and the Legal Profession in Hong Kong*, ed. R. Wacks (1990) 118.

34 op. cit., n. 32 (Cm. 570), para. 1.2.

35 General Council of the Bar, *Quality of Justice – The Bar's Response* (1989) para. 4.4.

36 *Times*, 3 July 1989.

37 *Times*, 26 January 1989.

38 *Times*, 15 April 1989.

39 *Judges' Response* (1989) para. 31.

40 *Guardian*, 17 February 1989.

41 *Guardian*, 2 February 1989.

42 *Legal Services: A Framework for the Future* (1989; Cm. 740) paras. 2.3 and 2.4.

43 The Law Society, *Solicitors in England and Wales: the private practice firm* (1991).

44 R. Abel, 'The Legal Profession in Turmoil' (1989) 52 *Modern Law Rev*. 294.

45 For detailed and compelling evidence of this statement the statistical work of R. Abel must be consulted. His most recent published data is found in op. cit., n. 43, p. 285. See, also, R. Abel, *The Legal Profession* (1988).

46 A newly qualified solicitor in London can expect a start salary equivalent to that of a full law professor at a British university. At this point the reader should be reminded that this paper is time-banded and ends in 1990. The economic recession badly affected recruitment by City firms. In 1991 a survey in the *Lawyer* showed that of the top 100 firms, just thirty-eight expected to have vacancies in 1991 for newly qualified solicitors (*Independent on Sunday*, 10 February 1991). The Young Solicitors Group stated that around 40 per cent of solicitors who had been made redundant in November 1990 had not found new employment in June 1991. A help line had been established (*Guardian*, 8 June 1991). Undergraduates are currently finding it exceedingly difficult to obtain places as trainee solicitors and, indeed, assured places are being cancelled by firms.

47 S.A. Scheingold, 'Radical Lawyers and Socialist Ideals' (1988) 15 *J. of Law and Society* 122.

48 *Law Society Gazette*, 1 March 1989, 40.

49 *Law Society Gazette*, 9 May 1990, 15.

50 *Law Society Gazette*, 23 November 1988, 29

51 *Law Society Gazette*, 30 January 1991, 11.

52 The Lord Chancellor has indicated that he will raise legal aid fees by no more than 1 per cent in April 1991. The Law Society has lodged a claim for 10.7 per cent. This represents an estimate that solicitors' overheads will rise this year by 8.7 per cent (*Law Society Gazette*, 8 January 1992). In Devon discontent reached such a level that in November 1991 participating members voted to withdraw from the statutory duty solicitor scheme.

53 *Guardian* 1 February 1991. 'In our experience, we found that civil legal aid was very difficult in the sense that we had to fund it as we went along and it took a long time to get the money after taxation.' John Cornillie, of Cornillie and Co., London, who took his firm out of legal aid, in *New Law J.*, 22 February 1991. 'We seriously believe that the profession will not be able to subsidise this type of work any longer.' Loraine Morgan, Southampton Criminal Courts Solicitors Association, in *Solicitors Journal*, 13 December 1991. See, 'Profit Margins Fell Last Year' *Law Society Gazette*, 13 March 1991; P. Thompson, 'Farewell Legal Aid' *Law Society Gazette*, 24 July 1991.

54 *Law Society Gazette*, 6 July 1988, 21.

55 *Labour Research*, August 1988, 16.

56 *The Lawyer*, 21 March 1989, 7.

57 *Law Society Gazette*, 28 March 1990, 12.

58 *Law Society Gazette*, 4 December 1991.

59 See C. Glasser, *Law Society Gazette* 9 March 1988; 5 and 20 April 1989; and M. Murphy, *Legal Action Group*, October 1989, 7.

60 Above, see section entitled 'The Social Legacy'.

61 Although this paper considers events between 1979 and 1990 it is clear that the early 1990s offer a different scenario for the profession. The deepening recession is affecting the City law firms. Assistant solicitors are being laid off; the articled clerk list is in 'its worst state ever' according to the Law Society's manager of recruitment (*Law Society Gazette*, 13 February 1991, 6); students who thought they had articling positions are receiving pay-off cheques from law firms along with a cancellation notice of articles; only two of the top fifteen law firms are recruiting (*Independent on Sunday*, 10 February 1991). In eighteen months, the profession has gone from boom to slump. The restructuring of the profession and legal services has provided no immunity from economic hardship arising out of recession.

62 In particular, note the type of positions that are sponsored and the absence of support for welfare law, civil liberties, jurisprudence, landlord and tenant, sociology of law, and so on. S. Bright and M. Sunkin, 'What Price Sponsorship?' (1991) 18 *J. of Law and Society* 475.

Information Technology in Legal Services

ANDREW CLARK*

INTRODUCTION

Developments in information technology provide a reference point for debates about the nature of contemporary social change.[1] For some observers, information technology is altering the fabric of modern society.[2] In particular, it underpins a set of structural transformations which mark a radical break with earlier forms of society and result in new opportunities for economic growth and social progress. In the emerging 'information society', knowledge and information are treated as the core economic variables and the dominant social actors are seen as those who process information in accordance with codified bodies of knowledge. Other commentators have rejected this notion of the 'information society', pointing instead to the continuities between past and present forms of society. While acknowledging the importance of technological change, these commentators have highlighted the role of information technology in preserving the established interests of corporate capital and the state.[3] In this context, the changing patterns of accumulation and control associated with the introduction and use of information technology are analysed within the framework of capitalist development. Thus, under 'information capitalism', accumulation proceeds through the private appropriation of social knowledge, and control over information adds a new dimension to existing forms of conflict.

More recent studies have focused on what Feenberg describes as the 'ambivalent potentialities' of information technology.[4] In this context, attention has centred on the ways in which new technical media influence the construction and control of knowledge and the configuration of communication in contemporary society.[5] Thus, Lyotard argues that 'along with the hegemony of computers comes a certain logic, and therefore a certain set of prescriptions determining which statements are accepted as 'knowledge' statements'.[6] As knowledge is defined increasingly in terms of its computability, it ceases to be legitimated by reference to principles of truth or justice. Instead, it is subjected to the requirement of 'performativity' which measures the value of knowledge in terms of its marketability or efficiency. Despite this rationalizing tendency, information technology also has a

* School of Law, University of Warwick, Coventry CV4 7AL, England

communicative dimension which opens up possibilities for new forms of social interaction and organization. Thus, in her historical study of telephone communication, Marvin interprets the introduction of new technical media in terms of the restructuring of 'arenas for negotiating issues crucial to the conduct of social life; among them, who is inside and outside, who may speak, who may not, and who has authority and may be believed'.[7]

This paper draws on these theoretical perspectives in analysing the development of information technology in legal services. As a symbolic domain, law is structured around specific forms of knowledge, flows of information, and networks of communication. Thus, Galanter has argued that law 'usually works not by exercise of force but by information transfer, by communication of what's expected, what forbidden, what allowable, what are the consequences of acting in certain ways'.[8] Teubner has ventured further to suggest that 'law is communication and nothing but communication'.[9] In this context, it is worth asking how the development and deployment of information technology in legal settings influences the organization of legal services and the activities of lawyers and legal advice workers. What are the implications of information technology for the contemporary restructuring of the field of legal services? How does the use of information technology affect the control of legal information and the construction of legal knowledge? What are the ramifications for the legal profession and what are the possibilities for progressive forms of legal practice?

In focusing on the use of information technology in legal services there is a risk of overstating its 'impact'. Recent studies in the sociology of technology have emphasized the extent to which the form and content of technology are shaped by a range of social, economic, and political influences.[10] In contrast to traditional conceptions of technology as the neutral application of scientific progress, technology is seen as the product of intentional processes of design, development and diffusion. New technologies are articulated and specified in relation to particular purposes and as they are implemented they become woven into broader patterns of social and economic activity. However, adopting a purposive construction of technology does not mean that it is possible to 'read off' how specific technologies will be taken up and used in practice or what consequences will flow from their use. In particular, the 'impact' of technology is always mediated by the social and institutional contexts in which it is implemented.

INFORMATION TECHNOLOGY AS ORGANIZATIONAL INFRASTRUCTURE

When it reported in 1979, the Royal Commission on Legal Services gave relatively little attention to the use of information technology in legal settings. However, the Commission did note the instrumental value of computerization in relation to the administration of law firms. In particular, it recommended that 'all solicitors should review their practices and office procedures to ensure

14

that they take full advantage of the efficiency and economy that can be obtained with the assistance of modern technology'.[11] During the intervening decade not only law firms,[12] but also law centres and legal advice agencies,[13] courts,[14] and government departments involved in processing legal information,[15] have taken advantage of the rapid decline in the relative cost of computing power. Much of the resulting investment in information technology has been directed towards the automation of routine clerical tasks. Typical examples would include the introduction of general purpose wordprocessing and accounting systems and the implementation of more specialized data processing systems, such as the 'automated summons production' system in the county court.[16] As Leith points out, these applications of information technology differ little in technical terms from those found in many non-legal settings.[17]

In most cases, the primary purpose of this type of technological development has been to increase the efficiency of legal offices and the productivity of clerical workers. However, office automation has also played an important part in enhancing the internal surveillance capacities of the organizations concerned.[18] In particular, administrative and accounting systems increasingly form part of sophisticated information systems designed to enable management to compare the performance of different departments and cost centres within an organization. Data derived from these systems is used to monitor the profitability or cost-effectiveness of different types of activity and to plan future organizational strategies. In this context, the introduction and use of information technology has significant implications for the organizational forms through which legal services and legal decision-making are mediated.

Although applications of information technology can be found in a wide variety of legal settings, there are significant disparities in the distribution of information and communication resources between different sectors of the market for legal services. As the élite law firms have grown in size, spread their activities across multiple sites and expanded the geographical scope of their services, computer-based systems have provided the mechanisms for co-ordinating and controlling their operations. These firms have invested heavily in the development of their information and communication infrastructures and have adopted styles of practice which depend on the use of new technology.[19] In particular, efficient information and communication systems compress the effects of space and time, linking lawyers to the global electronic networks of legal and commercial information which enable them to deliver fast and flexible services to their corporate and institutional clients.[20] Thus, information technology underpins the globalization of corporate legal practice and plays a strategic role for firms seeking to position themselves in increasingly competitive national and international markets for legal services.

The deployment of information and communication systems has also influenced the development of organizational infrastructures and modes of service delivery in other sectors of the market for legal services. Firms have merged or entered into resource-sharing arrangements with other firms to take

15

advantage of economies of scale, including those which relate to information technology. Other firms have adopted styles of practice pioneered by 'legal clinics' in the United States of America. These firms depend heavily on the use of technology to implement routine case-handling procedures and manage a high turnover of cases.[21] While part of the impetus for computerization has come from competition between firms striving to rationalize their operations in an effort to maintain or extend their market share, pressure has also been brought to bear from other sources. In relation to conveyancing services, firms risk losing business unless they comply with the standard operating requirements of financial institutions, including the use of information technology. The computerization of the Land Register and local authority land charges registers provides a further stimulus to the development of information and communication systems in this sector of the market for legal services.[22]

However, the disparities in the distribution of information and communication resources reflect and reinforce other tendencies towards polarization in the field of legal services. In particular, the financial constraints imposed on legal aid firms, law centres, and legal advice agencies over the last decade have restricted their ability to take full advantage of developments in technology. Even so, lawyers and legal advice workers involved in the practice of public interest law were among the first to make innovative use of computer technology in legal practice and have shown strong interest in the development of their information systems.[23] While individual agencies and groups have made extensive use of their limited technological resources, the development of information and communication networks spanning the field of public interest law could deliver benefits on a much larger scale. In this context, networking could serve as a means for legal aid firms, law centres, legal advice agencies, and social action groups to join in co-operative ventures, maintain strategic alliances, share information, and mobilize scarce resources.[24] The decentralizing potential of information technology would allow these organizations to develop new forms of practice and participate in collective activities without abandoning their existing commitments to autonomy and local accountability. Indeed, as Castells has argued, at a time when the 'space of places' is giving way to the 'space of flows', community-based organizations need to extend their horizons and establish their own networks of information and decision-making in order to counteract the increasingly fluid forms of capital and state power.[25]

LEGAL PROFESSIONALISM AND THE FLOW OF INFORMATION

If information technology has the capacity to influence the organizational structures of legal work, it also has implications for the construction of legal knowledge and the professional identity of legal practitioners. Apart from the practical significance of legal knowledge and information, the mysteries of the law library serve as a potent symbol of legal professional expertise. Therefore,

16

any changes in the methods used to organize, store and retrieve legal information are likely to have both instrumental and ideological consequences for the profession. More specifically, if the professional power of lawyers hinges on the capacity to control the construction of specialized legal knowledge, then the application of information technology may serve to weaken this control. In this context, several commentators have suggested that developments in legal databases and computer-assisted research techniques are likely to contribute to the 'de-professionalization' of law. For example, Rothman has argued that these developments 'reduce significantly the resources required for legal research' and 'open the previously esoteric and complicated area of legal research to anyone with access to the computer terminal'.[26]

In a recent attempt to elaborate this thesis, Katsh has highlighted the historical connection between the development of print media and the rise of legal professionalism.[27] The transition from manuscript to printed text was accompanied by the development of publishing as a distinct form of economic activity. Lawyers, with their existing culture of practical literacy, constituted a ready market for the emerging publishing industry of the fifteenth and sixteenth centuries.[28] However, the growth of legal publishing also encouraged the development of organized law libraries to serve as repositories for the expanding stocks of case reports and other legal material. As law libraries expanded in size, the capacity to locate relevant information came increasingly to depend on the methods used to categorize and index their contents. The techniques used to organize legal information also influenced the construction and transmission of legal knowledge. Therefore, although the printed text facilitated the spatial diffusion of legal information, it also became a focal point for the intellectual and social cohesion of the legal profession.

Although Katsh rejects the idea that knowledge itself constitutes a system of domination, he argues that 'the form in which knowledge appears can influence how it is organised, who has access to it, and how the profession that depends on it is perceived'.[29] Extrapolating from this argument, he maintains that the contemporary transition from print to electronic media has significant implications for the legal profession. In particular, he argues that it poses a threat to lawyers because 'what is considered "legal" and within the exclusive domain of the profession is shifting as a result of diminished control over a body of knowledge'.[30] By disrupting traditional methods of organizing and accessing legal information, electronic media serve to deconstruct the carefully erected barriers between legal and other forms of knowledge.

Katsh bases his argument on the development and use of 'on-line' legal database services, such as Lexis and Westlaw. These services provide users with access to the full text of a wide range of legal source material – case reports, statutes, delegated legislation, and so on – covering a number of different jurisdictions. The material is stored in remote computer databases, accessed via telecommunications links and retrieved by means of a variety of computerized search techniques. However, the use of these services differs

17

from the use of traditional law libraries in that it does not depend directly on knowledge of either the physical arrangement or the conceptual organization of the legal material contained in the database. Thus, users of legal database services are able to pursue creative research strategies free from the constraints imposed by conventional methods of ordering legal material.[31] In this context, the introduction of computerized legal research techniques has the potential to influence the reconstruction of legal categories and the reproduction of law itself. However, Katsh goes further in arguing that the removal of the constraints imposed by print contributes to the breakdown of the internal structures of legal thought and results in the emergence of 'disorganized law'. At the same time, he sees the development of electronic media as enhancing the accessibility of legal information to those outside the confines of the legal profession.

These further arguments misrecognize the significance of computer-assisted legal research. In particular, they fail to account for one of the central paradoxes of the 'information age', encapsulated in Baudrillard's observation that 'we are in a universe where there is more and more information, and less and less meaning'.[32] This paradox stems from the problematic character of information. The mathematical or cybernetic theory of information defines information in relation to selection among alternatives. It is that which destroys uncertainty or, in Bateson's formula, 'a difference which makes a difference'.[33] According to this approach, information is an intensional concept in that the status of any particular message as information depends on the knowledge and purposes of the receiver and the context in which it is received. However, information is commonly used in a much broader sense to refer to any data that have been organized and communicated. In this context, messages stand as information irrespective of the circumstances in which they are received. Hence, Jameson is able to argue that 'no society has ever been quite so mystified in quite so many ways as our own, saturated as it is with messages and information, the very vehicle of mystification'.[34] In situations where uncertainty stems from an excess rather than a lack of information, it is the capacity to encode and decode information that remains scarce.

The de-professionalization thesis fails to take account of these issues and, as a result, confuses the supply of legal information with the ability to gain knowledge and act effectively based on that knowledge.[35] Legal database services may enhance the flow of legal information within the legal professional community. They may also allow members of other professional groups, such as accountants, easier access to legal information. However, the distinction between the technical means used to conduct legal research and the frameworks of knowledge and skills of interpretation required to formulate research strategies and analyse their results remains intact. Therefore, although legal database services may have implications for the rivalry between professional groups, they do little to make legal information more accessible to those who lack sophisticated legal knowledge and skill. Indeed, to argue otherwise is to miss the point that legal database services are designed not to broaden access to legal information but to provide lawyers and other

18

professionals with the power of selection. Thus, as Freidson has argued, the deprofessionalizing influence of information technology is likely to be minimal 'so long as its programs and the evaluation of its printouts remain in the hands of the professions involved'.[36]

Katsh's suggestion that the use of computerized legal database services will result in the development of 'disorganised law' is equally misleading. It rests on an uncritical acceptance of the professional ideology of law as a systematic and coherent body of knowledge. In practice, the internal structures of legal thought, particularly within common law systems, exhibit only 'piecemeal' rationality and retain a significant degree of fluidity over time. As McBarnet has argued, 'the mystique of case law lies not only in the esoteric nature of professional knowledge; it lies in the very particularistic and *post hoc* form it takes'.[37] Ironically, attempts to formalize legal knowledge and reasoning for the purposes of implementing them in computer systems have served to confirm the indeterminacy of legal argument.[38] However, the notion of 'disorganized law' also overlooks the extent to which computer-assisted legal research techniques provide the professional élite with new means to reproduce the sphere of 'pure law'.[39] In particular, these techniques can be used to assist in the construction of increasingly elaborate taxonomies for codifying and rationalising legal knowledge.

These shortcomings of the de-professionalization thesis are compounded by lack of attention to the economic aspects of legal database services. Although the circulation of legal information has long been embedded in structures of economic exchange, the development of legal database services adds a new dimension to the commodification of legal information.[40] In particular, it forms part of a contemporary trend in which 'information and symbols are increasingly produced within industries, sold in markets and used as a means to accumulate capital.'[41] Thus, in its influential report entitled *Making a Business of Information*, the Information Technology Advisory Panel identified legal information as part of the 'tradeable information sector'.[42]

Despite the rapid growth of information markets, information does not fit neatly into traditional economic categories. For lawyers, the value of a legal database service lies in the combination of its contents and its search capabilities which together determine the scope for retrieving usable information. The economic value of any search can be measured by reference to the cost of locating the same information using other methods. However, this value bears no necessary relation to either the meaning of the information located or the cost of its production. In particular, whereas the development and maintenance of legal databases requires the allocation of scarce resources in the form of capital, labour, and technology, the marginal costs of reproducing the contents of a database or allowing access to additional users tend towards zero. In this context, legal databases provide the means to overcome the problems of scarcity associated with print. However, the introduction of legal database services has been accompanied by the development of a range of technical and legal constraints, in the form of computer access codes and copyright licensing agreements, designed to maintain the scarcity of legal information. When coupled with the pricing strategies of service providers, these constraints have effectively limited the use of these services to a small number of élite law firms.[43] Therefore, insofar as legal database services have affected the flow of legal information, they have done so by supplementing the control of the profession with the censorship of the market.

These developments raise significant questions about the value of legal information. Economic analysis of legal information entails a restricted notion of value precisely because the flow of legal information is linked to broader social and political values. In particular, access to legal information is an important component in realizing ideas about justice, citizenship, and democracy. Although computerized legal databases are unlikely to be of direct use to lay people, they could provide a means of promoting the availability and usability of legal information amongst public interest lawyers and legal advice workers.[44] Moreover, as the text of legislation and transcripts of court and tribunal decisions come to be produced in electronic form, the cost of maintaining legal databases will decline. In this context, there is scope for developing legal database services which cater for the needs of those working in the field of public interest law and which treat legal information as a social resource rather than a tradeable commodity.

While legal research is widely seen as an important aspect of legal work, the limited evidence available suggests that the majority of practitioners spend relatively little time engaged in research activities.[45] In contrast to more esoteric notions of what lawyers do, Campbell has suggested that legal practice comprises 'largely routinised, pragmatic, business-like work and attention to irritating and trivial logistical detail'.[46] Moreover, according to Rueschemeyer, 'organisational "know-how", economic experience, wisdom about personal relations, connections and "inside" knowledge are often as important for the lawyer's work as knowledge of the law'.[47] Indeed, law firms with access to on-line database services tend to use them more for the purposes of obtaining corporate and commercial information than for conducting legal research.[48] In recognition of these factors, attention has turned towards the development of systems which provide access to more immediately usable forms of legal information.

In this context, law firms have invested in the development of legal 'know-how' databases. In contrast to the type of material contained in conventional legal databases, 'know-how' databases are designed to make the accumulated knowledge and experience acquired within a firm readily available on a firm-wide basis. Although these databases are flexible and their precise contents vary, they typically include examples of standard documentation, records of past case work, copies of opinions, newsletters and briefings, and details of contacts. Legal 'know-how' databases may be likened to institutional memories. The desire to capture legal 'know-how' is motivated by the recognition that accumulated knowledge and experience represent valuable assets. In particular, as lawyers become involved in increasingly specialized

20

areas of work, they engage in forms of innovation which include the development of new legal knowledge and skill. Legal 'know-how' databases provide a means for firms to appropriate the benefits of this innovative activity.

Similar database facilities could be developed to support the work of public interest lawyers. However, in contrast to the private appropriation of knowledge and skill, these facilities would form part of broader strategies for preserving and sharing scarce information resources and mobilizing specialized knowledge and skill. By including details of the work undertaken by law centres, legal advice agencies, and social action groups, these facilities could also provide public interest lawyers with a means of 'counter-surveillance'. In particular, systems for recording and retrieving information about case work would enable agencies to monitor the operation of legal and social policies and contribute more effectively to policy development. Thus, database facilities could be used to underpin the development of strategic approaches to the practice of public interest law. Moreover, if developed on a co-operative basis with contributions from a wide range of participants, public interest law databases have the potential to become collective resources for all lawyers and legal advice workers involved in this field.

THE INDUSTRIALIZATION OF THE LEGAL MIND

The use of information technology to provide more structured support for different aspects of legal work has been pursued through the development of specialized legal practice systems. These range from relatively simple 'procedural support systems' designed to facilitate the processing of specific legal tasks and procedures, to more complex 'legal expert systems' which attempt to encode different forms of legal knowledge and skill. Thus, 'procedural suppport systems' have been developed to support the routine tasks involved in areas such as conveyancing, debt collection and litigation. These systems operate by breaking a particular type of procedure or transaction into a series of discrete stages. At each stage of the procedure, the user is prompted to supply relevant information. The system responds by automatically generating the appropriate standard letters and forms, recording the progress of transactions, and diarizing future events to remind the user of outstanding tasks. As well as facilitating the administration of individual transactions, these systems include reporting functions which simplify the management and control of case loads.

Computerized litigation support systems perform similar functions in relation to the administration and management of litigation. However, these systems also make use of database facilities for storing, indexing and retrieving the documentary evidence used in litigation. This approach offers considerable advantages over manual methods in terms of the efficiency of document handling and the techniques available for analysing complex factual evidence. More sophisticated forms of litigation support extend to the presentation of evidence in court, including the use of computer graphics and simulations.[49] Litigation support systems depend on advanced technology and require substantial capital investment. However, in cases involving large volumes of documentary evidence they can produce significant savings. Therefore, law firms with the capacity to offer litigation support services gain a competitive advantage in the market for large-scale litigation work. The use of computerized litigation support can also influence the outcome of litigation. In disputes between those who have access to litigation support and those who do not, the latter may be at a disadvantage and, therefore, more likely to accept settlement.[50] In these circumstances there is a risk that the outcome of disputes will increasingly revolve around the issue of technological superiority.

The development of these systems is taken a stage further with the addition of facilities designed to guide users through the various stages of a task or procedure, including the provision of 'context-sensitive' information for users and inference mechanisms which enable the systems to perform rudimentary decision-making functions. In this respect, procedural support systems begin to resemble so-called 'legal expert systems' or 'decision support systems' which draw on developments in the discipline of Artificial Intelligence. Designed to replicate the performance of legal 'experts' in the conduct of specific tasks, these systems operate on the basis of formalized representations of legal knowledge and rationalized reconstructions of legal problem-solving procedures.[51] Legal-expert and decision-support systems have been developed to support a wide range of activities, such as diagnosing and analysing problems in defined areas of law,[52] drafting specific types of legal document,[53] negotiating settlements in particular areas of dispute,[54] and supporting decision-making in the courts.[55]

The consequences of implementing these different kinds of legal practice system vary according to the purposes for which they are developed and the contexts in which they are deployed. However, an example of the possible implications can be found in a large firm of accountants which has recently implemented a number of 'legal expert systems'. These include a system known as VATIA which is based on representations of VAT legislation and relevant court and tribunal decisions. VATIA enables the user to assess the VAT liabilities of corporate clients and to give advice about the operation of VAT law. Before the system was introduced, much of this work was undertaken by the firm's VAT specialists. However, the system allows this type of work to be delegated to the firm's general auditors, leaving the VAT specialists free to concentrate on more profitable activities.[56]

As legal practice systems become more specialized and offer a wider range of facilities, they also become increasingly costly to develop. In particular, advanced systems require substantial investment in technology and skilled labour. In addition, if legal knowledge is encoded in a system and this is liable to change over time, the continuing utility of the system depends on a commitment to ongoing maintenance. In many cases, the deployment of legal practice systems also involves significant restructuring of legal service production, including the rationalization and routinization of work activities. These economic and organizational constraints suggest that the development and deployment of legal practice systems will be oriented either towards highly profitable areas of legal work where the rewards for mobilizing specialized legal knowledge and skill outweigh the costs of implementing systems, or towards 'mass-market' applications where rationalization yields both cost savings and increased control over service delivery. Therefore, while legal practice systems are likely to enhance the capacity of the élite law firms to provide creative legal services for their corporate and institutional clients, the deployment of these systems in other sectors of the market seems likely to encourage increasingly routinized and standardized forms of service delivery.

The development of legal practice systems rests on a form of cognitive-instrumental rationality which has implications for the manner in which legal knowledge is constructed and valorized in contemporary society. While these systems are designed to support rather than substitute for human decision-makers, the use of these systems on a routine basis seems likely to exert a subtle influence on legal reasoning and decision-making. In particular, it is reasonable to predict that the widespread use of rule-based representations of legal knowledge and algorithmic approaches to legal reasoning would promote a resurgence of formalism. More broadly, as media for transferring legal knowledge from small groups of 'experts' to larger groups of 'non-experts', legal practice systems may be associated with what Enzensberger has identified as the 'industrialisation of the mind'.[57] Thus, the introduction of legal practice systems influences the capacity of those occupying different locations in the professional hierarchy to exert control over the construction and application of legal knowledge. In addition, as the VATIA example indicates, these systems also provide means for transferring knowledge and skill across professional boundaries. In these circumstances, information technology is likely to play an increasingly prominent role in the processes whereby social relations of expertise are renegotiated within and between occupational groups. It is also possible that simplified legal practice systems could be developed and used to promote new forms of legal service provision for consumers. In particular, there is evidence to suggest that a market in consumer legal software is already established in the United States of America.[58]

The association between the introduction of legal practice systems and the restructuring of legal service production also indicates that these systems may be instrumental in relation to the so-called proletarianization of legal work. However, Derber has drawn an important distinction between *technical* proletarianization which entails loss of control over knowledge and technical decision-making and leads to de-skilling through the routinization of intellectual work, and *ideological* proletarianization which entails loss of control over the ends of professional work and leads to the role of the professional being limited to that of technical expert.[59] While lawyers and other professionals have experienced ideological proletarianization, Larson maintains that they have yet to become technically proletarianized.[60] For the

23

professions, technical proletarianization is associated not so much with the de-skilling of professionals as with the progressive delegation of less-skilled, newly automated tasks to lower-paid and lower-status occupational groups. This form of proletarianization has received a further stimulus from the institutional reforms introduced in the Courts and Legal Services Act 1990.[61] In the deregulated market for legal services, the use of legal practice systems to facilitate the automation and delegation of legal tasks is likely to play a prominent role in competition between legal service providers.

However, the automation and 'downgrading' of legal tasks are not inevitable consequences of the introduction and use of legal practice systems. As Cooley maintains, 'it is possible so to design systems as to enhance human beings rather than to diminish them and subordinate them to the machine'.[62] If designed and implemented with due care and attention, legal practice systems could play a role in facilitating the conduct of case work and mobilizing specialized legal knowledge and skill within law centres and legal advice agencies. Indeed, as the developers of a system designed to support debt advice work have argued, 'the problems and solutions within debt advice can and must be standardised and demystified if they are to become available to large numbers of people nationwide'.[63] This approach emphasizes that an element of routinization is necessary to secure the diffusion of legal knowledge and skill. In addition, it recognizes that routinization may also benefit clients by demystifying obscure legal rules and procedures.

The development of legal practice systems for use in law centres and legal advice agencies raises questions about the role of these systems in relation to the strategic objectives of community-based legal service agencies. Some areas of legal work may be more susceptible to support from legal practice systems than others. Therefore, it is important to ensure that developments are not 'technology-driven' and that areas of knowledge and skill which are less susceptible to technological support continue to be supported by other means. If lawyers, advice workers, and clients are not to be alienated by legal practice systems, careful attention needs to be given to the allocation of functions between users and systems to ensure that users retain control over decision-making processes. Moreover, it should be recognized that legal practice systems designed to support a particular type of task are unlikely to cover every instance of that task. Therefore, there is a continuing need for lawyers and legal-advice workers to develop their knowledge and skills in conjunction with any system. In these circumstances, as Lauritsen and others have shown, it is possible to harness the communicative potential of information technology to produce systems which enhance the delivery of public legal services.[64]

Information technology could also be considered as a means of delivering legal services. Relatively few attempts have been made to develop legal information systems for public use. By restricting the audience for these systems to those who possess legal knowledge and skill, developers have been able to make assumptions about the legal competence or 'tacit knowledge' of potential users. The advantage of this approach is that it limits the need to undertake the difficult and costly task of attempting to encode basic legal knowledge.[65] However, in the few cases where public access systems have been implemented, they have proved popular with lay users.[66] Thus, the developers of an expert system designed to provide members of the public with access to information and advice about social security claims have suggested that their system '. . . could contribute to the demystification of the claiming process, an increased take-up of benefits, and a partial reassessment of the public image of welfare'.[67]

An example of what can be achieved in this direction is the 'Courtguide Information System' developed by the Law Foundation for New South Wales and the State Attorney General's department.[68] This system forms part of a larger project designed to make the operation of the civil courts intelligible to potential litigants. It uses interactive video technology to provide users with information about the work of the courts and the role of court staff, the procedural steps involved in different types of court action, and the consequences of different court orders. It contains information about proceedings relating to child custody, domestic violence, neighbour disputes, and a range of other legal matters. The system is installed in court buildings and community centres and also includes information about local sources of legal advice and assistance.

This analysis suggests a distinctive role for information technology in mobilizing legal knowledge and skill within the field of public-interest law and making legal information more readily accessible to those participating in legal processes. In contrast to technologies designed to rationalize legal knowledge and control its application, the successful implementation of information systems in public-interest legal practice rests on attention to the communicative dimension of the new technical media. It also depends upon the integration of information systems into existing forms of service delivery. As such, information technology may be used to augment rather than displace existing requirements for legal services and reduce some of the information inequalities and asymmetries currently associated with the provision of legal services.

THE AMBIVALENT POTENTIALITIES OF TECHNOLOGY IN LEGAL PRACTICE

Developments in information technology are influencing not only the organizational structures through which the provision of legal services is mediated, but also the processes whereby these services are constructed and delivered. The adoption of information technology in legal settings has been associated most closely with developments in the élite law firms where sophisticated systems are used to enhance the provision of creative and flexible legal services for corporate and institutional clients. In other sectors of the market for legal services, the introduction of information technology is one of a number of factors which appear likely to promote an increasingly routinized form of service delivery for the majority of individual consumers. Information technology may also encourage the development of alternative forms of service delivery, for example, through the production and marketing of 'self-help' legal software. Insofar as these developments enhance the availability of affordable legal services for consumers they may be welcomed. However, disparities in the distribution of information technology in legal settings also have implications for the quality of legal services available to different social groups.

There is an appreciable risk that the development and deployment of information technology in legal settings will exacerbate existing divisions between 'information rich' and 'information poor'. Those whose legal representatives have sophisticated information and communication systems at their disposal may gain significant advantages over others. In addition, as technology is developed to support some areas of legal work, the relative cost of providing services in other areas is likely to increase. Therefore, in areas which are less susceptible to computerization or where there are fewer incentives to invest in the development of appropriate information systems, the availability of services may be adversely affected. This risk is compounded if information technology is seen as a means of further extending the logic of the market into the sphere of public provision. In particular, if public funding is withdrawn from services which are seen as candidates for computerization or emphasis is switched towards what Gorz describes as the 'auto-production' of consumers, public sector legal services will inevitably remain technologically impoverished.[69]

Despite the dominant uses of information technology, the trajectories of technological development in legal services are neither fixed nor immutable. Public interest lawyers and legal advice workers could take advantage of the decentralizing potential of information technology to strengthen their existing forms of organization and promote the formation of a collective identity. They could also utilize the communicative dimension of information technology to enhance the mobilization of scarce legal resources, the availability of legal services, and the accessibility of legal information. Clearly, the realization of these objectives will depend on investment in appropriate technological infrastructures. However, it will also depend on the formulation and implementation of coherent information and communication policies which take account of the different requirements of public-interest lawyers and legal advice workers, as well as the groups and individuals they represent. In addition to maintaining a critical awareness of both the potential and the limitations of information technology, future development entails looking beyond the automation of existing practices towards new ways of communicating about law.

NOTES AND REFERENCES

1 D. Lyon, *The Information Society: Issues and Illusions* (1988).
2 D. Bell, 'The Social Framework of the Information Society' in *The Microelectronics*

26

Revolution, ed. T. Forester (1980); T. Stonier, *The Wealth of Information: A Profile of the Post-Industrial Economy* (1983); Y. Masuda, 'Computopia' in *The Information Technology Revolution*, ed. T. Forester (1985).

3 T. Morris-Suzuki, 'Capitalism in the computer age' (1986) 160 *New Left Rev.* 81; G. Locksley, 'Information technology and capitalist development; (1986) 27 *Capital and Class* 81; M. Castells, *The Informational City: Information Technology, Economic Restructuring and the Urban-Regional Process* (1989); D. Harvey, *The Condition of Postmodernity* (1989).

4 A. Feenberg, 'Post-industrial discourses' (1990) 19 *Theory and Society* 709.

5 J-F. Lyotard, *The Postmodern Condition: A Report on Knowledge* (1984); M. Poster, *The Mode of Information: Poststructuralism and Social Context* (1990); S. White, *Political Theory and Postmodernism* (1991); B. Smart, *Modern Conditions, Postmodern Controversies* (1992).

7 C. Marvin, *When Old Technologies were New: Thinking about Electronic Communication in the Late Nineteenth Century* (1988) 4.

8 M. Galanter, 'The legal malaise, or justice observed' (1985) 19 *Law and Society Rev.* 537.

9 G. Teubner, 'How the law thinks: toward a constructivist epistemology of law' (1989) 23 *Law and Society Rev.* 727.

10 D. MacKenzie and J. Wajcman (eds.), *The Social Shaping of Technology* (1985); W. Bijker, T. Hughes, and T. Pinch (eds.), *The Social Construction of Technological Systems* (1987).

11 The Royal Commission on Legal Services, *Final Report* (1979; Cmnd. 7648) ch. 22, para. 53.

12 National Law Library, *Lawyers and Technology: Report on a Study of the Use of Technology by Solicitors* (1983); N. Faulkner and T. Saunders, 'Solicitors and information technology: a survey' (1985) 135 *New Law J.* 326; M. Blacksell, K. Economides, and C. Watkins, *Solicitors and Access to Legal Services in Rural Areas: Evidence from Devon and Cornwall* (1986); Robson Rhodes, *IT Use Amongst the Legal 500* (1990); Touche Ross, *Solicitors' Use of Information Technology* (1990); Bar Council, *Review of Chambers Administration* (1989).

13 National Association of Citizens' Advice Bureaux, *Microcomputer Project: Final Report* (1987); J. Ryan and G. Sheridan, *Computers in Non-Commercial Organisations* (1987); E. Kempson, *Computerising London's Advice Agencies* (1988).

14 C. Hedderman, *Computers in the Courtroom* (1988); S. Overend, N. Bellord, and J. Bishop, *Computers in the Official Referees' Court* (1988); J. Plotnikoff, *Future Trends in Technology for the Courts* (1990); P. Waugh, 'The use of computers in the administration of justice in the United Kingdom' (1991) 5 *Yearbook of Law Computers and Technology* 26.

15 For example, on the development of information technology in the Department of Social Security, see M. O'Higgins, 'Computerising the social security system, an operational strategy in lieu of a policy strategy' in *The Computer Revolution in Public Administration*, eds. D.C. Pitt and B. Smith (1984); R. Geary and P. Leith, 'Law in a Changing Technological Society' in *Law, Society and Change*, eds. S. Livingstone and J. Morison (1990); M. Adler and R. Sainsbury, 'The social shaping of information technology: computerisation and the administration of social security' in *The Sociology of Social Security*, eds. M. Adler, C. Bell, J. Clasen, and A. Sinfield (1991).

16 'A Nice Little Earner' *Guardian*, 4 January 1990.

17 P. Leith, *The Computerised Lawyer: A Guide to the Use of Computers in the Legal Profession* (1991) 139.

18 On the development of the management information systems in the magistrates' court, see D. Massey and P. Morgan, 'A management informations system for the magistrates' court' (1988) 25 *Home Office Research and Planning Unit Research Bull.* 37; P. Morgan, 'Management information system for the magistrates' court: measuring court workloads' (1989) 26 *Home Office Research and Planning Unit Research Bull.* 45; T. Treasdale, 'Management information system for the magistrates' court: performance indicators for fine enforcement' (1990) 27 *Home Office Research and Planning Unit Research Bull.* 46. More generally, see C. Dandeker, *Surveillance, Power and Modernity: Bureaucracy and Discipline from 1700 to the Present Day* (1990).

19 M. Galanter, 'Mega-law and mega-lawyering in the contemporary United States' in *The Sociology of the Professions*, eds. R. Dingwall and P. Lewis (1983); Y. Dezalay, 'The "Big Bang" and the law: the internationalization and restructuration of the legal

field' in *Global Culture: Nationalism, Globalization and Modernity*, ed. M. Featherstone (1991).

20 On the concept of 'time-space compression', see D. Harvey, *The Condition of Postmodernity* (1989) 220.

21 G. Bindman, 'Legal clinics: can we learn from the USA?', *Law Society Gazette*, 22 September 1982; J. Dirks, *Making Legal Aid Pay* (1989).

22 'Buying and selling property in 2001' (1985) 43 *Computers and Law* 14; A. Restorick, 'HM Land Registry and the conveyancing community' (1989) 62 *Computers and Law* 23; 'Search system that warrants inspection', *Guardian*, 19 September 1991.

23 On 'public interest law', see J. Cooper and R. Dhavan (eds.), *Public Interest Law* (1986). Early examples of technical innovation in this area would include the Welfare Rights Assessment Programme developed during the early 1980s by Cardiff Citizens Advice Bureau to support welfare rights research work (G. Morgan, 'Welfare benefits computing' in *Research Highlights in Social Work: New Information Technology in Management and Practice*, eds. G. Horobin and S. Montgomery (1986)); and the implementation of a microcomputer network at Brent Law Centre (P. Lefevre, 'One computer per desk?' (1986) 22 *Computanews* 4).

24 For opposing views on 'networking' of law centre activities, see R. Campbell, 'The role of law centres', *Legal Action*, February 1989, and K. Hatton, 'Law centres: another view', *Legal Action*, June 1989.

25 Castells, op. cit., n. 3., p. 352.

26 R.A. Rothman, 'Deprofessionalization: The case of law in America' (1984) 11 *Work and Occupations* 191. See also N. Toren, 'Deprofessionalization and its sources' (1975) 2 *Sociology of Work and Occupations* 323; M. Haug, 'Computer technology and the obsolescence of the concept of profession' in *Work and Technology*, eds. M. Haug and J. Dofny (1977).

27 M.E. Katch, *The Electronic Media and the Transformation of Law* (1989) 210.

28 E. Eisenstein, *The Printing Press as an Agent of Change* (1979); L. Febvre and H-J. Martin, *The Coming of the Book* (1976); N. Thrift, 'Flies and germs: a geography of knowledge' in *Social Relations and Spatial Structures*, eds. D. Gregory and J. Urry (1985).

29 Katch, op. cit., n. 27, p. 213.

30 id., p. 220.

31 A. Paliwala, 'Creating an academic environment: the development of technology in legal education' (1991) 5 *Yearbook of Law, Computers and Technology* 136.

32 J. Baudrillard, *In the Shadow of the Silent Majorities* (1983) 95.

33 G. Bateson, *Steps to an Ecology of Mind* (1973) 428.

34 F. Jameson, *The Political Unconscious* (1981) 60.

35 L. Winner, *The Whale and the Reactor: A Search for Limits in an Age of High Technology* (1984) 108.

36 E. Friedson, *Professional Powers: A Study of the Institutionalisation of Formal Knowledge* (1986) 112.

37 D. McBarnet, 'Legal form and legal mystification' (1982) 10 *International J. of the Sociology of Law* 409.

38 D. Berman and C. Hafner, 'Indeterminacy: a challenge to logic-based models of legal reasoning' (1987) 3 *Yearbook of Law Computers and Technology* 1; P. Leith, 'The application of A1 to law' (1988) 2 *A1 and Society* 31; P. Leith, *Formalism in A1 and Computer Science* (1990) ch. 5.

39 Y. Dezalay, 'From mediation to pure law: practice and scholarly representation within the legal sphere' (1986) 14 *International J. of the Sociology of Law* 89.

40 P. von Nessen, 'Law reporting: another case for deregulation' (1985) 48 *Modern Law Rev.* 412; P. Clinch, 'The Establishment v. Butterworths' (1991) *Anglo-Am. Law Rev.* 209.

41 G.J. Mulgan, *Communications and Control: Networks and the New Economies of Communication* (1991) 170.

42 Cabinet Office Information Technology Advisory Panel, *Making a Business of Information: A Survey of New Opportunities* (1983).

43 For example, in the United Kingdom Lexis is used extensively by approximately fifty of the largest law firms (F. Sharman, 'Developments in legal databases' (1991) 1 *Law Technology J.* 43.)

44 Preliminary steps in the development of on-line databases for use in the field of public interest law include a pilot project involving the use of Lawtel – an on-line database of legal abstracts – in Citizens Advice Bureaux ('NACAB to decide on Lawtel' (1987) 29 *Computanews* 8) and the recent development of the Statewatch on-line database (further information available from Statewatch, PO Box 1516, London).

45 J.E. Carlin, *Lawyers on their Own: A Study of Individual Practitioners in Chicago* (1962); C.M. Campbell, 'Lawyers and their public' in *Lawyers in their Social Setting*, ed. D.N. MacCormick (1976).

46 C. Campbell, 'Research into legal services: response and reappraisal' in *Law in the Balance: Legal Services in the Eighties*, ed. P.A. Thomas (1982) 224.

47 D. Rueschemeyer, *Lawyers and their Society: A Comparative Study of the Legal Profession in the United States and Germany* (1973) 23.

48 'Law libraries increase use of on-line databases', *The Lawyer*, 13 November 1990.

49 M. Tantum, 'The impact of the computer on the investigation of fraud' (1989) 2 *LTC and BILETA Newletter* 50; P. Marcotte, 'Animated evidence', *ABA J.*, December 1989.

50 M. Tantum, 'The lawyer and the war' (1991) 5 *Yearbook of Law Computers and Technology* 65.

51 R. Susskind, *Expert Systems in Law: A Jurisprudential Inquiry* (1987); A. Gardner, *An Artificial Intelligence Approach to Legal Reasoning* (1987); T. Bench-Capon (ed.), *Knowledge-Based Systems and Legal Applications* (1991).

52 P. Capper and R. Susskind, *Latent Damage Law – The Expert System: A Study of Computers in Legal Reasoning* (1988); R. Widdison and F. Pritchard, 'The EC Competition Adviser', *Computers and Law*, February 1991.

53 J. Sprowl, 'The automated assembly of legal documents' in *Computer Science and Law: An Advanced Course*, ed. B. Niblett (1980); D. B. Evans, 'Artificial intelligence and document assembly' (1990) 16 *Law Practice Management* 18.

54 D. Waterman and M. Peterson, 'Evaluating civil claims: an expert systems approach' (1984) 1 *Expert Systems* 65; D. Waterman, J. Paul, and M. Peterson, 'Expert systems for legal decision-making' (1986) 3 *Expert Systems* 212.

55 D. Bainbridge, *The Basis, Development and Potential of a Computer System to Assist with the Sentencing of Offenders* (1989), unpublished PhD thesis, Birmingham Polytechnic; R.S. Gruner, 'Sentencing Advisor: an expert computer system for federal sentencing analyses' (1989) 5 *Santa Clara Computer and High Technology Law J.* 51.

56 Department of Trade and Industry, *Expert System Opportunities – Legislation and Regulations: Professional VAT Advice – Ernst & Young VATIA Application* (1990).

57 H.M. Enzenberger, *Dreamers of the Absolute* (1988) 1.

58 'Where there's a will, there's a new way with law' *Guardian*, 29 September 1988; 'Lawyers on a disk', *ABA J.*, July 1990.

59 C. Derber, 'Towards a new theory of professionals as workers: advanced capitalism and postindustrial labor' in *Professionals as Workers: Mental Labor in Advanced Capitalism*, ed. C. Derber (1982).

60 M.S. Larson, 'Proletarianization and educated labor' (1980) 9 *Theory and Society* 131.

61 C. Stanley, 'Justice enters the marketplace: enterprise culture and the provision of legal services' in *Enterprise Culture*, eds. R. Keat amd N. Abercrombie (1991).

62 M. Cooley, *Architect or Bee? The Human Price of Technology* (1987) 176.

63 M. Wolfe and T. Jones, 'Moneyspinner replies' (1990) 49 *Computanews* 1.

64 M. Lauritsen, 'Representing lawyering knowledge in practice systems' in *Proceedings of the Third International Conference on Logica, Informatica, Diritto*, ed. A.A. Martino (1989); M. Lauritsen, 'Delivering legal services with computer-based practice systems' (1990) 23 *Clearinghouse Rev.* 1532; J. Rafferty, E. Smith, and B. Glastonbury, 'Welfare benefits packages' (1990) 2 *LTC and BILETA Newsletter* 124; 'Thumbs up for Debt Alert' (1991) 55 *Computanews* 1.

65 H. Collins, *Artifical Experts: Social Knowledge and Intelligent Machines* (1990) 103.

66 J. Epstein, *New Technology – New Entitlement? An Experience in Public-Access Computers to Assess Entitlement to Benefit* (1984).

67 P. Dawson, S. Buckland, and N. Gilbert, 'Expert systems and the public provision of welfare benefit advice' (1990) 18 *Policy and Politics* 52.

68 Law Foundation for New South Wales, *Annual Report* (1989) 23. See also J. Plotnikoff, *Future Trends in Technology for the Courts* (1990) 6, describing the introduction of similar 'access centres' at courts in Colorado.

69 A. Gorz, *Paths to Paradise: On the Liberation from Work* (1985).

From Profession to Business : The Rise and Rise of the City Law Firm

R. G. Lee*

THE MARKET FOR LEGAL SERVICES

The Green Paper on Legal Services[1] published in 1989 was a radical document; far more radical than the reform which it eventually engendered.[2] In its very first paragraph it promised to ensure that 'a market providing legal services operates freely and efficiently so as to give clients the widest possible choice of cost effective services'. By the third paragraph it stated that consumers should be entitled to 'choose from the largest possible number and spread of . . . competent providers. Depending on the area of legal services in question, such providers may or may not need to be lawyers.'[3] It is beyond question that this was meant. The reaction by the legal profession to the Green Paper was intriguing. It was denounced by the Bar. Indeed the Bar and the judiciary spent considerable time and effort opposing the threat of competition by other lawyers, to such monopolistic rights as advocacy, that it barely seemed to acknowledge the wider point that non-lawyers may provide equally efficient services.[4] Smaller solicitors' practices also showed concern at the potential loss of work,[5] already hard pressed by competition in traditional areas of work and hit by the residualization of legal aid and the threat of fixed fees. Yet the one arena in which the sentiments of the Green Paper were supported and even welcomed was in the large law firm – and certainly the City of London law firm.

Understanding this reaction is important for it can signify much about the nature of such firms. One reason why they may not fear the market is that they know that the market has failed. This may seem a large claim to make, but a perfectly competitive market, sufficient to achieve allocative efficiency for legal services, is not, and is not likely to be present. There are a number of obstacles. For the market to work, the clients would have to be able to assess their own welfare. Legal services are technical. They are provided to those who find themselves in difficulty. They consist of a range of options and strategies which can produce a series of results, some more and some less advantageous – and the advantages may vary from client to client. Most lawyers are familiar with clients – even large corporate clients – who are happy enough to leave

* Director of Research and Development, Wilde Sapte, Queensbridge House, Upper Thames Street, London EC4V 3BD, England

31

decisions to them. Indeed, the freedom from such decisions is what they may wish to purchase.

Thus an agency relationship may develop between lawyer and client. Both parties may be happy with this, but it is not a model in which the parties typically trade. Client loyalty demonstrates that the agency relationship is often preserved past the point when one might expect the client to re-contract with another provider. Besides which, at any point in time, clients may have lengthy on-going legal matters with their chosen provider. Changing lawyers may itself be costly, and the informational asymmetries make it difficult to guarantee a technically better service. Moreover, client choices are narrow. The client may be able to acquire the services in another form, but this is not easy. Few other providers will possess the technical skill and knowledge. For corporate clients, in-house provision may be possible. However, as legal regulation becomes more pervasive and legal rules more complex, it is difficult to obtain the specialist services, especially where these are required only on an occasional basis.[6] So it is to the law firm that the client turns, and informational asymmetry suggests: 'better the devil you know . . .'.

The above offers a generalized account, but I suggest that a review of Galanter's table on contrasting styles of lawyers indicates that the failure in market provision will advantage what he describes as 'mega-law firms'.[7] This is largely because of the specialized nature of the services which they offer and their organization of those services. Although they deal with a large corporate client base, the services which they sell are more diverse, they relate to their clients more frequently, and solidify this relationship, working on longer assignments and from an earlier stage. They offer a wider range of potential solutions which, according to Galanter include greater innovation and more exhaustive exploration.[8] In other words, the greater sophistication of the client in making choices is off-set by the increasing complexity and diversity of the choices to be made.

Such problems of information, together with the growth of the agency relationship, allow the law firm the potential to exploit the client. The realization of this possibility has led to self-regulation by the profession. The professional qualification, continuing education, and practice rules offer certain assurances to the client. Indeed, the very problem with the rhetoric of the Green Paper is that it can only talk of competition among 'competent providers'.[9] If the market worked as it should, incompetent providers would be regulated out. The promise of maintenance of professional standards is itself an admission of market failure. Yet once professional standards are required, supply is reduced. Not anyone can enter the market as 'a solicitor', so that the self-regulation restricts supply. The extent to which it should be permitted to restrict supply is no small issue. It is, of course, possible to place seemingly meaningless steps to qualification – such as eating dinners – in the way of would-be entrants. Nevertheless, some guarantee of minimum standards and of ethical behaviour may be necessary to secure the agency relationship.

32

Because the preservation of this relationship may be seen as in the interest of the lawyers, generally such guarantees will be forthcoming. Moreover, we might suppose that where agency relationships are continuing and strong, the trust and reliance would be at its greatest. Thus, there develops a closeness of relationship between corporate client and large law firm which is reflected in the 'client-care' programmes of the law firm (about which more later). Where ethical issues arise, these more frequently concern the vigour with which a client's interest may be promoted rather than any lack of care in their promotion. This is reflected in the growing dissatisfaction of the larger law firms with professional indemnity processes,[10] for which, they feel, their subscription vastly outweighs the claims made or likely to be made against them in comparison to smaller-sized firms.

This indicates a problem which is implied in the work of Galanter. On almost every front, the interests of the larger law firm diverge from those of the small firm. Increasingly, the split profession must refer not only to solicitors and barristers but also to what Galanter refers to as 'mega' and 'ordinary' lawyering. (Notably, many larger firms recruit from the Bar as well as other solicitors' firms, diluting the significance of the traditional 'split'.)[11] It is necessary to address the intriguing question of how and why such firms have grown so rapidly in order that one can understand their culture and the marketing of their services.

THE GROWTH OF THE LARGER LAW FIRM

External Factors Influencing Growth

In their work of late, Galanter and Palay have suggested that the growth of 'the mega-law firm' rests largely upon an internal dynamic which dictates growth at an exponential rate.[12] This analysis is not disputed here and is considered in greater depth below. Yet, at the same time, Galanter and Palay assert that the role of exogenous factors in explaining growth have been overstated. The United Kingdom differs historically from the United States of America, however, in important respects. Whereas, in the 1950s, there were some thirty-eight law firms there with over fifty lawyers, the typical unit here was kept smaller for longer by the restriction, which held until 1967, that partnerships could not exceed twenty members.[13] At this stage my own fifty-five partner firm had only nine partners.[14] In addition, one can point to firms established by single individuals such as S.J. Berwin or D.J. Freeman,[15] whose growth has outstripped that of most competitors, growing into large firms from small beginnings in a limited time frame. Finally, the geographical spread is somewhat different. Even though New York houses more mega-law firms than elsewhere in the country, it does not reflect the dominance of the City of London, home to nineteen of the twenty largest law firms in the United Kingdom.[16]

33

To ignore location is to disregard the fact that growth has followed on the back of London's standing as an international financial centre. It also implicitly denies a vital factor in recent British history – that one of the prime beneficiaries of Thatcherism was the City law firm. This is not the place to review the history of the Thatcher governments. Since memories are short, however, it is possible to encapsulate the trends of the eighties as the era of the North/South divide; of the yuppy, the filofax, and the Porsche; of public expenditure cuts; of privatization. The restructuring of older industries and the rapid escalation of large-scale unemployment in the older industrial areas gave way to considerable growth in the service sector. Nowhere was this more true than for financial services, which were deregulated and reregulated under Thatcher. The abolition of barriers to the provision of such services ('Big Bang'), of exchange controls, of distinctions between market makers and brokers, and of fixed commissions all contributed to a hive of activity within the City of London.[17] Where banks moved into the London markets seeking to provide comprehensive financial services, City law firms were there to assist.

Work followed too on the back of the re-regulation in the form of the Financial Services Act 1986. Similar stories can be told of privatizations; of the work involved in privatizing and of how privatized industries have become massive consumers of legal services in their own right.[18] This is in addition to London's traditional strengths in areas such as insurance and shipping. Because this analysis concentrates on factors peculiar to London, it will ignore the growth of highly leveraged acquisitions which became part of a world-wide commercial trend in the late eighties. Even so, in the United Kingdom, that work largely came to the City, as has the corporate rescue activity which has followed in its wake in the nineties.

The internationalization of legal work is significant, however, from another dimension. The last few years have seen considerable inward investment into Europe, especially from the United States of America and Japan. Large London law firms have been at a considerable advantage in attracting this work. Apart from linguistic attractions, they are much larger as units than any of their European counterparts. Even today, only the Dutch come anywhere to rivalling the London firms in terms of size.[19] For investors into the single market, City of London law firms provided one-stop shopping for all legal services – referring on as necessary into particular jurisdictions, often through their own office within the member-state in question.[20] Meanwhile, for domestic clients, the growth of European Community law with its imposition of technical standards, stricter liabilities, pan-European supervision and ever-more detailed regulation, has provided a perfect platform from which to sell legal services.

All of this demonstrates exogenous factors towards growth with the market which City law firms have been best placed to reach. It does not, however, explain the growth of units as large as the typical large City firm, since there may be a variety of models by which such demand may be met. To address this question, it is necessary to examine the nature of the firms themselves.

Central to the understanding of large law firms is their corporate structure. They are partnerships. There is a good deal of ignorance as to how such partnerships work, not assisted by the positive refusal of law firms to enlighten people as to their internal organization. Such internal organization differs from firm to firm. For example, some firms recognize the position of salaried partner. Such partners are generally admitted to the partners' meetings, although they will not usually have a vote. Most importantly, they may be liable for partnership's debts, but will not receive a share of the profits. In contrast, an equity partner will have a profit share. Some of the larger firms have equity partners only, and indeed some small firms will admit straight to equity rather than bothering with salaried partners. On the other hand, some firms will have quite high percentages of salaried partners. In the *Lawyer* 'Top One Hundred' for the autumn of 1991, salaried partners constituted almost 30 per cent of partner numbers in eleventh-place Denton Hall Burgin & Warren, and 38.5 per cent of thirteenth-place Dibb Lupton Broomhead & Prior.[21] Inevitably, eight of the top twenty firms declined to give the ratio of salaried to equity partners. Part of the sensitivity regarding this information concerns overall numbers of equity partners. Unless one knows the overall number of equity partners, it is impossible to make any assessment of the shares of the partnership profits. This is difficult enough in any case. Most law firms operate a lockstep structure. There are many variants of this structure, but essentially it will operate on a points basis with the greater number of points going to the more senior of the partners. However, at some stage the maximum points score will be reached, and thereafter the increase in a partner's income will depend upon the firm's increased profitability. It is much less usual in the United Kingdom system for partnership shares to be allocated in accordance with the business actually brought in, but there may have been some modification of lockstep systems over recent years to take some account of the need to reward exceptional effort or success on the part of individual partners.

According to a recent article in the *Financial Times*: the top six firms are mooted to have growth revenues equivalent to between £900,000 and £1m per partner. Senior equity partners in these firms are said to 'draw' between £300,000 and £400,000 in salary a year with individual lawyers earning more.[22] Note that these figures are difficult to interpret. The figures for gross revenue do not assist greatly in assessing profitability. The press focus on these because they are reasonably easy to assess. This can be done by working through the number of partners and solicitors within a firm, and making an assessment of fees generated by each. It is much less easy, however, to assess profits which would form a more usual measure of financial performance. It follows that in the absence of a profits per partner figure, the drawing figure given above can only be estimated. Moreover, this figure does not represent partner pay. Some proportion of this figure will have to be reinvested in the business, and, like any other business, expenditure will vary from year to year depending on the firm's accommodation needs, overseas expansion, investment in technology, and so on.[23]

Nonetheless it can be seen that the rewards are considerable, and their level is significant in permitting the law firm to function in a particular manner. An unusual feature of any law firm, as opposed to most other corporate activity, is that the staff can themselves identify reasonably well their own contribution to the firm's financial health. Depending on the area of work and the experience of the solicitors, they will have a 'bill-out rate' which is fixed in pounds per hour. At the end of every year it is open to fee earners to assess the money earned for the firm and to compare it with their salary figure. To take a simple example, suppose that a junior solicitor bills out at £100 per hour[24] and that the target number of working hours demanded of that solicitor in a year is 1,400. If the solicitor actually works 1,500 hours per annum, and assuming that all bills are paid, then the income generated will be £150,000 for the firm. At the same time, the salary figure for that solicitor may be £25,000.[25]

This raises the question of why non-partners should forego the bulk of income earned. Obviously some proportion of this figure will be defrayed against overheads, which, within City law firms, are undoubtedly costly. Nevertheless, part of what remains will constitute profit. On the other hand, newly qualified solicitors are in no position to earn this income alone. Their ability to do so is dependent on a regular source of work. At this stage in their career, the solicitors cannot establish this. It is therefore possible to view the payment back to the partnership, as a rent upon what Galanter and Palay describe as the human capital investment of the partnership.[26] This refers to the investment already made by partners in establishing the agency relationship with clients, and expending time in establishing detailed knowledge of the client organization. Indeed, it is this surplus of human capital which allows the equity partner to hire solicitors to work as assistants, and convert the human capital investment into profit.

From the equity partner's point of view, the system seems admirable. Their efforts early in their career enable them later to retain profits which someone else effectively earns for them. This phenomenon means that a significant indicator of the financial health of any firm is its ratio of partners to solicitors – commonly known as its leverage. Thus it is possible to look at the 'Top One Hundred' and see that Slaughter and May have ninety-seven partners to 335 other solicitors.[27] This gives a ratio of partners to solicitors of almost exactly 1:3.5. This healthy ratio means that each partner can supervise the work of 3 or 4 assistant solicitors within his or her team. All in this team will bill-out at rates lower than the partner. Indeed, in their first one or two years, the billing rates of these solicitors will appear very competitive. Providing that they are well trained and adequately supervised, they will be able to discharge much of the work leaving the partner some spare capacity to invest further in the generation of human capital. This produces a spiralling effect in which the continuing effort in business development produces more and more work which the partners must in turn delegate down to the assistants working alongside them. Thus there is some truth in the tendency of the larger firm to generate exponential growth, providing the firm is well managed.

However, this process is not risk-free. This is because it cannot be held frozen in time. The assistant solicitors themselves gain experience, and develop their own human capital on the back of contacts, opportunities and experience with which they are provided. There must, therefore, be some chance that they will quit the firm to realize these opportunities in their own right, unless they are eventually given reward or recognition. Equally, it is possible that assistant solicitors may become disaffected with the process of enhancing the profitability of the partners. For this or other reasons, they may fail to develop the necessary competencies to bring in business in their own right. This may lead to some drop off in the work rate and effectiveness of such solicitors, and clearly they are unlikely to receive the reward or recognition conferred on others.

A major difficulty which faces law firms is that the only available process of reward or recognition is partnership. Not all three or four assistants working alongside a partner will be made partners. Therefore, the reward will be given to some, and not to others. This poses a problem of reward for those solicitors whom a firm may wish to retain, but upon whom it is not proposed to confer a partnership. There are no established mechanisms to cope with this. Salaried partnerships can occasionally be used, but the usual expectations of salaried partners is that they will achieve, in time, full equity partnership. It follows that there is a continual fall-out of personnel from the large firms, as they realize that they are unlikely to achieve partnership status. Because persons will already have acquired some human capital, they will generally be able to relocate to another law firm in which they can more effectively exploit that legal capital. This is generally possible. Apart from the bigger law firms, few law firms have the necessary expertise in all areas. It follows that a smaller law firm may well be willing to hire and confer partnership status upon a solicitor who brings the rate of contacts and experience gained from a larger law firm.[28] This represents a wastage rate to the larger law firm, but there is little that can be done short of dividing the partnership shares into ever-smaller proportions.

TOWARDS CORPORATE STRUCTURES

It is possible to overcome some of the dilemmas of the partnership race by seeking to lengthen the time within which a solicitor will become a partner. However, this is problematic. Salaried partnerships have already increased the length of this period, and although most law firms would like to extend the period leading to partnership, this may be difficult to achieve if smaller competitive firms are willing to offer partnerships in order to attract senior solicitors from larger firms. Moreover, as the post-qualification experience of solicitors is extended, differentials between the 'bill-out' rate of the solicitor and of the partner are eroded, so that it becomes difficult to justify to the client why a senior solicitor should be used on a particular task when, for comparatively little more outlay, a partner could be available. At

37

the same time a firm may wish to reduce the 'charge-out' hours of its partners to allow greater time for client development and the like.

Problems are also caused by the horizontal shape of the management structure within partnerships. This is to say that amongst legal staff, the worker is either a solicitor (or training to be a solicitor) or is a partner. This profile is maintained by the general secrecy that surrounds whether or not a partner has achieved equity status. A more vertical structure would make it possible to build in rewards by placing people within a more clearly defined hierarchy. As it is, some of the larger firms are having to provide titles such as 'senior solicitor' in order to confer some recognition of status upon those persons who are not likely to achieve partnership.

Added to this, there is a further, and potentially enormous problem connected with the partnership structure. This is that the range of partners can legitimately claim to be the business owners. In smaller partnerships, these business owners are also the business managers, and partnership meetings can effectively govern the firm. As practices grow, this becomes unwieldly, and in order to discharge the management of the firm, responsibility for particular functions is devolved to particular partners. At a further stage of growth, committee structures emerge to offer representation to the greater number of partners, but eventually the bureaucracy which this entails leads to a corporate structure being adopted. This may take the form of appointing one partner to occupy the role as managing partner,[29] and reporting to that managing partner will be a team of persons with full-time responsibility for areas of practice management.[30] These include areas such as finance, office administration, marketing, training, and information technology. The involvement of professionals in these areas makes for more efficient management. Not only can these people pursue a single area of specialism, but partner time is freed to work on client development, and supervising and discharging the legal work as such.

There then develops an ambiguous, even enigmatic, structure. The large law firm adopts the body of a partnership but with the mind of a corporation. Its operation depends upon partners conceding autonomy and authority over large areas of the firm's practice in the interests of efficiency and profitability. Where such goals are realized, then these corporate structures will be supported, but there may follow a difficult and tense period as the partnership as a whole takes on its new persona. Nonetheless, with one or two notable exceptions, most of the larger United Kingdom law firms have adapted to something like this structure and it is difficult to see that, having done so, they would find it easy to return to previous forms of management or administration.

Having said that, it is clear that the partnership system is enduring. Professional requirements apart, there seems to be no great will to follow a corporate structure.[31] This is probably a result of the direct financial rewards which the partnership structure delivers. Moreover, even though the voice of partners in the partnership meetings begins to carry less and less authority, the structure itself still seeks to promote team endeavour and entrepreneurial spirit. It offers incentives for the partners themselves to achieve in the interest of the profitability of the partnership, and offers further incentives down the line to those wishing to share such profits. In the future, one might expect the proportion of solicitors to partners to increase, along the lines of the accountancy practices.[32] However, it is difficult to predict the death of partnership as such. On the other hand, it is clear that there are new challenges ahead in the form of both multi-disciplinary and multi-national partnerships.

MULTI-DISCIPLINARY AND MULTINATIONAL PARTNERSHIPS

The limitations on the formation of a partnership have existed since the Joint Stock Companies Act of 1844 which obliged partnerships above a specified number to incorporate. Because most professions adopt partnership as their traditional business form, the Jenkins Company Law Committee's report of 1962[33] recognized the limitations which partnerships imposed. In the view of the committee, the restriction that partnerships could not exceed twenty partners constituted a major impediment to economic growth and expansion. The subsequent Companies Act 1967 implemented some of the major recommendations of this report in relation to professional partnerships. Section 120 exempted partnerships of solicitors, stockbrokers, and accountants from the limit of twenty members. In all cases, the exemptions have been granted only where the partners are members of an accredited professional body. In recent years pressure has grown for the introduction of a more general exemption which would allow for the formation of large 'multi-disciplinary' partnerships (MDPs).[34]

This pressure led to a Department of Trade and Industry request that the Office of Fair Trading consider the formation of such partnerships. The Director General, in his report of August 1986,[35] suggested that section 716 of the Companies Act 1985 should be revised with a view to removing the obstacles to MDPs. The DTI has responded to this report and in a consultative document has made a number of proposals.[36] In particular, the department suggests that MDPs, without restrictions on size, should be permitted as long as they are adequately regulated by professional bodies. The primary criteria for considering whether a professional body should be included is whether its disciplinary arrangements would allow it to exercise effective control over members of MDPs. This would include control of the minority of partners who would be otherwise unregulated by a professional body.

In the past, exemptions have only been granted where partners belonged to a single professional body formed for the purpose of carrying on one or a small range of activities. Specific criteria for exemption have not been devised, with particular applications considered on the merits. It has not been necessary for all members to belong to the professional body, but, as a rule of thumb, more than 75 per cent within a requisite professional body is thought to allow for adequate regulation. The problem which arises in respect of MDPs is that no individual body will necessarily control a majority of the partners. Consequently, minimum standards are likely to be specified for all professional bodies relating to such matters as discipline, indemnity, ethical conduct, and so on.

This may lead to slight modifications of the rules of some professional bodies. Subject to this, a single general exemption could then allow MDPs to be formed from combinations of members of specified professional bodies. It is proposed that MDPs will be subject to a joint minimum proportion of partners who will have to be members of one or more of the specified bodies. The Department of Trade and Industry considers that this should be in the range of 51 per cent to 75 per cent. The professional bodies must have enough members to ensure that proper professional standards are maintained so that those who deal with such partnerships are properly protected. However, the DTI view is that this percentage figure should be no higher than is reasonably necessary. Once such an exemption is in place it will be for the Law Society to decide whether they wish to retain within their rules restrictions on their members in respect of the formation of MDPs alongside members of other professional bodies. However, the maintenance of such restrictions may be regarded as anti-competitive and subject to investigation by the Office of Fair Trading as a matter of competition law. Consequently there will be a two-tier approach. Statutory exemption may need to be accompanied by changes in professional rules.

It seems clear that the government, driven in part by the European Commission, are committed to MDPs as a mode of regulating restrictive trade practices within the professions. However, many significant issues of policy remain to be decided. These include the range of options for MDPs in terms of the disciplines which may be matched, and the extent to which persons who are not members of any professional body will be allowed to become partners within an MDP. The models for MDPs may vary. High-street practices may wish to look towards MDPs with the surveying professional to provide one-stop services for house purchase. The growth of the solicitor/estate agent relationship over recent years makes this a logical progression. Whether it provides the most acceptable model of independent legal advice remains to be seen. However this pattern is somewhat different from the possibility of accountancy and law MDPs involving commercial law firms. If MDPs become a possibility, certain law firms with a strong financing-based practice may well become targets for larger accountancy predators. The impact of this would be considerable, giving rise both to national law firms, which have been hitherto unknown,[37] and the potential for 'mega-law' on a scale previously unimagined.

Alongside such weighty considerations is the development of yet another species of firm – the multinational partnership (MNP). It can be assumed that the government will meet Community law requirements by exempting, from section 716, MNPs of more than twenty solicitor and foreign lawyer partners. It will be interesting to see the extent to which MNPs are permitted across other professional disciplines, and to involve law firms established outside the European Community.

It is the non-European Community jurisdictions for which MNPs are attractive. In relation to other Community law firms, the European Community provides a form of corporate structure – the European Economic Interest Group[38] – which may serve the needs of law firms wishing to collaborate across borders for the near future. It is safer to assume, in any case, that law firms would probably prefer some looser form of association initially, before integrating fully into a MNP. However, for associations of firms between member and non-member states, all that can be done at the moment is to announce the fact of the association. In effect, an announced association becomes a form of exclusive referral. This is because, whether or not it is intended, once an announcement is made of a tie-up with a law firm in another jurisdiction, it is unlikely that other referral work will flow in from elsewhere within that jurisdiction. Referral work across borders, between law firms, is always made in the expectation that there may be some reciprocity. Once a law firm announces that this is not likely to be so, it may expect that other referral work will dry up.

For some firms, MNPs may remain an attractive option. It is noticeable that many of the larger law firms have begun to open offices across western Europe, and into central and eastern Europe. The strategy, even among the largest firms, is not uniform. This reflects doubt as to its efficiency. In general, the best way to service the needs of a client with a legal problem outside the jurisdiction will be to instruct local lawyers. Thus, access to reliable local advice may prove more significant than representation within the jurisdiction. On the other hand, a local office may be seen by the client wishing to deal in that country as a sign of proficiency. Unless a foreign office brings in a steady stream of work, however, it can prove a drain upon the partnership resources. It may be for this reason that, in longer term, the trend will be towards networks of firms, and perhaps the MNP, rather than the individual international law firms. Certainly, where an international network includes a number of large firms in different jurisdictions, there may be considerable gains through cross referrals.

As with MDPs, it is difficult to predict the precise future shape of MNPs. Much will depend not only upon the nature of any detailed regulation introduced both by government and the profession itself, but also upon the policies pursued by the larger law firms. Just as in relation to international operations no uniform pattern has emerged, so to in relation to expanded partnerships, there will be no obvious path to follow. Nonetheless, certain trends are obvious. Whether by MNPs, exclusive referrals, or international offices, most of the larger players within the City seek now to sell themselves as international law firms. If MNPs should prove successful, they may achieve internationalization at far less cost than that of establishing international offices. On the other hand, the opening of international offices in jurisdictions with limited experience of private law, such as those of central and eastern Europe, although initially very costly, may bring long-term rewards.

In relation to strategies concerning MDPs, attitudes of lawyers may vary according to age and experience in practice. Many younger lawyers see no real objection to MDPs, even in the knowledge that this may produce con-

41

glomerate accountancy and law practices. In their view, the organization within which they work is already large and diverse, and comparatively little of their time is spent on problems which can be categorized as purely legal. It is the older practitioner that retains the loyalty to the particular law firm, and the concept of the law firm in general. This has both to do with the perception of MDPs as faceless conglomerates (denying that their own firm has already become such) and the notion of arm's length dealing with accountants as either clients or expert advisers.

IS SIZE IMPORTANT?

The discussion of MDPs and MNPs is significant because it is likely to effect the strategies of a large number of firms within the next decade. These firms will not necessarily be the very largest firms which often have already established their international associations/offices. Moreover, that group is, on the whole, large enough and rich enough to withstand any enforced mergers with other professions. However, the pressure may fall upon firms outside the very largest group. In an influential article in the *Financial Times*,[39] based on a 'poll of polls', Robert Rice makes the following claim:

> even within the biggest ten law firms ranked by the number of lawyers some have fared less well than others. A gap has opened up between the top six in the accompanying poll of polls and the rest.

> This leading group characterised by their size, their expertise across a broad range of specialist areas of law and their international work are set to change the face of the legal profession in the UK and across Europe. As they expand and tighten their grip of international legal work, they will force smaller competitors to rethink their business strategy.

This suggestion is premised on the assumption that certain firms within the top ten are performing better than their competitors, and that this places enormous pressure upon the firms outside the top firms to bridge the gap. In the 1980s, many law firms merged, or sought quickly to acquire new ranges of expertise. This drive was dictated by a need to become 'full service'. Arguably, in the 1980s, size was not important for its own sake, but simply in order to provide a range of services to the clients such that an important client need not look outside the single law firm for the entire range of its required legal services. Thus, the ability to cater for all needs of a large corporate entity gave a firm a better chance to retain that client by allowing fewer opportunities for rivals to market their services to that client. During this time few law firms seem to wish to retain the identity of a 'boutique' practice[40] offering services within a particular niche in the market. Some mergers were certainly more successful than others, the merger of Clifford Turner & Coward Chance being the most significant, projecting two medium-size firms into a far superior position within the market.[41]

The recession, however, has cast doubt upon some of the strategies of the 1980s. Some of the newly merged firms have found themselves with excess capacity at a time of economic downturn, leading to some restructuring within the newly merged firm, all merged firms that have subsequently broken up, in whole or in part. It appears that the larger firms have ridden the recession with comparatively more ease than their smaller competitors. It is quite possible that partner drawings within the larger firms will have been reduced. Nonetheless, they will remain at a staggeringly high level in comparison with most industrial salaries. At the same time, these firms have been able to manage their way through the recession partly because of their size. They have not sought to make wholesale redundancies whilst maintaining the level of the partnership share. To this extent, they have proved themselves to be the best managed firms, although they tend to be the firms where much of the management devolves away from fee-earning partners. At the same time, they had achieved, prior to the recession, some helpful economies of scale. They were also able to continue to market their services throughout the recession on the basis of their scope and quality. As they have continued to invest in areas such as recruitment, or information technology (which suffered early cuts outside the larger firms),[42] they have continued to attract highly desired corporate clients. Indeed, it could be argued that there may have been a flow of clients into the larger firms during the recession, even though the overall workload has dropped.

The question of whether size is important arises in another context: should we worry on a professional or ethical level that firms may grow too big? Fears of this kind may be more apparent than real. Certainly, in relation to most professional issues, the larger law firms have mechanisms to monitor the requirements of, and compliance with, Law Society rules. This is not to say that such procedures never break down, but size may dictate sophisticated measures to guard against conflicts, oversee the continuing education status of its staff, control money into and out of the firm, and the like. Information technology makes much of this feasible, and it is generally worth the investment to appoint persons with particular responsibility for these matters. In fact, in relation to many of these requirements, the driving force in meeting them will be the demands of good and efficient management rather than the mere fact of the practice rule.

There do seem to be some levels on which there could be genuine concern. Since 1989, it has become apparent that there has been a fall in recruitment into the profession generally.[43] The decline has been sharper outside the City of London, where, with some exceptions, levels of recruitment of trainees have at least been maintained. Thus, the major route into training is rapidly becoming the large law firm. Yet no large firm offers a complete range of legal services. There are whole areas of private client, welfare law, and legal aid work which are ignored. The danger is that there may arise severe skills shortages in these areas – many of them already hard-pressed by the residualization of legal aid, and the loss of traditional monopolies (such as conveyancing) which may have provided a cross-subsidy for other areas of work. These trends may become exacerbated if the Law Society proceeds with

43

plans to license firms to take trainees, and possibly place the cost of monitoring on licensed firms only.

The other major area of concern is in relation to certain types of litigation. Much of the litigation conducted in City firms is between major commercial interests, but some takes the form of defendant work in multiple plaintiff or 'disaster' litigation. Great strides have been made by plaintiff lawyers both managerially and procedurally to present effective lead cases by teams of lawyers working in a consortium. However, in the nature of things, the uninformed plaintiff may choose lawyers not well-versed in such techniques, and facing the mighty resources, technical and technological of the large law firm.[44] The uneven nature of this contest remains a worry. On the other hand, both issues provide no reason for restricting the growth of law firms. Rather, they suggest that the fact of 'mega-lawyering' must be recognized, and its consequences better managed.

CONCLUSION: THE FUTURE

In summary, some law firms seem to have emerged with a considerable lead over their competitors. Although they charge the highest rates for their legal services, they are not generally under challenge. Difficulties in evaluating the technical quality of their legal work leads to clients assessing 'client care' elements of their work, and these firms have invested substantial resources in ensuring the support elements of their legal service are exemplary. While there is some fragmentation of client loyalty, there is a strong chance that clients will remain within the very largest firms to ensure full service. Meanwhile, the exponential growth of these firms will ensure their size advantage. Size will doubtless pose managerial problems but by adapting corporate models these can be tackled, without necessarily prejudicing the professional conduct of the firm's business. The immediate expansion of these firms is likely to be on a multinational and multi-disciplinary basis, and having survived the pressures of recession, it is possible to anticipate further growth.

Anyone who has worked in the City from the mid-to-late eighties through to the nineties must fight shy of attempting to predict the future, given the changes over that short period. Law firms may face difficult times in the near future. Large law firms are no exception. Nonetheless, the ability of the largest units to manage their way through recession, thus far, augurs well, in business terms, for their future. Doubtless they will continue to face tough competition, chipping away at clients which have already abandoned traditional notions of loyalty and show increasing consumer resistance to fee levels. Yet, in the longer term, growth across the single market should provide a steady supply of inward investment and other work – especially if London can retain its pre-eminence as a financial centre. These firms are already increasingly international (and European) enterprises.

The position of the 'boutique' firms does not seem to be in long-term doubt. Their health throughout the recession has depended on the nature of the

44

speciality. However, in the longer term, they should maintain their market share if only because such firms tend to gain referral work from larger firms who do not regard them as competitors for the full service work which larger firms provide for their clients. The more specialist the boutique firm becomes, the stronger its market identity within that sector. This implies that the boutique firm could grow, providing it continues to service an identifiable group of clients or client needs.

This leaves the medium-sized firm, which may fall under severe pressure in the nineties. Assuming that the medium-sized firm is not a boutique provider, the question arises whether it can compete for business against its larger competitors. The difficulty which it will face is that there is never any doubt that the largest firms can provide a full service to meet the needs of corporate clients. A medium-sized firm may have strengths but is likely to have areas of weakness or even of no facility. In the eighties, certain medium-sized firms attempted to resolve these difficulties by a carefully planned merger. The climate which permitted merger has changed. In the immediate future, financial worries may inhibit such activity. In the longer term, however, the medium-sized firm may need to provide a full and comprehensive service to compete, and this implies growth. The alternative may be to slim down back to boutique provision. This alternative may be forced on some firms by recession. As it becomes apparent in certain areas of work that a firm is never likely to achieve a core strength in a particular area, solicitors may leave, perhaps as a team, to move to another practice.

This flaking away of groups of people is a growing trend. Advertisements regularly incite experienced partners to defect.[45] The attraction for a partner may be the more favourable remuneration package, or it may simply be the opportunity to feed off the existing client list of the firm to which the partner wishes to transfer in order to extend the range and quality of his or her workload. All this suggests a tendency for a small number of large firms to continue to grow, probably at the expense of those firms in the next size sector. All these terms such as 'large' and 'medium' are vague, but the *Financial Times* suggested that a break-away group of six firms or so are already some way ahead of competitors in turn-over.[46] City solicitors may dispute precisely where the line should be drawn, but few would argue with the general analysis. It would take some years if the analysis of the erosion of the middle sector is correct. Meanwhile, we remain a long way from the national presence which the large accountancy firms exhibit, but, in spite of recessionary pressures, we seem nearer to the 'Big Six'[47] model than ever before.

NOTES AND REFERENCES

1 Lord Chancellor's Department *The Work and Organisation of the Legal Profession* (1989; Cm. 570) issued together with *Contingency Fees* (1989; Cm. 571), and *Conveyancing by Authorised Practitioners* (1989; Cm. 572). The first of these Green Papers should be read alongside the Lord Chancellor's Department's *Civil Justice Review* (1988; Cm. 394). The Green Papers led to a later White Paper: *Legal Services: A Framework for the Future* (1989; Cm. 740).

2 The Courts and Legal Services Act 1990; for a critique of the Act see M. Partington, 'Change or no-change? Reflections on the Courts and Legal Services Act 1990' (1991) 54 *Modern Law R.* 702; and R. White, *A Guide to the Courts and Legal Services Act 1990* (1991). For the background to some of the Act see F. Cownie, 'The Reform of the Legal Profession' in *The Changing Law* (1990) eds. F. Patfield and R. White.

3 *The Work and Organisation of the Legal Profession*, op. cit., n. 1, para. 1.3., and see also para 1.1. On this element of the Green Paper see L. Benson, 'A Sacrifice to Competition' *Financial Times*, 1 March 1989.

4 'Lord Halisham criticises legal profession plans' *Financial Times*, 15 April 1989; 'Judges poised to snub Mackay' *Guardian*, 11 April 1989; 'Courts to close while judges discuss reforms' *Times*, 12 April 1989; 'The establishment fights back' *Observer*, 12 March 1989; 'Charges are inconsistent with independent Bar' *Independent*, 3 May 1989; 'Bar rejects reforms packages' *Times*, 3 May 1989; 'Bar chief rejects state control' *Guardian*, 1 May 1989. F. Maher, 'Practising in partnership' (1991) *Law Society Gazette*, 18 September, 2; 'Choice should not be limited in the public interest' *Financial Times*, 26 January 1991; 'Mixed practice appears harder than theory' *Financial Times*, 6 February 1991.

5 E. Fennel, 'Singing a different Hymn' *Times*, 11 April 1989 points to the difference between the views on the reforms expressed by smaller, regional practices and those expressed by the Law Society (as outlined in Law Society, *Striking the Balance: Legal Reforms Briefing Papers* and *Striking the Balance: The Final Response* (1989)). Also see T. Shaw, 'Law Reforms "threaten small solicitors' firms" '*Daily Telegraph*, 2 May 1989, and R. Ford, 'Pressure may "squeeze out" some law firms' *Times*, 30 May 1989.

6 Some consideration of these issues is to be found in K. Mackie, *Lawyers in Business* (1989) ch. 3; and see also D. Chan and C. Wilson, 'The Rise of the In-house Lawyer' *International Financial Law Rev.* May 1983, 4.

7 M. Galanter, 'Mega-Law and Mega-Lawyering in the Contemporary United States' in *The Sociology of the Professions: Lawyers, Doctors and Others* (1983) eds. R. Dingwall and P. Lewis) 152. For some of the other literature on this topic see B. Garth, 'Legal Education and Large Law Firms: Delivering Legality or Solving Problems' (1989) 64 *Indiana Law Rev.* 433; J. Fitzpatrick, 'Legal Future Shock: The Role of Large Law Firms by the End of the Century' (1989) 64 *Indiana Law Rev.* 461; D. MacDonald 'Speculations by a Customer About the Future of Large Law Firms' (1989) 64 *Indiana Law Rev.* 593; J. Heinz and E. Laumann, *Chicago Lawyers: The Social Structure of the Bar* (1982); B. Buchholz, 'When Firms Branch Out' (1991) *Am. Bar Association J.* (March) 49; D. Cantor 'Law Firms are Getting Bigger . . . and More Complex' (1978) *Am. Bar Association J.* (February) 215 and see n. 12 below.

8 id.

9 Above, n. 3.

10 'City firms set up PIA study group' *Lawyer*, 2 April 1989. This article reviews the work of the City Working Party on Professional Indemnity Assurance.

11 E. Fennell, 'Solicitors get set to make a star appearance' *Times*, 16 July 1991.

12 M. Galanter and T. Palay, 'Why the Big Get Bigger: The Promotion-to-Partner Tournament and the Growing Large Law Firms' (1990) 76 *Virginia Law Rev.* 747; and M. Galanter and T. Palay, *Tournament of Lawyers: The Transformation of the Big Law Firm* (1991) 87 and following; and see J. Pritchard, 'Law firm growth is an inevitability' (1991) *Legal Business* October, 3.

13 This limitation, which originated in the Joint Stock Companies Act 1844, is now contained in s. 716 Companies Act 1985.

14 A. Salmon, *The History of Wilde Sapte 1785–1985* (1985).

15 'D. J. Freeman: Chapters 1, 2 and 3 but not 11' (1991) *Legal Business*, September, 33. 'Mr S J Berwin: Obituary' *Times*, 8 July 1988.

16 'The Legal Business 100 London' and 'The Legal Business 100 Regions' *Legal Business*, April 1990, 16 & 18, and see 'Lawyers' Top 100' *Lawyer*, 24 September 1991. Note that if the analysis is in terms of gross fee income, all of the top twenty firms are based in London, see 'Lawyers' League Table confirms late 1980s as years of strength' *Financial Times*, 18 June

1990. Other indications as to size of law firms can be found in Chambers and Partners, *Chambers and Partners' Directory* (1991); J. Pritchard (ed.), *The Legal 500* (1991).

17 AGCAS Working Party on the Legal Profession, *Opportunities for Lawyers in Legal Departments in Government and Industry* (1984), and R. Sandar and D. Douglas, 'Why are There So Many Lawyers? Perspectives and Turbulent Market' (1989) 14 *Law and Social Enquiry* 431.

18 N. Page 'A Private Function' (1990) *Legal Business* 24. S. Cirell, 'The Complexities of Competitive Tendering' *Lawyer*, 16 April 1991. This drive for privatization work also extends to central and eastern Europe – see E. Fennell, 'English join the East's velvet revolution' *Times*, 2 July 1991; R. Rice, 'Big New York firms follow the trail of eastern promise' *Financial Times*, 17 December 1990.

19 For an analysis of comparative size of European law firms see J. Pritchard (ed.), *Law Firms in Europe* (1991).

20 'Different Ways to the World' *Times*, 6 March 1990; 'Advising British Businessmen on Legal Matters Overseas' *Corporate Money*, 10 August 1990; [?] Stewart, 'International Image Making' (1991) *International Financial Law Rev.* 9. For a review of access to Europe, see P. Walters, 'Uncertain Steps Towards a European Legal Profession' (1978) 3 *European Law Rev.* 265; N. Foster, 'European Community Law and the Freedom of Lawyers in the United Kingdom and Germany' (1991) 40 *International and Comparative Law Q.* 607; and A. Wegenbaur 'Free Movement in the Professions: The New EEC Proposal on Professional Qualifications' (1986) 23 *Common Market Law Rev.* 91; J. Lonbay 'Diplomas Directive: Recognising Legal Qualifications in the EC' (1991) 1 *Lawyers in Europe* no. 7., p. 10 and no. 8., p. 5. For the current state of play on admission to United Kingdom practice see the Law Society's *Qualified Lawyers Transfer Regulations* (1990) as reviewed in (1990) *Law Society's Gazette* no. 36, p. 7.

21 op. cit., n. 16.

22 R. Rice, 'Ups and Downs of Legal Life' *Financial Times*, 1 October 1992.

23 'Pressure Mounts on firms to declare revenue and earnings' *Financial Times*, 5 March 1990; 'Jumping on the IT Bandwagon' *Times*, 13 March 1990.

24 For an actual indication of 'bill-out' rates see Chambers and Partners, op. cit., n. 16, p. 10. The average rate for 1990 for an assistant solicitor in London undertaking company/ commercial work was £140 per hour.

25 id., p. 12, for the actual figures for 1990: £28,000–£32,000 for the average one-year qualified solicitor.

26 Galanter and Paley (1991), op. cit., n. 12, p. 89 and following, and see R. Gilson and R. Mnookin 'Sharing among the Human Capitalists: An Economic Inquiry into the Corporate Law firm and How Partners Split Profits' (1985) 37 *Stanford Law Rev.* 313.

27 op. cit., n. 16.

28 P. Sinnett and A. Scivener, 'Barristers Practising in Law Firms; Barristers as Solicitors – A Good Thing' *Legal Business*, April 1991, 45. F. Bawdon, 'The Mental Leap from City to High Street' *Lawyer*, 4 June 1991; M. Gwinner, 'The Case of Headhunters in Today's Market' *Legal Business*, October 1991, 49.

29 J. Aylwin, 'The Importance of being the Managing Partner' (1991) *Law Society's Gazette*, 13 February; M. Read, 'Partners Please' (1991) *Solicitors' J.*, 27 September, 11 October.

30 Galanter and Palay (1991), op. cit., n. 12, ch. 4; V. Eliot Smith, 'Has Marketing made its Mark' *Times*, 14 August 1990; C. Wilson 'Managing for Success at Skadden Arps' *International Financial Law Rev.*, November 1984, 31.

31 Under s. 9, Administration of Justice Act 1985, which comes into force on 1 January 1992, solicitors firms will be able to incorporate as limited companies. It remains unclear how likely it is that firms will choose this option. The transaction and taxation costs of dismantling partnerships could prove prohibitive.

32 See the table in *Accountancy*, July 1991, 14; Coopers and Lybrand Deloitte had 735 partners to 7,807 professional staff and KPMG 591 partners to 7,793 professional staff.

33 *Report of the Company Law Committee*, (1962; Cmnd. 1749).

34 The restriction is now contained in s. 716, Companies Act 1985 – see R. Lee, 'Multi-disciplinary partnerships' (1991) *Professional Negligence* 168.

35 Director General of Fair Trading, *Restrictions on the kind of Organisations through which Members of Professions may offer their Services* (1986).

36 Department of Trade and Industry, *Proposal for a General Exemption Permitting the Formation of Multi-disciplinary Partnerships with more than 20 Members* (1991).

37 Some law firms based in London, such as Davies, Arnold Cooper have opened northern offices, and others such as Norton Rose have joined national networks (M5 group). The real challenge may come from non-London firms opening city offices: see J. Pritchard, 'The Best-kept Secret: Fees and Profits outside the City' *Legal Business*, September 1991, 3.

38 Directive 2137/85, OJ 31.7.85 L 199.

39 Rice, op. cit., n. 22.

40 G. Appelson, 'Boutique Firms hold their Own' *National Law J.*, 1 March 1983; Galanter and Palay (1991), op. cit., n. 12, pp. 125 forward.

41 K. Dillon, 'Can they Skaddenize Europe?' *The Am. Lawyer*, December 1989, 40. For a review of the effect of the recession on merged firms in Canada, see 'Canadian Law Firms: Every Which Way but Loose' *International Financial Law Rev.*, October 1991, 11.

42 'D. J. Freeman . . .', op. cit., n. 15; S. Shuaib, 'Too much of a good thing' (1991) *Lawyer*, 1 October 1991, 3; 'Evidence mounts of job crisis' *Law Society's Gazette*, 10 October 1990, 8; R. Clayton, 'In the Jaws of Redundancy' (1991) 135 *Solicitors' J.* 78.

43 id.

44 'Modern technology is threatening to tip the scales of justice' *Independent*, 6 March 1990; 'Jumping the IT bandwagon', op cit., n. 23; M. Middleton, 'Getting Support' *National Law J.*, June 1984, 26.

45 Gwinner, op. cit., n. 28.

46 Rice, op. cit., n. 22.

47 The 'Big Six' – formerly the 'Big Eight' – is often used to describe the breakaway of an élite group of accountancy firms whose size and profitability greatly outstrips all competitors; see *Accountancy* table, op. cit., n. 32; 'Big Six Target of EC Probe', *The European Accountant*, February 1990, 11; and 'Slowdown in Listed Client Moves after "Hectic" Reshuffling', *Accountancy Age*, 5 December 1991.

Lawyers in the Market: Delivering Legal Services in Europe

CHRISTOPHER WHELAN* AND DOREEN MCBARNET**

INTRODUCTION

The creation of the Single European Market (SEM) presents lawyers with both an opportunity – to provide legal services – and a challenge – to meet legal needs and to be competitive domestically and internationally. The stimulation of competition and trade in Europe and beyond, encouraged by a burgeoning of national and European regulation, is likely to lead to an increased demand for legal services across a wide field of legal practice.

The opportunity to provide legal services and the challenge of meeting the demand for legal services are not new. In the last two decades or so, the way law firms are organized and the nature of services provided have been transformed in the United Kingdom, the United States of America, and western society generally.[1] Several contrasting viewpoints on this transformation have emerged. Some have focussed mainly on the profession and its response to an increasingly competitive market;[2] others on the conjunction between organizational imperatives within the law firm and changes in the legal and business environment;[3] others still have put the main spotlight on the market for legal services itself.

This chapter focuses on lawyers and the market, in the context of the Single European Market. The creation of the SEM promises a great expansion in the market for legal services. The declared goals of the SEM, combined with the use of law to achieve them; the emphasis on the need to create competitive advantage; and the likely increase in the size of the SEM all point in this direction. These will be considered in the first part. Law firms have begun re-structuring in response. Some examples are presented in the second part. At the same time, barriers still exist in the market for legal services in Europe. These will be considered in the third part. In the final part, some implications of lawyers in the SEM will be reviewed.

EXPANDING THE MARKET FOR LEGAL SERVICES

One of the elements in the process of professional transformation has been the

* *School of Law, University of Warwick, Coventry CV4 7AL, England*
** *Centre for Socio-Legal Studies, Wolfson College, Oxford OX2 6UD, England*

creation of a deregulatory and free market environment.[4] During the 1980s, the United Kingdom government expressly extended one of its 'fundamental' policies – the promotion of competition[5] – to the provision of legal services. It expressed its belief that, as long as the public is assured of the competence of the providers of legal services, 'free competition between the providers of legal services will, through the discipline of the market, ensure that the public is provided with the most efficient and effective network of legal services at the most economical price.'[6] For the government, competition is promoted primarily by the process of *de*regulation and the removal of barriers on trade including, in the context of legal services, restrictive practices.[7] The most obvious example of this is the loosening of statutory regulations restricting the conduct of conveyancing. The threat this posed to solicitors prompted further deregulation, this time professional, for example, of advertising restrictions.

In the SEM, the underlying objectives have been similar. Major goals include the fostering of competition, the removal of obstacles to the free movement of goods, services, people, and capital (the four freedoms) and facilitating free trade. The government has itself pointed to the European Community Treaty and declared that 'the UK must ensure that it avoids introducing any new restrictions which might breach it.'[8] Thus, in relation to legal services, the creation of the SEM should help to protect the Thatcher legacy by reinforcing the trends already visible in the United Kingdom.

However, in the context of the SEM, there is a second major element which will probably serve to expand the market for legal services and accelerate the transformation of the legal profession. While the declared approach of the Thatcher government to promoting competition was to deregulate, the approach of the European Commission is predominantly to *regulate* – particularly in relation to economic activities affecting the corporate and commercial sectors.

For lawyers, both deregulation and regulation represent an opportunity and a challenge. While deregulation opens up the legal profession to intra- and inter- and even international professional competition, it also frees them to take advantage of the opportunities created by the method adopted in the European Community to achieve the same purpose. The deregulatory climate removes barriers to the development of legal services throughout the Community. At the same time, the regulatory method elevates the importance of law and, potentially, of lawyers' services in economic and social life. As former EC Commissioner Peter Sutherland put it: 'law lies at the heart of the European Community'. The Community was created by law; it is a source of law; it is a legal order – pursuing its objectives purely by means of law; and it is based on a Community of law where rights and obligations are equally shared.[9] As a result, a lawyer in the SEM is confronted not only with his or her national law, institutions, and system but, increasingly, with a European jurisdiction, European law and institutions such as the European Court of Justice and, potentially, with the legal systems and laws of the other member states. In short, the breakdown of barriers which is the goal of the SEM will result in a multiplication in the raw material with which lawyers work and, potentially, a vast increase in the scope of legal 'work' and practice: an 'immense corpus of law . . . a massive challenge and workload for the legal profession which will be called upon to transform the single market programme into living law.'[10]

This points to a third reason why the SEM may expand the legal market. The declared goal of the SEM is to foster competition. Law is the tool being used to achieve this. Our research on corporate responses to the SEM suggests there is an irony in this:[11] one way to secure competitive advantage is to use legal creativity to escape legal controls. The competitive climate of the 1980s financial world spawned creative devices to manipulate financial information.[12] Competition and regulation have likewise stimulated legal creativity more generally, and for a long time, in the United States of America,[13] the United Kingdom[14] and indeed, despite claims that civil law countries are less open to creativity,[15] in other parts of Europe.[16]

In the SEM, the co-existence of a vast new body of legal 'material' and the reinforcement of a competitive environment both in the SEM and in the legal profession has elevated the role of law throughout the European Community. The opportunities for innovative enterprise have increased for lawyers as they have for others: 'Contingency and discretion increase as rules and institutions grow in bulk.'[17] The Treaty of Rome is like a 'kaleidoscope':[18] the image changes whenever you shake it. The European Court of Justice, unlike United Kingdom courts, (in theory) can strike down common law or statute on the yardstick of compatibility with Community treaties. The SEM thus provides 'powerful inducements to lively mindedness, efficiency and creativity, if one's training and legal background are conducive to them.'[19] Globalization will extend it further. In this context, the creativity of lawyers and others will be sought by those with the motivation and resources to use them in order to obtain the competitive advantage it offers. In short, if the SEM succeeds in stimulating a competitive market then creative legal services are likely to be in demand.

Finally, developments in Europe are only part of a wider expansion in the market for legal services. The creation of the SEM is also a major step in the process of globalization and internationalization of capital movements, trade, and human mobility. 1 January 1993 marks not only the day when the twelve member states, 325 million people, and 250,000 lawyers of the European Community will form the SEM; it is also the date the European Economic Area (EEA) is intended to come into effect. The creation of the EEA – following the agreement made in October 1991 between the European Community and the European Free Trade Association (EFTA) – will lead to the expansion of the single market to the seven affluent EFTA countries and the establishment of the four freedoms throughout the Community and EFTA. It will also lead to the adoption by EFTA of some 12,000 pages of existing Community legislation (known as *acquis*)[20] and of relevant new legislation, and to the creation of a European Economic Area court.[21]

In any case, the European Community is likely to expand. The former German Democratic Republic has been incorporated. Some of the EFTA

51

countries have applied for membership; others plan to follow. In addition, the Community is talking about admitting Poland, Czechoslovakia, and Hungary – Central Europe's three strongest economies – around the year 2000. In the meantime, it has initialled 'association agreements' with these countries to establish a free trade area in 1992, and is negotiating similar agreements with Romania and Bulgaria. Thus, by the year 2000, the European Community may well have expanded to include at least twenty-five countries and 450 million people.

In short, the SEM combines several elements that promise to transform the market for legal services. How have law firms responded to the new legal environment?

RESPONDING TO MARKET CHANGE: TOWARDS THE EUROPEAN LAW FIRM

There are numerous ways in which United Kingdom lawyers and law firms can seek to market their services to clients in the context of the legal environment of the SEM. Law firms have responded to the creation of the SEM by developing, in a variety of forms, what may be described as embryonic versions of the 'European law firm.' Three of these, the multi-national partnership, the creation of networks and the European Economic Interest Groupings are considered here.

1. *Multinational Partnerships*

Until 1990, a United Kingdom solicitor who formed a partnership with a foreign lawyer could not, as a partner of the foreign firm, perform any of the functions reserved by statute to qualified persons, unless he or she established his or her own firm. While this restricted multinational practice based in the United Kingdom, it also protected domestic lawyers from foreign-dominated competitors.

Both statutory and professional barriers to the formation of partnerships between United Kingdom lawyers and those from another jurisdiction were removed in 1990.[22] It was argued that the role for these partnerships would be 'significantly enlarged' for United Kingdom lawyers after the implementation of the 1988 mutual recognition directive.[23] Fear was also expressed that solicitors subject to restrictions might lose out to more flexible foreign lawyers as commercial organizations become more international. In any case, national competition policy prevents anti-competitive mergers or monopolies.[24] In addition, according to Eidenmuller, 'Major efficiency gains can be achieved by multinational partnerships with homogeneous office structures throughout the EC.'[25]

Accordingly, 'safeguards' are now purely a matter for professional self-regulation. In its Solicitors' Overseas Practice Rules 1990, which came into force on 1 September 1990, the Law Society permits a solicitor to share fees

52

with lawyers in other jurisdictions and to practice through a company in which all the directors and owners of all shares are persons with whom a solicitor is permitted to share his or her fee.[26] Whether the non-European Community partners and lawyers in a United Kingdom-based multinational law firm could rely on the 1988 directive to work elsewhere in the Community is not yet clear.

2. *Networks*

As domestic clients become more international in outlook, law firms throughout the European Community have to consider creating an international network and, via competition, will have to ensure that network is not only viable but strong. This may favour large law firms, particularly North American and English ones, because many large companies, including multinationals, may use only large 'household name' firms. Moreover, to the extent that the creation of the SEM produces market pressures for change and rationalization, any resistance on the continent to large 'name' firms or, indeed, to the intrusion of Anglo-American law may be weakened. This must be one of the hopes behind the creation of networks involving British and United States firms, such as the 'strategic alliance' announced in 1989 between Macfarlanes and O'Melveny & Myers.

However, smaller firms are also involved in networks or other 'pooling' arrangements to provide commercial services to clients. Their role in the European market is boosted by the 'segmentation' of the legal services market (contrasted, for example, with the dominance of the auditing market by the 'Big Six' accountancy firms) and the growing problem of 'conflict of interest' which prevents some 'mega-firms' from accepting work and yields it to the 'second division' firms. The most 'visible' is probably 'Eurolink for Lawyers', an international legal network which after only one year of operation covered fourteen European countries (fifty cities) and the United States of America. It includes ninety firms, one third of which are British, employing 2,000 commercial lawyers. Members have access to a database to find an associate in another country. Through such networks, smaller firms may obtain the benefits of the large firm without the need for formal integration and an elaborate internal organization.

Networks can seek to develop an identity, similar to a brand name. It should perhaps be remembered that four of the 'Big Six' accountancy firms (that is, with the exception of Arthur Anderson and Price Waterhouse) are actually networks of national practices bound together with different degrees of cohesion. They share services and systems as well as clients. They are multinational, multi-disciplinary and close to the model of a 'one-stop shop.' They also supply corporate legal services through large legal departments. The international law firm Baker & McKenzie is organized on a similar basis.

3. *European Economic Interest Groupings*

On an international level, the rapid development of law firm consortia, affiliates, and associations, as well as the opening up of branches overseas, are alternatives to mergers and acquisitions. However, there are disadvantages. Opening a branch is an expensive option. Although networks are cheap and flexible, their real purpose is to encourage the referral of business among the members. But firms cannot remain in business by developing work for other firms. In the context of the European Community, there is another option: the European Economic Interest Grouping.

In order to free groups who wish to engage in cross-border co-operation from having to master the intricacies of more than one legal system, and to comply with their legal requirements, the European Community has created a new form of legal entity to operate at Community level, the European Economic Interest Grouping (EEIG). The EEIG offers a specially designed legal entity with rules governing its creation and operation which are common to partners throughout the Community. Each member must be engaged in economic activity prior to the creation of the EEIG and it must have at least two members, based in the Community, but must not employ more than 500 people. Any business, whether a company, a partnership or a sole trader, may be a member.

The EEIG offers a flexible structure for cross-border co-operation free of national law obstacles, at least in relation to its formation. The formation of an EEIG depends on a contract drawn up by its members rather than such company law concepts as the memorandum or articles of association. There is no minimum capital requirement; members have to come from more than one member-state, and there is unlimited liability. As a result of the latter, the EEIG is under no duty to disclose financial information about its activities and performance, unlike companies and limited partnerships throughout the Community. This gives the EEIG a number of advantages. It can use flexible forms of funding – there is no capital requirement. Members can finance its activities through subscriptions or borrowings. They decide what proportion and in what manner each member is to bear its share of the financing of the operation. There are no requirements for formal meetings of members. Members have unlimited joint and several liability for all liabilities. The EEIG registers in one member-state, and becomes subject to the law of that state with regard to matters not covered by the Community regulation.

It was designed to be particularly useful for groups such as lawyers who might find it difficult to form more complete links with professionals in other states. Members of an EEIG can integrate part of their commercial activities whilst retaining their legal and economic independence. Activities can be pursued which each member has in common.

The EEIG first became available in July 1989. By December 1990, nearly ninety EEIGs had been registered. One of these was Pannone de Backer, which registered on the 9 September 1989. It consists of five law firms across Europe providing cross-border legal services. Members pool their services within the EEIG to develop their existing activities, to explore areas of co-operation and to increase the profits of each member. Lawyers are free to participate in an EEIG and provide services for its members which relate to the

54

practice of law, as long as the EEIG does not itself engage in practice directly with third parties.

An EEIG offers several practical advantages. It is a way of engaging in cross-border activity without significant risk or complex and expensive legal procedures. It can be used to gain access at low cost to advice and to resources across frontiers: 'its flexibility and scope present opportunities and advantages for many firms.'[27]

Re-structuring of law firms and legal practice is thus one way for lawyers to take advantage of the opportunities of the SEM. However, there remain barriers within the market to the establishment of the 'European law firm.' There is a maze of prescriptions and proscriptions involved in opening or expanding a branch office in a European Community country. Paradoxically, some of these barriers are the result of using the very law said to be aimed at their removal.

MARKET BARRIERS

The removal of barriers to individuals and firms offering services throughout the Community is one of the aims of the SEM. According to Jacques Delors, President of the European Commission, freedom of movement and the freedom to work anywhere in the European Community 'implies the right to exercise one's occupational or professional activity anywhere in Europe – for firms, professions and wage-earners alike.'[28] Subject to only a few exceptions, all Community nationals are entitled to work, to seek work, to set up business, and to provide services in any member-state, and to be treated on the same terms as any national of the 'host' country. Translating these entitlements into reality, however, has not proved easy.

Entry to the practice of law is restricted in each member-state, mainly by requirements related to the education and training of lawyers. For lawyers (and law firms) wishing to engage in practice elsewhere in the Community, the key questions are whether the qualification to practice in one member state is recognized or not by another; whether they have to undergo a period of re-qualification in whole or in part, before they can work; and whether additional barriers have been placed in their way. For the profession too, there are implications concerning their role in the establishment of a market for legal services throughout the European Community (and beyond).

The European Community has adopted a series of directives to deal with these questions. The underlying principle appears to be that lawyers who have trained and are qualified to practice in one member state can practice in another. The legal services directive[29] sets out general principles governing the provision of legal services by lawyers of one member-state in another. Any self-employed person may offer services on a temporary stay in another member-state if the home-state titles are used and, subject to requirements to work in conjunction with a practising lawyer of that state, may represent clients in legal proceedings.

The EC directive on the recognition of higher-education diplomas,[30] which was supposed to come into effect by 4 January 1991, goes much further. This provides that lawyers (and others whose access to work is restricted by state requirements that they have at least three years' university level education or equivalent, plus any appropriate job-based training) who have qualified in one member-state will have the opportunity of obtaining full access to the legal profession in another member-state.

The principle underlying this directive is that of mutual recognition: professional education and training may vary in detail between member states, but any fully trained professional in a given field is as likely to have much the same knowledge as that required of his or her counterpart in a different Community state. Accordingly, a fully qualified professional in one member-state is deemed to be a fully qualified professional in another and has the right to use the relevant professional title. This approach avoids the need to agree a common curriculum for all professionals in a given sector and to harmonize entrance requirements.[31]

However, further problems have emerged. Not only has implementation of these principles in practice lacked uniformity throughout the European Community but the regulations can also be used to undermine the very principles on which they are said to be based. As a result, barriers remain and, indeed, some new ones have been created. The conflict between attempts to protect domestic 'markets' and the aims of the SEM to promote competition, free trade, and deregulation are visible in the market for legal services.

The 1977 directive, although modest in its scope, opened the door to multinational practice. It thereby posed the first threat of foreign competition to 'host' lawyers. In Germany, attempts were made to minimize this threat and to 'circumvent the legal services directive'[32] by requiring that visiting lawyers always be accompanied by a 'host' lawyer in all proceedings. This provision was struck down by the European Court of Justice.[33]

The 1988 directive poses a more significant threat to protectionist-minded states. It provides that persons with diplomas obtained in one member state can claim to have those diplomas recognized in another where he or she wishes to be established and take up the practice of law. However, the directive also contains two safeguards which may be used by member states to restrict access to their professions. The first is relatively minor in scope. If the length of education and training in one state is shorter than that required in the country to which they wish to move, the professional may be required to produce evidence of up to four years experience as a fully qualified professional in another Community country. The second may offer more opportunities to discourage foreign lawyers. Where there is a substantial difference in the content of education and training, incoming professionals may be required to undergo a procedure designed to ensure that they have acquired the extra knowledge required. The content may differ because of differences in the boundaries of a profession in different states or because there are individual subjects which are specific to one member-state and which are essential in order to operate as a fully qualified professional in that state.

The procedure may comprise either an examination – the aptitude test – or a period of assessed supervised practice not exceeding three years – the adaptation test. While many incoming professionals wishing to obtain the benefit of this directive can choose between the two, for professions whose practice requires a precise knowledge of national law and involves providing advice and/or assistance on national law as an essential and constant aspect of the professional activity (in the United Kingdom, these professions are the legal professions, patent agents, patent attorneys, accountants, and auditors), the member state can derogate from this principle and specify either an aptitude test or an adaptation period. However, such professionals should not be re-tested on or asked to re-qualify in areas their training has already covered. Germany, France, and the United Kingdom require aptitude tests comprising written and oral examinations.[34]

Although the aim of the directive is to remove barriers to the proper practice of law throughout the European Community, there is still scope for obstructing such freedom and it remains to be seen whether – and, if so, how – barriers are re-built. After all, the directive does not mean that member states are required to accept qualifications gained in other member states. They are merely prevented from rejecting such qualifications without good reason.[35] Good reasons can be found not in any qualitative difference between one lawyer and another, but on the grounds that the professional body (probably with a view to protecting the interests of the 'host' profession) can re-construct the education and training requirements so that the content of the foreign lawyer's education and training is likely to be significantly different from that of the 'host' country. Even if there is a challenge before the European Court of Justice, sufficient disincentives will have been created to deter prospective foreign lawyers during a period when the 'host' lawyers can adjust to the new realities of the SEM after 1992. The directive was framed deliberately in fairly general terms so as to ensure that its provisions could apply to a large number and wide variety of professions. This has left open the possibility of different interpretation. It is not surprising, therefore, that significant discretion – some would say 'too much'[36] – is likely to remain with the examiners.

How serious can the obstruction be? It has been argued that it 'seems doubtful whether the aptitude test will have much practical relevance.'[37] While United Kingdom firms may want branch offices, for example, in Germany and to collaborate with local firms, 'few will want to staff those offices with UK lawyers, admitted both in the UK *and* as 'integrated lawyers' in Germany.'[38] While specialists on United Kingdom law will be needed in the Frankfurt office, and on German law in the London office, 'when it comes to pleading in court or advising on local law, the home state lawyer, more familiar with professional customs and rules, will probably do a better job than the 'integrated lawyer'.'[39] A United Kingdom lawyer can, in any case, appear in a German court, accompanied by a German lawyer – perhaps a colleague in a multi-national partnership – under the terms of the legal services directive.[40] On the other hand, a recent survey of British professional bodies suggested that the need for qualifications achieved in higher education which would enable their members to get jobs in other member states was of 'paramount importance.'[41] And in the SEM, it has been argued that European Community law will be 'the most transferable of law as well as the one where there is likely to be the greatest volume increase in legal proceedings.'[42]

However, the directive may be used to undermine the goals of the SEM. The regulation of professions in various states remains 'untouched'[43] by the directive; the European Court of Justice has recognized that each member state is free to regulate its own legal profession;[44] and individuals still have to meet the requirements of the particular body regulating the profession. Thus, in France, an aptitude test will also determine whether foreign lawyers can join the French profession. But from 1 January 1992, all foreign lawyers are banned from practising unless they do become members. This is because, in December 1990, the professions (*conseils juridiques* and *avocats*) have been unified into a single profession – *avocats* – and a monopoly on the provision of all legal services created for its members. Foreign lawyers who are not members of the new French legal profession will thus be prohibited from giving legal advice, even on foreign and European law: 'A Greek lawyer advising a Dutch client on Greek law in Paris is breaking French law unless he has re-qualified.'[45] Foreign law firms will also be prohibited from establishing branch offices.[46] These changes turn 'the right to join the French profession into an obligation to do so,'[47] regardless of the law he or she intends to practice. The only exceptions are lawyers and firms established before 31 December 1990 who will automatically become members of the French legal profession. So, rather than open up legal practice to European Community nationals (and others), the French approach has been to re-define the requirements of the French lawyer and the legal services which are the monopoly of lawyers. A similar approach to France is said to exist in Luxembourg and Greece.[48]

France has used a 'clever interpretation'[49] of the 1988 directive to retain a competitive advantage for its lawyers in relation to practice in France by its new law. This is an irony since that law was designed to create an SEM 'Open for Professions.'[50] Proving that the French law is in breach of the Treaty of Rome may not be easy: restrictions on practice can be justified if they are for the public good and what this is remains undefined when it comes to legal services.

The 1988 directive applies only to 'regulated' professions. In the United Kingdom, the designated regulatory authorities include the Law Societies of England and Wales, Scotland, and Northern Ireland, the General Council of the Bar for England and Wales, The Faculty of Advocates, the Executive Council of the Inn of Court of Northern Ireland and the Chartered Institute of Patent Agents. This means that a qualified lawyer from the United Kingdom will only be eligible for entry to engage in activities in another member-state if those activities are regulated in another member-state and where the local professional body is included in the annex to the directive. There is the possibility, then, that, rather than promote the goals of the SEM, the 1988 directive 'enshrines the anti-competitive practices to be found in each national market and does nothing to bring the profession up to a common standard throughout Europe.'[51] Each profession can make its own rules – on the methods of providing services, the structure and organization of the firm, relationships with others inside and out of the profession and country, and so forth – with which all its members must comply. Each member-state can define the scope of the lawyers' monopoly and, indeed, of the work that the lawyer is regulated to do.

In practice, as Eidenmuller points out, the main impact of the directives will be to force each member state to 'reassess the whole body of law governing their own legal professions.'[52] Thus, in Germany, lawyers are normally admitted to one civil court only – the 'localization' rule. But if Community lawyers use their freedom to provide legal services throughout Germany under the legal services directive, for example as part of a multi-national partnership, not tied to a particular court, this will discriminate against German lawyers. As Eidenmuller concludes: 'International deregulation is bound to have a feedback on the national level.'[53] It may, for example, be inequitable that an English lawyer can qualify in France and be able to provide all legal services whereas a French lawyer has to qualify in accordance with the requirements of several designated authorities in the United Kingdom (although there may be free movement within certain parts of the country for certain professionals). This situation exists despite the fact that the United Kingdom market can be described as pro-competitive.

In short, the Delors declaration on professional freedom of movement has not yet been achieved and its future is uncertain. The market for legal services in the SEM remains in a process of dynamic change. There will be 'winners' and 'losers' and battles will be played out both within and outside the profession. That is the nature of a market. What are some of the implications for lawyers in the market?

IMPLICATIONS: LAWYERS IN THE EUROPEAN MARKET

There are many implications and questions. Three will be tackled here. First, what kind of law firm will emerge in the context of the legal environment of the SEM? What will 'tomorrow's European lawyer' look like? Secondly, what are the implications of the apparent emphasis placed by the market on commercial rather than professional goals? Finally, what are the implications of the opening up of competition for legal services?

1. *Towards the Large Law Firm?*

In the United States of America, the dominant player in the legal profession is the large law firm. The development there of the large law firm and the distinctive style of lawyering associated with it has been described as the 'great innovation in lawyering in the past century.'[54] In their study of the 'Big Law Firm' in the United States, Galanter and Palay identify three periods in the century-long history of the large firm: the origins of the big firm; the golden age, circa 1960; and the transformation of the big firm since then. It is the latter period which best mirrors developments in Europe. In the United States since the 1960s, there has been a transformation of the legal environment which has affected the large firm:

> the amount and complexity of legal regulation; the frequency of litigation; the amount and tenet of authoritative legal material; the number, co-ordination, and productivity of lawyers; the number of legal actors and the resources they devote to legal activity; the amount of information about law and the velocity with which it circulates.[55]

Large law firms are undergoing the transformation in an environment:

> with more lawyers, competing with more large firms like themselves, all supplied with more technological infrastructure, involved in more contested activity in more varied arenas with more contenders, using a larger, more indeterminate and more diffusely bounded body of legal knowledge.[56]

What has been the effect of this environment on United States law firms? According to Galanter and Palay (echoing many other commentators, particularly Nelson), there have been shifts to larger units of practice with more large and larger firms. This has led to more intense specialization within the firms and the work of various levels being more differentiated. In Nelson's phrase, there are 'finders' who bring in work, 'minders' who manage it and 'grinders' who do it.[57] The work that big firms do has 'changed dramatically'[58] due to an increase in the number, size, and responsibility of in-house legal departments and a surge in corporate litigation since the 1970s. As 'much routine work has been retracted into corporate law departments there has been a great surge of litigation and other risk-prone high-stake transactions.'[59] There has been a 'dramatic turnabout' in the last quarter century:

> A business environment that is more competitive, more insecure, and more uncertain – in which there are more large risk-prone deals, with higher stakes and more regulation to take into account, amid more volatile fluctuations of interest and exchange rates – generates new demand for intensive lawyering.[60]

Moreover:

> The large, contested, and/or risk-prone one-of-a-kind transaction – litigation, takeovers, bankruptcies, and such – makes up a larger portion of what big law firms do.[61]

Firms have become 'more openly commercial'[62]: they engage professional managers and consultants; they engage in aggressive marketing and some take on marketing directors; they use 'rainmakers' to generate business; there is 'lateral movement' between firms' lawyers (and 'headhunters'' firms to facilitate this) and between firms (via mergers). Recruitment activity has intensified; and some firms have adopted the strategy of hiring non-lawyer professionals in order to provide diversified services and, where appropriate, 'one-stop shopping.'[63] As with any business the 'down-side' of this is bankruptcy, de-mergers and, ultimately, dissolution and break-up.

In the United Kingdom, the foundation of a similar legal environment has been laid in the last twenty years. There has been an increase in the size and number of large law firms since the ban on firms with more than twenty partners was removed in 1967. The need for specialist advice, enough 'critical mass' – human and technical resources – to tackle 'heavyweight deals', the creation of a host of initials – TSA, FSA, DTI, SEC – has meant not only that 'everyone wants their own lawyer around' but that the firms have to be large and experienced enough to compete.[64] 'Merger-mania' gripped the profession in the late 1980s; mergers produced the first United Kingdom 'mega-firms' such as Lovell White Durrant, which, when it merged in 1988 became the second largest law firm in Europe, and Clifford Chance. Some of these were a response to the internationalization of legal practice. Thus, one of the main attractions of the merger between Coward Chance and Clifford Turner in 1987 was, according to David Maunder, managing partner at Clifford Turner, 'the excellence of the international 'fit' between the firms, which presents the chance to throw together existing resources to provide a substantial global presence.' He cited the 'opportunities to strengthen the resources available for back-up and support' as the other one.[65] In-house corporate legal departments have also grown rapidly: in 1990 four British companies employed more than fifty lawyers.[66] The picture painted by Galanter and Palay is very similar to the situation in the United Kingdom.[67]

A 'transactions-costs' approach 'illuminates the reasons for the acceleration of merger activity among law firms.'[68] In a market where business is channelled through personal referral networks, a broader net can be cast, by hiring lawyers who have their own networks: 'The acquisition of new partners and the opening of branch offices is like the acquisition of lightning rods who can attract business to their own field as well as to other areas of the firm's practice.'[69] Thus, the spread of firms wishing to set up operations in several countries or to offer services in a number of different states from a United Kingdom base can be seen as an attempt both to offer a greater range of services to domestic clients and to compete with 'host' country lawyers in the national and international legal market-place. When Freshfields opened their Frankfurt office in November 1990, they hired a team of German lawyers. This will allow them to practice local law for German clients as well as United Kingdom and European Community law.

The opening up of the legal services market in Europe, particularly the corporate and commercial sectors, has resulted in a number of claims asserting the actual or impending 'dominant influence' of large United States law firms. There is, undoubtedly, a lively turf war engendered by United States law firms' interest in Europe. This is manifest, for example, in France with the law which restricts legal services to members of the French legal profession, and in Germany with the restructuring of law firms. The creation, in 1990, of Germany's largest law firm with 100 lawyers[70] was stated to be a response not only to the changed demands of German and international business, 'but also to the competition of foreign law firms with many hundreds of lawyers.'[71] There have been longstanding links between the 'élite' American practitioners and Europe. By the mid-1880s, the 'main work of this practice was to

61

serve as legal brokers and intermediaries between large American corporations trying to attract new capital . . . and the investment banking communities of Wall Street and Europe.'[72] More contentious, however, is the claim that 'legal professions in other countries have increasingly emulated the American big firm.'[73] Whether or not this is true, in practice, the SEM is likely to see a disproportionate role played by the individual or firm which is able to dominate the market for private legal services and to meet the needs of the SEM corporate client.

2. *Professionalism versus Commercialism: Tensions within the Profession*

In the United Kingdom of the 1980s and the SEM of the 1990s, the demand for legal services from the corporate and commercial sector has grown at the same time that access to lawyers has been placed on the altar of market forces. Thus, while the United Kingdom government has expressed its belief that 'access to legal services by those who need them is fundamental to the rule of law and the preservation of liberty'[74] there is a danger that competing demands for services may be sacrificed on this altar. The underlying ethos of the SEM, and indeed of the Thatcher government, regarding the reform of legal service provision, has been that of the market. Thus, in the government Green Paper on the work and organization of the legal profession there was no acknowledgment of the public service performed by lawyers.[75] The deregulation of lawyers' services has been aimed at achieving a 'market providing legal services [which] operates freely and efficiently so as to give clients the widest possible choice of cost effective services.'[76]

A market ethos emphasizes the high earnings available to lawyers rather than the public service lawyers can offer, and the need to re-structure to meet the demands of higher paying corporate clients and commercial work. While this largely ignores the fact that the interests, expectations, and needs of different groups of clients in relation to their lawyers are diverse,[77] it means also that in the context of the legal environment of the SEM the dominant 'player' will most probably be 'a creature of private market forces.'[78] The profession's services are available to the highest bidder, but only major corporate actors can afford the price.

Thus, while the SEM and globalization generally provide virtually all lawyers with opportunities, there will be winners and losers. Those who are able to re-organize and re-structure their practices to offer more services to a wider constituency of clients and who can respond more effectively to clients' demands will obtain a competitive advantage in the legal environment of the SEM. Those who wish to hang on to traditional restrictive practices and to suppress competition will lose out. Those who benefit significantly from the expansion of activities in the corporate and commercial sectors will gain. It is a context in which the process of professional transformation is likely to accelerate.

In the United States of America and elsewhere, these issues have fuelled debates on whether law is a profession or a business: has professionalism been

62

sacrificed to commercialism? As Galanter and Palay point out, these debates are as old as the profession itself. However, they believe there are differences now: 'First, the exponential character of growth means that the magnitude of the inevitable structural changes will be far greater than earlier adjustments. Second, changes in the state of knowledge, information, and belief about the legal system make it more difficult to avoid challenge to long-accepted models of professional life':[79] this time, the 'crisis' is the real thing.'[80] In a context of growth, 'collegiality, independence, and public service are likely to be jeopardized.'[81] According to Abel, in the United Kingdom 'the age of professionalism is ending.'[82]

One particular implication of the creation of the SEM is that it is likely to reinforce the existing division of the profession into 'hemispheres.'[83] The legal profession in the United Kingdom is not just made up of two branches, solicitors and barristers. There are many different segments and stratified layers of practice. The finding of Heinz and Laumann[84] in Chicago that there are two 'hemispheres' of legal practice – those who represent corporate clients and large organizations and those who represent individuals – fragmented in terms of social status and client interests, is reflected in predictions in the United Kingdom that large legal aid firms will increasingly take a 'different path of development from the rest of the legal profession, which is already splitting between firms and barristers dependent on commercial work and those dependent on public funds.'[85]

3. Competition for Legal Services

The European market raises other issues with implications for lawyers. For example, as law becomes increasingly international in its scope and operation, there will 'inevitably develop forum shopping.'[86] If the English legal system offers an attractive base for dispute resolution it may thereby become one of the main centres. The move to European regulation may also have the effect of reducing national state controls over the profession, not only through the move to Brussels-based regulation but because the corporate and commercial hemisphere is less dependent on state-created markets such as that based on legal aid.

Another question which the opening up of national frontiers has posed is what are the 'lines of demarcation between the spheres of competence of different forms of know-how.'[87] Historical and comparative reviews of the role played by lawyers[88] reveal quite clearly that 'the work lawyers do within any given society is not preordained';[89] the domains over which different kinds of know-how have jurisdiction depend on various contingencies:

> Although lawyers may seek to claim certain tasks as uniquely their own, these claims are often disputed by competing occupational groups and rejected by society at large.[90]

Dezalay has recently referred to these disputes as 'territorial battles and tribal disputes.'[91]

In the United Kingdom, the Lord Chancellor's department has observed, it is 'important to recognise . . . that . . . access [to legal services] does not necessarily mean access to a lawyer.'[92] Other professions, such as accountants, have been willing to step into the breach left by lawyers in areas such as tax and corporate bankruptcy, while government deregulation has created competition from rival occupations such as licensed conveyancers. Although different types of expertise may be offered by various professions and the 'knowledge which lawyers use in their work is a knowledge of law',[93] that is a knowledge which is not restricted to them.

This is explicitly recognized in the 1988 mutual recognition directive, which allows derogation in the case of a 'legal' profession. This is defined as one which requires a precise knowledge of national law and involves providing advice on national law as a constant and essential aspect of professional activity. In the United Kingdom, the Department of Trade and Industry has made use of this derogation in relation to accountants, patent agents, patent attorneys and auditors.[94]

European lawyers may thus face 'unprecedented competition in the market for advice concerning the law of corporate and public finance' not only from the lawyers of other countries, but from other professions. This, in turn, may stimulate responses within the legal profession. Thus, in the United Kingdom, it has been predicted that there may be some 'innovative developments in fields such as debt restructuring, syndicated money lending and leasing as some solicitors decide to go for non-traditional markets because they face competition from accountants on their own territory.'[95]

One thing is clear. The market for legal services in the new Europe is set for expansion. However, markets involve winners and losers. In the new and wider market lawyers are not simply being presented with the demand for legal work inherent in both deregulation and regulation. They are also being confronted by market barriers and enhanced inter-professional competition. All three factors will shape future developments in the organization of the profession.

These developments, in turn, will affect the nature of legal services on offer. Locating lawyers, and other providers of legal services, squarely in the context of the market also has implications for winners and losers among potential clients. Any move to mega-firms, further emphasis on corporate rather than personal services, enhancement of the tensions between professionalism and commercialism, all will affect the nature of legal services. Where professional services are available to the highest bidder, it may be that only major corporate actors can afford the price. Not just the legal profession but legal services will be affected by being placed on the altar of the market.

NOTES AND REFERENCES

1 See, for example, in the United Kingdom: R. Abel, *The Legal Profession in England and Wales* (1988) (a); R. Abel, 'England and Wales: A Comparison of the Professional Projects of Barristers and Solicitors' in *Lawyers in Society, Vol. I: The Common Law World*, eds. R. Abel and P. Lewis (1988) (b); R. Abel, 'Between Market and State: The Legal Profession in

Turmoil' (1989) (a) 52 *Modern Law Rev.* 285; in the United States of America: R. Nelson, *Partners with Power: The Social Transformation of the Large Law Firm* (1988); R. Abel, *American Lawyers* (1989) (b); M. Galanter and T. Palay, *Tournament of Lawyers: The Transformation of the Big Law Firm* (1991); in western societies: R. Abel and P. Lewis, *Lawyers in Society Vol. I: The Common Law World* (1988) (a); R. Abel and P. Lewis, *Lawyers in Society Vol. II: The Civil Law World* (1988) (b); R. Abel and P. Lewis, *Lawyers in Society Vol. III: Comparative Theories* (1989).

2　Abel, id., 1988(a), 1989(b); Y. Dezalay, 'Putting Justice 'Into Play' on the Global Market: Law, Lawyers, Accountants and the Competition for Financial Services' (1989) 6 *Tidskrift for Rattssociologi* 9; Y. Dezalay, 'Teritorial Battles and Tribal Disputes' (1991) 54 *Modern Law Rev.* 792; M. Burrage, 'Revolution and the Collective Action of the French, American, and English Legal Professions' (1988) 13 *Law and Social Inquiry* 225.

3　Galanter and Palay, op. cit., n. 1.

4　M. J. Osiel, 'Lawyers as Monopolists, Aristocrats, and Entrepreneurs' (1990) 103 *Harvard Law Rev.* 2009; Nelson, op. cit., n. 1; R. Sander and D. Williams, 'Why are There So Many Lawyers? Perspectives on a Turbulent Market' (1989) 14 *Law and Social Inquiry* 431.

5　Lord Chancellor's Department, *The Work and Organisation of the Legal Profession* (1989; Cm. 570) 1.5.

6　id., para. 1.1.

7　In its White Paper *Opening Markets: New Policy on Restrictive Trade Practices* (1989; Cm. 727) the government proposed that there be a prohibition on anti-competitive agreements in professional rules (with the exception of rules on advocacy in court, the conduct of litigation and associated training) in new restrictive trade practices legislation.

8　Lord Chancellor's Department, op. cit., n. 5, para. 1.11.

9　P. Sutherland, 'Address by Mr Peter D. Sutherland' in *The Legal Implications of 1992*, ed. Irish Centre for European Law (1990).

10　id., p. 4. If the European Free Trade Association and the European Community form the European Economic Area (see text below), it will implement 950 directives, 160 regulations, 120 decisions and 300 non-binding instruments.

11　D. J. McBarnet and C. J. Whelan, *Beyond Control? The Regulation of Financial Risk, Corporate Activity and the Single European Market* (forthcoming); D. J. McBarnet and C. J. Whelan, 'Regulating a Competitive Market: The Challenge of Creative Compliance' in *The Internationalisation of the Capital Market and the Regulatory Response*, ed. J. Fingleton (1992).

12　D.J. McBarnet and C.J. Whelan, 'Beyond Control: Law Management and Corporate Governance' in *Corporate Control and Accountability*, eds. J. McCahery, S. Picciotto, and C. Scott (1992); D.J. McBarnet and C.J. Whelan, 'The Elusive Spirit of the Law: Formalism and the Struggle for Legal Control' (1991) 54 *Modern Law Rev.* 848.

13　See, for example, Nelson, op. cit., n. 1; Osiel, op. cit., n. 1; J. Schumpeter, *Capitalism, Socialism and Democracy* (1950); J.W. Hurst, *The Legitimacy of the Business Corporation in the Law of the United States* (1970); R. Gordon, 'Legal Thought and Legal Practice in the Age of American Enterprise 1870–1920' in *Professions and Professional Ideologies in America*, ed. G. Geison (1983).

14　D.J. McBarnet, 'Law, Policy and Legal Avoidance' (1988) *J. of Law and Society* 113; D.J. McBarnet and C.J. Whelan, 'Leapfrog Law: The Development of Priority in Bankruptcy' presented at the Law and Society Association Conference, Washington D.C. (1987).

15　Osiel, for example, has argued (op. cit., n. 4, p. 2060) that 'while civil lawyers have been intolerant of ambiguity, practitioners of common law have reveled in it, seeing it merely as revealing the indispensability of imagination and ingenuity in practical judgment.' He argues (id., pp. 2060–61) that 'differing attitudes of common and civil lawyers toward ambiguity in legal reasoning have led to corresponding differences in the degree of social prominence that they have accepted.'

16　McBarnet and Whelan, op. cit., n. 11.

17　Galanter and Palay, op. cit., n. 1, p. 45.

18　A. Hermann, *Financial Times*, 17 May 1989.

19 Sutherland, op. cit., n. 9, p. 23.

20 Department of Trade and Industry, *Single Market News* (Winter 1991) 1.

21 The timetable may be affected. Three days before the 'initialling' of the EEA treaty in November 1991 (after which changes to it could not be made), the European Court of Justice asked for clarification of the treaty, in particular, its relationship with the proposed EEA court. For example, would the ECJ be bound by decisions of the new court? The ECJ will delivered an opinion in mid-December, after this article was written.

22 Following proposals in the Green Paper, *The Work and Organisation of the Legal Profession*, op. cit., n. 5, and the White Paper, *Legal Services: A Framework for the Future* (1989; Cm. 740). See the Courts and Legal Services Act 1990, s. 60.

23 id. (White Paper), para. 13.2.

24 Lord Chancellor's Department, op. cit., n. 5, para. 12.17.

25 H. Eidenmuller, 'Deregulating the Market for Legal Services in the European Community: Freedom of Establishment and Freedom to Provide Services for EC Lawyers in the Federal Republic of Germany' (1990) 53 *Modern Law Rev*. 604.

26 Under the six categories in Rule 8 (1) (a) to (f). Rule 4 states that solicitors must comply with the *Conseil Consultat des Barraux Européens* (*CCBE* – Council for the Bars and Law Societies of Europe) Code of Conduct for Lawyers in the European Community.

27 Institute of Chartered Accountants in England and Wales, *File Notes 1992 No. 2 – European Economic Interest Groupings* (1990).

28 Quoted in Department of Trade and Industry, *Europe Open for Professions* (1991).

29 Directive 77/249 OJ 22.3.77 L 78/17.

30 Directive 89/48 OJ 21.12.88 L 19/16. This will also apply in the EFTA.

31 This has been done to a greater or lesser extent for doctors, dentists, nurses, midwives, vets, pharmacists, and architects (the latter taking nineteen years to be adopted).

32 Eidenmuller, op. cit., n. 24, p. 607.

33 The court held that working in conjunction with a 'host' lawyer can only be required where representation by a lawyer is mandatory under domestic law: *Re Lawyers Services: EC Commission* v. *Germany* Case 427/85, [1989] 2 CMLR 677. See Eidenmuller, id.

34 In the United Kingdom, the Law Society, under the Solicitors' Act 1974 ss. 2 and 80, introduced the Qualified Lawyers Transfer Regulations 1990. These make provision for two three-hour examinations, on property law and litigation, and a one-and-a-half-hour paper on professional conduct and accounts, and an oral test on the principles of common law with special reference to contract and tort, and a choice of either criminal or commercial law. The test will not be imposed on every Community lawyer seeking to practice in the United Kingdom; only those who have not studied the common law will have to take the whole test. The rationale for preferring an aptitude test over an adaptation test according to the General Council of the Bar was that the latter would amount to 'simple "flying hours"' . . . however poor the pilot.' (General Council of the Bar, *Quality of Justice – The Bar's Response* (1989) 134.

35 Department of Trade and Industry, op. cit., n. 28; see also, *Irene Vlassopoulou* v. *Ministerium fur Justiz, Bundes-und Europaan-gelegenheiten, Baden-Wurttemberg* Case C-340/89, European Court of Justice.

36 Eidenmuller, op cit, n. 24, p. 607.

37 id.

38 id.

39 id.

40 id., p. 608.

41 Pickup Europe Unit, *Trade Associations and Professional Bodies: Facing the Single European Market* (1991).

42 Sutherland, op. cit., n. 9, p. 6.

43 EC fact sheet no. 8, 1991.

44 See *Unectef* v. *Heylens* Case 222/86 European Court of Justice [1987] ECR 4097.

45 J. Carr, 'A lucrative law unto themselves', *Times*, 26 March 1991.

46 This would appear to overturn the decision in 1988 of *Claude Gullung* v. *Conseil de l'Ordre des Advocats du Barreau de Colmar* (1988), Case 292/86 which suggested that a British firm could

open an office in Paris and would have the right of establishment without registering and without becoming subject to French professional rules.

47 R. Rice 'Difficulty in defining a European legal eagle', *Financial Times*, 11 February 1991.
48 id.
49 Carr, op. cit., n. 44.
50 Department of Trade and Industry, op. cit., n. 27.
51 D. Waller, 'Accountancy: The Challenge of Europe', *Financial Times*, 30 November 1990.
52 Eidenmuller, op. cit., n. 24, p. 608.
53 id.
54 Galanter and Palay, op. cit., n. 1, p. 1.
55 id., p. 37.
56 id., p. 45.
57 Nelson, op. cit., n. 1, p. 69.
58 Galanter and Palay, op. cit., n. 1, p. 48.
59 id., p. 51.
60 id.
61 id., p. 52.
62 id.
63 The District of Columbia was the first to allow multi-disciplinary partnerships in the United States of America: Galanter and Palay, op. cit., n. 1, pp. 66, 124.
64 D. Blackhurst, 'The Lawyers Take Over' *Sunday Times*, 20 August 1989.
65 *New Law J.*, 24 April 1987, 377.
66 *The Lawyer*, 9 October 1990.
67 See also Abel, op. cit., n. 1, 1988 (a).
68 Nelson, op. cit., n. 1, p. 68.
69 id.
70 Following the merger of Bruckhaus Kreifels Winkhaus & Lieberknecht, Westrick & Eckholdt, and Stegemann Sieveking Lutteroth & Steeger.
71 *Times*, 20 November 1990
72 G. Gawalt, *The New High Priests: Lawyers in the Post Civil War America* (1984) 59, quoted in Galanter and Palay, op. cit., n. 1, p. 6.
73 Galanter and Palay, op. cit., n. 1, p. 2.
74 Lord Chancellor's Department, op. cit., n. 5, para. 2.3.
75 R. Smith, 'The Green Papers and Legal Services' (1989) 52 *Modern Law Rev.* 527.
76 Lord Chancellor's Department, op. cit., n. 5, para. 1.1.
77 Smith, op. cit., n. 75.
78 Nelson, op. cit., n. 1, p. 287. This assumes that the principles of the SEM will operate in due course in countries like France.
79 Galanter and Palay, op. cit., n. 1, p. 69.
80 id., p. 3.
81 id.
82 Abel, op. cit., n. 1, 1988 (b), p. 66.
83 J.P. Heinz and E.O. Laumann, *Chicago Lawyers: The Social Structure of the Bar* (1982).
84 id., p. 219.
85 Smith, op. cit., n. 75, p. 538. See also Osiel, op. cit., n. 4, p. 2047: 'the greater autonomy from commercial interests sought by current critics of the profession has historically been obtained by lawyers only through greater dependence upon the state and landed interests or through significant sacrifices in social prominence.'
86 Sutherland, op. cit., n. 9, p. 6.
87 Dezalay, op. cit., n. 2, 1991.
88 Such as A. Abbott, *The System of Professions: An Essay on the Division of Expert Labour* (1988); Abel and Lewis, op. cit., n. 1, 1988 (a), (b), 1989.
89 Osiel, op. cit., n. 4, p. 2025.
90 id.
91 Dezalay, op. cit., n. 2 (1991).

92 Lord Chancellor's Department, op. cit., n. 5, para. 2.3.
93 Osiel, op. cit., n. 4, p. 2053.
94 The directive allows member states in these circumstances to *require* other nationals to pass an aptitude test.
95 E. Fennell, 'Silver Linings among the Clouds', *Times*, 8 January 1991.

Local Government Lawyers: The 1980s and Beyond

MARK STALLWORTHY*

As the climate of local government service provision has changed radically in the 1980s, so has the role and function of local government lawyers. They are increasingly required to be more than service providers within a public service ethos. Other roles have burgeoned, particularly those relating to corporate advice, at a time of significant corporate change. I argue that competing policy pressures have placed local government lawyers in the invidious position of holding the middle ground, with a view to what local government members and officers would like to achieve and to what can be achieved within the often shifting parameters of the law.

THE WIDER CANVAS

Constitutional structures proved inadequate to deal with what was often a breakdown of relations between central and local government during the 1980s. One author has sketched a constitutional settlement which has preferred 'to entrust the protection of rights to the ordinary law of the land and the due processes of the courts, and to leave our institutions to evolve experimentally under the guiding principle of parliamentary sovereignty'.[1] Such an *ad hoc* constitutional approach has in turn left the institution of local government exposed to the dictates of central executive dominance.

Moreover, some of the clashes between local and central government played out in the courts have increased pressures on local government lawyers. The contribution of the courts has at times shown a notable lack of understanding of local government policy priorities, seen for instance in the now infamous case of *Bromley London Borough Council* v. *Greater London Council*[2] which, in view of the approach of most of the appellate judges involved, arguably provided a modern-day model of *Roberts* v. *Hopwood*.[3] That said, and despite the litigious atmosphere of the 1980s, judicial modes of dispute resolution are perhaps inappropriate to the operation of central-local relations. The increasingly formalized nature of legal control over local government has resulted in further legal constraints upon local decision-making and wider ministerial powers of intervention. This effect has been

* *Solicitor, Research and Development Unit, Wilde Sapte, Queensbridge House, Upper Thames Street, London EC4V 3BD, England*

69

widespread, although the mounting restraint upon the raising of local revenues and on borrowing powers is especially indicative of this development. In relation to the nexus between finance and autonomy, two separate developments have now been combined. First, reliance upon central grant has led to enforced constraint at a time of retrenchment. This confirmed the trend envisaged as far back as 1954 whereby 'as the Treasury came to provide more and more money for the local councils, the voices of Whitehall would speak more often and with greater insistence'.[4] Secondly, as regards the 'dominium' of local financial resources, there has been a series of measures restricting local expenditure levels as well as the raising of capital. Writing in 1981, one writer warned that such a development would mean that 'to all intents and purposes (local government) would have no legal independence from the centre'.[5]

The resulting dynamic of change can be seen in the increased application of market forces into traditional areas of public service provision. For example, in housing, central policies have included mandatory sales of housing stock, and capital restrictions including those upon the application of proceeds. In bus transport, activities have been opened up to the commercial sector. In other key areas, such as planning and inner city regeneration, the role of local government has been constrained and in some instances residualized. The application of a market rationale is of course all part of a broader picture. The policies reflect a central commitment to market forces as an effective allocator of resources.

In constitutional terms, the diminution of the role of local government is a sharp illustration of how far the centre may go in unravelling (as indeed in extending) a communitarian philosophy of service provision. Local government is most noticeably active in the areas of public service provision and of wealth transfers. It may be that local government is destined to have 'fewer functions and responsibilities . . . less ambitious aspirations . . . and would be more supportive of, perhaps even dependent on, the local private sector, and so must require, raise and receive less finance'.[6] In circumstances where the centre has pursued policies espousing freedom of choice, local government service provision has been seen as a constraint upon this objective. There is also perhaps an inherent distrust of devolved power bases. In contrast, it has been argued that local government:

> however inconvenient, foolish or inefficient . . . (is) essential to the system of limited government. Any central government, intent on increasing its own powers and decreasing opportunities for dissent from alternative approaches to its policies, will sooner or later feel the need to attack and emasculate these alternative governments, the alternative centres of power, at their electoral and financial roots.[7]

Local government lawyers have accordingly been faced with a series of new challenges. In some ways local government has benefited, for instance, in the move towards greater openness.[8] Moreover, the arrival of compulsory competitive tendering has led to a more structured approach at local government level to the costs of service provision.[9] This has infiltrated beyond the level of direct service organizations, whose activities have been compulsorily put out to tender, to central service departments such as legal departments. The government has now produced a consultation paper looking towards a future reform of municipal management structures. This envisages the possibility of cabinet-style executives, and other suggestions with a view to improving the efficiency of decision-making and the efficacy of local government. It contains a declaration of a theme much developed in recent years, namely that:

> councils should be looking to contract out work to whoever can deliver services most efficiently and effectively, thus enabling the authority to be more responsive to the wishes of their electorate. . . . local councils increasingly need different skills to meet the challenge of their developing role as enablers rather than providers.[10]

In this so called enabling role, local authorities would consist essentially of tight units of operation, contracting services out to, and monitoring the performance of, independent contractors. Much depends upon chosen objectives – and the evenness of the playing field. It is noteworthy that the controversial report of the Archbishop of Canterbury's commission on urban priority areas emphasized the need to return to a 'common-sense view that what matters is whether expenditure utilises available resources to meet genuine needs, irrespective of whether it is undertaken in the private sector or through government provision'.[11] Whatever the balance of public provision and private provision, clearly a mix now exists and is unlikely to be unscrambled. The local government lawyer remains crucial to the process. Indeed, some now involved in local government may be engaged working in the private sector in the future and this may be one indicator of how far, in the atmosphere of competition, private sector law firms make progress into areas particularly of service provision.

Whilst lawyers operating in local government do not themselves provide (or ordinarily provide) a service direct to the public, the services of local government generally are amongst the most visible. The Thatcher years saw over one hundred pieces of legislation directly relating to local government. These included sixteen major statutes, including the Rates Act 1984, which introduced rate capping, and, latterly, the Local Government Finance Act 1988 which introduced in England and Wales the community charge, or poll tax. Then, in pursuit of the policy objective that local authorities be required to undertake certain activities on a competitive basis, the government produced the Local Government Act 1988. The initial sally into this field was the Local Government Planning and Land Act 1980, with respect to certain maintenance and construction contracts. In the 1988 Act, a number of direct service activities became designated activities for the purposes of compulsory competitive tendering. Defined activities were the collection of refuse, cleaning of buildings, street cleansing, catering for purposes of schools and welfare as well as other catering, the maintenance of grounds, and the repair and maintenance of vehicles.[12] To these, the management of sports and leisure activities has subsequently been added.[13]

The 1988 Act also contained a number of sweeper-up provisions designed to further other policy objectives. Thus, for example, provision was made, according to the long title to the Act, 'to prohibit the promotion of

71

homosexuality by local authorities'. There was also further control placed upon local authorities' powers of 'propaganda' with regard to political issues, this being a process which had been started especially in the Local Government Act 1986.[14] A significant piece of legislation has been the Local Government and Housing Act 1989. In part I of this Act, for example, in accordance with recommendations made in the Widdicombe report,[15] provisions were made restricting political activities on the part of holders of certain posts. Thus, it is provided that the holders of what are defined as politically restricted posts, are disqualified from becoming a member of another local authority or the House of Commons or the European Parliament. The contract of employment of every such person is deemed to incorporate certain provisions restricting such political activities. This particular reform dealt with the issue of so called twin-tracking, much criticized in the Widdicombe Report. A financial minimum salary provision for those to be affected was also made.[16] Officers giving regular advice to the authority or its committees or speaking on behalf of the authority on a regular basis to journalists and broadcasters must be included in the restricted list. The 1989 Act also contained, in parts IV and V, major reforms of the finance and expenditure controls on local authorities and important alterations to discretionary expenditure powers and to the availability of municipal interests in private companies.

For this sector to be subjected constantly to further arrangements and re-arrangements is no new thing. What is new is the context of law-making: a major cumulative change in the ways of operation of local government brought about in an incremental fashion. There has been surprisingly little structural change. To date, in terms of structure, the Local Government Act 1985 saw the abolition of the Greater London Council and the six Metropolitan County Councils. A more broad-ranging structural overhaul is awaited.[17] Given the climate of change, it is unsurprising that the body of local government lawyers has increased markedly in recent times – although, as the Audit Commission has recently pointed out, not at the rate of lawyers in private practice.[18] The larger firms in the field of private practice have gone for high levels of growth during the 1980s, especially those situated in the City of London, where significant new areas of fee-earning have emerged. High levels of expenditure control have meant that the same flexibility of response has not been available to local government.

Increased demands have been met in other ways. For instance, the use of para-legal staff has been of particular value. This can be illustrated in two specific areas. As a result of the Housing Act 1980, the discretionary element was taken out of local government council house sales policies. The impact of the central government policy of council house sales, aimed at creating a 'property-owning democracy' upon a wider basis, has been profound. Indeed, a famous initial and unsuccessful challenge to the Secretary of State's powers under the 1980 Act is an interesting example of the pressures on local government lawyers in areas of inter-governmental conflict.[19] Nevertheless, the resulting extra administrative responsibilities have mainly been met by in-

72

house provision. Given the nature of the property-holding portfolio, and its ready amenability to a standardized system, para-legal staff have proved an invaluable resource. An illustration of a less novel kind is the use of para-legal staff for court work. By section 223 of the Local Government Act 1972, any member or officer, authorized by the authority to prosecute or defend on the authority's behalf or to appear on the authority's behalf in proceedings before a magistrates court, is entitled to prosecute or defend or to appear there notwithstanding anything contained in other legislation, and to conduct any such proceedings, although not a solicitor holding a current practising certificate.[20]

Some changes have had less of an impact throughout the local government legal service than might have been expected. The principles and processes of local government finance have undergone the most sustained series of changes during the Thatcher years. Arguably, indeed, legal developments in this were the harbinger of much that has changed elsewhere. Certainly, the alterations in the early 1980s as well as the (temporary) introduction of targets and penalties into the rate support grant mechanism, betokened a move to increased central control.[21] The apotheosis of this process was perhaps the introduction of rate-capping and thereafter the introduction of the community charge.[22] It must be noted however that the numbers working within local government legal departments are dwarfed by those working within the equivalent finance departments. Thus, at the level of service provision, up to and including the enforcement of the legislation, local government finance officers have generally played the larger role.

LAWYERS AS SERVICE PROVIDERS

Local government lawyers require a wide variety of skills, going well beyond the bounds of specialist practice in substantive law fields. It is recognized that those in private practice, say as sole practitioners, may have to develop an array of abilities other than dealing with the legal caseload. Moreover, as regards the larger City-type practices, the required skills must reflect a more sophisticated corporate structure. A key distinctive feature of the role of local government lawyers within the organization is that it operates upon three essential layers. There is the level which is concerned with service provision, but there are also important monitoring and corporate roles.

Lawyers will operate in a multiplicity of fields of service provision, and most pursue individual specialisms. These increasingly include areas of social welfare (the newly introduced Children Act 1989 is of major significance and will likely increase workloads). Planning law offers an illustration of an area of growth in recent years. Planning activity has been economy-driven, for, despite the Local Government Planning and Land Act 1980, and what effectively amounted to a consolidation in the Town and Country Planning Act 1990, the first significant piece of planning legislation of the present government is the Planning and Compensation Act 1991.

Many local government lawyers have had to acquaint themselves with a new application of commercial and contract law skills, in the emerging field of compulsory competitive tendering. This development is crucial to an understanding of the changing roles of local government lawyers. Moreover, it impacts significantly upon the nature of the operational structure in which they will continue to work, and will be considered further below. The whole process of compulsory tendering has required lawyers to develop a more sophisticated understanding of the operations of other service departments and of the needs of the client authority.

It has been necessary to produce contract documentation within the wider context of other policy pressures, respectively within the home authority and from central government. These arise, for instance, in the operation of the fair competition provisions in the Local Government Act 1988.[23] Thus, where it is intended to contract with the authority's own direct services organization, in entering into the contract and in doing anything else in connection with the contract before entering into it, the authority must not act in a manner likely to restrict, distort or prevent competition. This has proved particularly contentious as the government has sought to flesh out what might be considered to be fair competition by means of separate guidance.[24] Construction of such a general provision has not surprisingly proved a matter of difficulty. This is an important incident of compulsory competitive tendering legislation and has made stern demands upon local government lawyers, say, as to the likelihood of enforcement action being taken by the Secretary of State for the Environment.[25]

LAWYERS AS CORPORATE ADVISERS

Lawyers also play a central role at the corporate level of local government activity. By this is meant the operation of the authority as an elected and policy making body. Accordingly, lawyers are called upon to advise the council and also its committees and sub-committees which operate under delegated authority. This involves a welter of drafting work, in particular, for committee reports prepared by lay officers are likely to be scrutinized by lawyers or, indeed, drafted in whole or in part by them. Local government leaders and committee chairs require the direct support of senior local government officers, and lawyers are crucial to this process.

There are a variety of ways in which this can be accomplished. For example, in the smaller authorities in particular, the chief executive may well be a lawyer. More likely, there will be a separate department, say, a department of law and administration, where a lawyer may fulfil the function of secretary and lawyer to the council. It may be that the legal role is separated from the administrative, or secretary's, load.[26] Whichever arrangement is in place, not only will a lawyer be a central member of the authority's management team but other senior lawyers are likely to have important roles servicing

74

committees and other groups, and preparing documentation for consideration by elected members and chief officers.

In fulfilling this corporate role, lawyers operate within a sphere of activity which is the creation of statute. As statutory corporations, it remains essential that local authorities comply with the doctrine of *ultra vires* in carrying out their activities. The interest rate swap case of *Hazell* v. *London Borough of Hammersmith and Fulham*[27] points up how inter-dependent are significant players in the private and public sectors. The case illustrates also the continuing constraints operating upon local authorities. In that case, lawyers have had to wrestle with the apparatus for financial management of local authorities as contained in schedule 13 of the Local Government Act 1972. The mechanism, known as interest-rate swaps, in its multitudinous forms, was initially set up as a hedge, and a widely recognized one at that, against risks attendant on the movement of interest rates. The London Borough of Hammersmith and Fulham developed a major exposure, beyond that of other authorities.

The final judgment of the House of Lords was that such transactions were beyond the legal power of the authority. The House would not take a lead from the less restrictive approach of the Court of Appeal (especially as regards activities devoted to putting things right once the *ultra vires* spectre had been raised by the district auditor). The 1972 Act (which pre-dated this particular market) was construed so as not to extend the powers of local authorities to operate in this field. Thus, a major flexibility of response open to those, say, in the private sector was denied. This confirmation was to some unsurprising in view of the common law's strict line on *ultra vires* throughout its rather turbulent history.[28] This came at a time ironically when the Companies Act of 1989 was coming into force, section 108 in effect abolishing the doctrine in company law.[29]

Generally, as a result, local authority lawyers must continue to tread carefully due to the continuing limitations caused by the status of the authority as a statutory corporation. One particular result, in the light of the new competitive market, is the impact of the prohibition upon local authority 'trading'. It has long been recognized that local authorities can only trade with specified statutory authorization. Some exceptions to this have developed and, for example, many local authority lawyers are happy to sanction the selling off of, say, products which are genuinely residual surplus to the carrying out of an *intra vires* operation. Conversely, a number of local authorities have apparently set up businesses as sidelines and have looked at these as a way of augmenting revenues. This issue is by no means resolved and the *Hazell* case brings a clear resolution of the question no nearer. Of most concern to local government lawyers are the pressures to think of innovative ways of dealing with this problem. Direct service organizations are having to operate in a competitive environment and commonly now have the experience of seeing their activities put out to tender either voluntarily or in accordance with statutory requirements. Not surprisingly, many direct service organization officers feel that they have to operate with one hand tied behind their back in circumstances where they are unable to look for economies of scale, and so on, in the same way that other operators in the market can.

INSTITUTIONAL INCOHERENCE

The direct service organizations have been the first to find themselves facing genuine economic competition. Strangely, despite the creation of these, and their increasing separation from the client authority, there is no coherent legal regime applied to them. At law, these organizations carry out certain of the functions of local authorities, although statutory grants of power make no reference to them as identifiably separate. The doctrine of *ultra vires* applies to their activities. In the preparation of business plans, it has accordingly been necessary to look for statutory authority and test the relevant activity against this. This, therefore, has been a source of perplexity, and even potentially of conflict between lawyers and other local government officers. The recent legislation requiring exposure to competition with especially the private sector has seen the greater recognition of the new entity with references to the separation of functions. There does exist a requirement for separate accounting as well as for a rate of return on capital, the 1980 Act and the 1988 Act enabling the Secretary of State to determine required rates of return on capital.[30] Even such requirements, however, have been introduced in a low-key way.[31]

Therefore, in terms of its activities, it still cannot be said that the direct service organization can be viewed separately from the authority. As a result, any consideration of what may be a lawful function, crucial to the problem of survival in a climate of economic competition, is hindered. Not all local authority functions require this specific recognition of statute. Exceptions include the creation of agency agreements authorized by the Local Government Act 1972.[32] A further extension enabling the provision of certain goods and services to other public authorities is contained in the Local Authorities (Goods and Services) Act 1970. The most contentious potential foundation for extending local authority activities is contained in the 1972 Act whereby local authorities may 'do anything . . . which is calculated to facilitate, or is conducive or incidental to, the discharge of any of their functions'.[33] It is this residual provision which is commonly looked to by local authorities in seeking to justify activities as lawful. There are many occasions on which the legal skills as well as the innovative abilities of local government lawyers have been put to the test, with the position at common law not always providing sufficient guidance.[34]

What is clear is that, in its reforms in 1980 and 1988, the government has not reshaped permitted legal structures to allow local authorities free rein in market competition with the private sector. For the lawyer involved in advising client departments and direct service organizations, this exercise in policy priorities creates obvious difficulties. The fact is that legislation such as the Local Government Act 1988 was passed for specific purposes, and in that a line can be taken to have been drawn under those priorities, it was inevitable that commercial and legal problems should emerge.

THE CORPORATE LAWYER IN LOCAL GOVERNMENT

The corporate role can be illustrated in a number of ways. The obvious factor which must weigh heavily on the mind of a local government lawyer is the financial impact of policy decisions. These decisions may be taken by council or by committee or by chief officers under schemes of delegated authority. At a time of stricter control of revenue spending and of capital budget allocations and capital expenditure, this can be a major constraint. This paper does not devote attention to the intricacies of controls on local government spending. However, beyond this, there are financial implications in many day-to-day decisions.

For instance, it has not always been clear what the financial implications might be for a local authority upon a successful application for an interlocutory injunction. Local authorities have a specific statutory power to seek injunctions as part of the machinery of enforcement under otherwise empowering legislation.[35] In effect, therefore, enforcement can be over the whole range of local government activity. Thus, for example, it may be necessary to consider seeking an injunction against a statutory nuisance under the Environmental Protection Act 1990, where it is considered that the criminal remedies are insufficient, in the circumstances of the case, to ensure compliance and there is indeed a specific power to this effect.[36] Another example of local authority fire-fighting arose with regard to the phenomenon of acid house parties. Once again, the authorities often had, in principle, a right of action in the criminal court, perhaps under the Local Government (Miscellaneous Provisions) Act 1976 (or, for example, for public nuisance). Similarly, whilst the heat may have been taken out of the Euro-argument regarding Sunday trading, for the present (although confusion remains as to the precise impact of the European Court of Justice decision in *Torfaen District Council* v. *B & Q Stores*),[37] the local authorities involved have become engaged in disputed applications for interlocutory injunctions.

A major problem faced by local authorities in this area has been the possibility of a defeat upon a full hearing. Upon such an event, the exposure under any obligation to indemnify a successful defendant, in accordance with undertakings given in court at the time of the interlocutory hearing, is a very real constraint. The application for an injunction, accordingly, involves a weighing of the risks of cases proceeding to a full hearing and any interlocutory injunction being overturned. The courts have given out confused messages on this issue in the recent past. Thus, it has been held that local government bodies, unlike the Crown, are required to give an undertaking as to such an indemnity in respect of lost profits upon the grant of an interlocutory injunction. In *Kirklees* v. *Wickes Building Supplies Limited* the local authority had applied for an interlocutory injunction to restrain the defendant from using its premises for retail trade on Sundays.[38] In effect, the authority was enforcing section 47 of the Shops Act in accordance with the authorization under section 222 of the Local Government Act 1972. Justice Mervyn Davies granted the application, on the usual basis that the balance of convenience lay in that direction, damages being an inadequate remedy. As to whether an undertaking should be given to indemnify against any damage occasioned by the order should the defendant succeed at trial, it was held that there was a discretion in the court to dispense with such an undertaking. If it was not necessarily required of the Crown in such circumstances of law enforcement action, then it ought not to apply as a matter of course against a local authority.

The Court of Appeal, however, in the same case took a very different line. The interlocutory injunction was discharged. Lord Justice Dillon noted the exception available to the Crown. As a matter of domestic law, it was held that it would be wrong to extend to local authorities the Crown immunity from giving the cross-undertaking. Local authorities would more readily apply for interlocutory injunctions if they knew that upon failure at full trial they would still be free from liability to compensate the other party for loss occasioned. A further reason was given, namely, that should the defendant succeed at the full trial, without right to unrestricted retroactive effect, the right to trade on a Sunday would have been adversely affected pending trial without compensation and a cross-undertaking should therefore be required under Community law. Whilst there may be some sympathy for the view of the Court of Appeal in this case, on practical grounds (and the injunction may have draconian consequences much as a Mareva order might have), it has to be said that a requirement for an undertaking in cases such as this is likely to have by its very nature a restrictive effect upon the policy decisions of local authorities to seek injunctions. This is particularly the case in the light of the confused position on the legality of Sunday trading, notwithstanding that local authorities remain under a statutory duty to enforce the law. The financial implications must weigh heavily when local government lawyers are called upon for advice.

MONITORING ROLE

Another identifiable role of local government lawyers is that of monitoring. Arguably this merges into the corporate role, for it is a major task of local government lawyers to keep abreast of changes in the law, and potential changes, briefing the management team and elected members in order that efficient and appropriate choices can be made. Clearly, such a role is of crucial importance in a climate of change, as can be seen from the discussion of competitive tendering.

However, monitoring has a more formal structure now under the Local Government and Housing Act 1989. This has made a number of changes in the control mechanism for authorities and is ostensibly part of central government's plans to make authorities more responsive to the needs of the chargepayer. Thus, the 1989 Act provides for the creation of a monitoring officer (and also provides for the creation of a head of the paid service).[39] This monitoring role is often performed by the senior lawyer in the authority. It remains to be seen how the role will develop, through some kind of internal regulatory structure, obligations being laid upon the regulator.

CONTRACTING OUT OF LEGAL SERVICES

The spectre of contracting out which has applied to certain activities may now be extended, as the attention of central government turns towards the provision of so-called white-collar services. The government has produced a consultation paper setting out proposals for extending competition to professional and technical services.[40] Most discussion has surrounded the split of local government legal departments into the corporate side, the monitoring side, and the services side. Indeed, this has already been done voluntarily, to one extent or another, by a number of authorities. For example, Lincolnshire County Council is to subject all its legal services to outside competition, with in-house corporate legal advice in support of this process being provided by a private sector firm. Berkshire County Council has chosen to expose parts of the legal service to outside competition. Certain authorities, for example, Berkshire and Northamptonshire County Councils, are separating direct services from the corporate/client function.

All these methods are available, although it must be asked how far local authority lawyers will be able to operate in a regime which would rigorously separate the layers of local government service. Moreover, the idea of a corporate legal adviser having no role with regard to the provision of legal services must prompt questions as to the efficiency of such a process and as to whether the quality personnel required for such a corporate role might be found. However, this is the way in which events seem to be leading. The Audit Commission, in a recent paper, has suggested that before any compulsory legislation is extended to legal services, it would be beneficial for local authorities to take steps to expose legal functions to outside competition.[41]

The environment has changed, as the Audit Commission has pointed out, with increased demand for legal services, changing organizational frameworks, staffing changes and an emphasis on managerial leadership, all of which have impacted upon the role of lawyers.[42] Yet, the separation of the corporate from the monitoring role and, again, of each from the service provision/contractor role is not necessarily so clearly beneficial. Indeed, the line is difficult to draw in many circumstances and the creation of artificial barriers between clients and contractors can also create difficulties. There is, nevertheless, now an ethos of contracting out and this may sweep into the structure of local government legal service itself. Customers, and we may assume these to be such bodies as direct service organizations as well as other customers within the local authority umbrella, are more concerned about cash-limited budgets, and will accordingly exert pressures for support functions such as law services to be cost-conscious and competitive.

The problems, however, that will follow upon any proposals for compulsory contracting out are significant. In terms of the operation of legal controls, there are immediate difficulties. It is doubtful whether legal services can be treated in a manner analogous to other services contracted out to date. The mechanism of detailed specification will be quite inappropriate in the context of many legal services.[43] Moreover, private practitioners looking to tender may have to engage in a high degree of lateral thinking, in circumstances where a straightforward time-costing formula may be unacceptable. Beyond this, the technical and financial evaluation may cause serious difficulties for private firms. The 1988 Act's prohibition of anti-competitive criteria, such as questions concerning terms and conditions of the tenderer's staff, may lead to interesting questions in the light of the less restrictive view elsewhere of the managerial role.[44] On the broader canvas, common contractual terms, for instance, regarding default procedures and events of default, will be problematic in their application to the provision of legal services.

IN-HOUSE AND OUT-OF-HOUSE ALTERNATIVES

A number of alternatives offer themselves, not only as regards the splitting up of the various layers as mentioned above. Service provision may be carried on in-house without outside competition, and to date, a policy arrangement such as this has been a perfectly lawful solution. Even within an in-house arrangement, local government lawyers have participated in the changed ethos. Accordingly, it is now an increasingly common practice for service-level agreements to be entered into, setting out the extent of services to be required and arrangements for review as well as the powers and accountabilities of individual officers. Such service-level agreements may even extend to in-house charging arrangements. Much local authority legal work is already contracted out and the Audit Commission estimated that the buy-in is around £19 million worth of work per annum.[45] This is stated to be equivalent to about 10 per cent of total local authority legal costs. The Audit Commission recognized certain problems in contracting out, for example, with regard to control and conflicts of interest arising:

> Quality control of legal services therefore requires the involvement of someone who enjoys both the confidence of the client departments and the professional respect of those whose work he or she is judging. It would normally be best to entrust this important task to the council's corporate legal adviser, who should exercise this role for any in-house and bought-in services.[46]

Problems in this context come from both directions. First, it may increasingly prove difficult for the corporate legal adviser to have a sufficiently broad range of either talent or resources to control the service provider, especially perhaps one operating out-of-house. Secondly, client departments are not always in a position to judge the quality of service provision. This perspective might indeed become increasingly appropriate. Due to the pressures, particularly upon direct service organizations, the level of demand for necessary legal services may suffer. Moreover, care is needed with regard to the charging of costs to departments and other bodies. Precisely where does the corporate (and monitoring) role begin and end?

A further problem has been created by management buy-outs. The most infamous instance has concerned West Wiltshire District Council, the subject of criticism by the District Auditor. The council has subsequently taken action, for example, taking legal services back in-house, using (as do many authorities) private firms as necessary.[47] Management buy-outs may be efficacious, particularly in accordance with new Audit Commission guidelines, which seek to ensure competitive bidding and arm's-length negotiations as well as adequate monitoring and control thereafter.[48] The Audit Commission recognized in its guidelines that even the legality of allowing staff paid time-off to organize a buy-out should be open to considerable doubt. Furthermore, certain of the incentives which could be provided in a more consumer-orientated attitude to carrying out local government services again might be open to question. In the aftermath of the experience of West Wiltshire District Council,[49] it is to be hoped that, in accordance with the Audit Commission guidelines, management buy-outs will be less controversial. Nevertheless, even a successful buy-out should pose questions about the level and impact of outside provision to the local authority, of the sort considered in this paper.

Over the past decade, the level of acceleration in job opportunities in the private sector has not been mirrored in the local government sector. Whilst steps have been taken to make local government lawyers' salaries more realistic, in comparison with other sectors, there have clearly been difficulties in attracting applicants for posts in sufficient quantities. The tide is however beginning to turn, with the early 1990s seeing the onset of a deeply recessionary period in the economy generally. This has had an impact upon the private sector and there are signs at the time of writing that the provincial firms, which have previously had major difficulties in recruiting sufficient quality staff, have themselves become less avid participants in the jobs market.

This all leaves more opportunities for local authorities, which have been emphasizing the broad-based nature of local government legal work as well as all the other opportunities which supposedly sell the notion of working as a local government lawyer, such as job satisfaction, the honing of management skills, and career progression. Indeed, whilst pressures upon local government lawyers have increased, so have the skills demanded of them. Edward Fennell, writing in the *Times*, opined that while many lawyers in private practice 'are like medieval knights surrounded by squires and attendants, the local government lawyer often has to draw on a pool of clerks and administrators. This makes them more self-reliant'.[50] Whilst this may be arguable, the fact that a wide cross-section of lawyers are responding in greater numbers to local government vacancies is a significant development of late. For the lawyers themselves, the question of in-house or out-of-house provision will result simply in a change of site for many service providers. Whatever the impact

81

upon career patterns, the results for the viability and efficiency of local government service provision must form the criteria for evaluation of developments to date and of further changes anticipated. If recent signs of increased dialogue between central and local government are auguries of future treatment of such issues, then prospects for considered reform must be the brighter. For this there will be much relief, as the prospect of the single-tier authority hoves into view.

The immediate future includes the introduction of a new 'council tax', the broad restructuring of local government itself, and the extension of contracting out in areas more complex than previously.[51] It would be a mistake, however, to dismiss the continuing dynamic of change as a question of '*plus ça change . . .*'. Local government has undergone a revolution, albeit brought about incrementally, and to some extent by chance. Only some incidents of this revolution could be charted here. The role of local government lawyers reflects the changed culture. The development of a compulsory scheme for competitive tendering of legal services, or even of voluntary contracting out schemes, might be seen by central government as providing a welcome neutrality in legal provision. Certainly, legal advisers would be less pressured to hold competing forces in tension. Even if political change in Westminster were to lead to an abandonment of present central priorities, the benefits of recent developments, in terms, for example, of accountability and cost awareness, are likely to be sustained. For all the pressures on the local government lawyer in recent years, such benefits, in whatever economic structure he or she eventually practises, may prove of lasting value.

NOTES AND REFERENCES

1   N. Johnson, 'Dicey And His Influence on Public Law' [1985] *Public Law* 717, at 720.
2   [1983] 1 AC 768.
3   [1925] AC 578.
4   W.A. Robson, *The Development of Local Government* (3rd ed., 1954) 42.
5   M. Elliott, *The Role of Law in Central-Local Relations* (1981) 90.
6   J. Gyford, *Local Politics in Britain* (2nd ed., 1984) 144.
7   P. McAuslan and J.F. McEldowney, 'Legitimacy and the Constitution: The Dissonance between Theory and Practice' in *Law, Legitimacy and the Constitution*, eds. P. McAuslan and J. F. McEldowney (1985) 17.
8   See, for example, the Local Government (Access to Information) Act 1985.
9   This process has been accelerated by the provisions in the Local Government Act 1988. Extensions to a wider range of services are proposed in the Local Government Bill 1991.
10 Department of the Environment, *The Internal Management of Local Government in England* (1991) 2.
11 Archbishop of Canterbury's Commission on Urban Priority Areas, *Faith in the City* (1985) paras. 9.49 and 9.50.
12 Local Government Act 1988 s. 2(2).
13 Local Government Act 1988 (Competition in Sports and Leisure Facilities) Order 1989, S.I. No. 2488.
14 Above, n. 12, ss. 27, 28. See, also, P.A. Thomas and R. Costigan, *Promoting Homosexuality: Section 28 of the Local Government Act 1988* (1990).
15 Widdicombe Committee, *Report on the Conduct of Local Authority Business* (1986; Cmnd. 9797).

16 Set at £19,500 per annum – see the Local Government (Politically Restricted Posts) Regulations 1990, S.I. No. 42 and Local Government (Politically Restricted Posts) No. 2 Regulations 1990, S.I. No.1447.

17 This process is to commence in accordance with the review provisions contained in part II of the Local Government Bill 1991, which puts structural change on the agenda.

18 See, for example, the Audit Commission, *Competitive Counsel? Using Lawyers in Local Government* (1991).

19 See *Norwich City Council* v. *Secretary of State for the Environment* [1982] 1 All ER 734.

20 Examples of situations in which such representation can prove economically attractive are prosecutions upon non-payment of car parking fines and prosecutions upon non-compliance with other enforcement procedures, such as statutory nuisance abatement notices.

21 The Local Government Planning and Land Act 1980 has been followed by a stream of legislative measures. See, for example, in particular part V of the Local Government Finance Act 1988.

22 See the Rates Act 1984; also part I of the Local Government Finance Act 1988, together with its own 'capping' measure, contained in part VII.

23 See part I of the Act and in particular section 4(5).

24 For example, under Department of the Environment Circular 1/91.

25 The power to give directions vested in the Secretary of State is contained in s. 14 of the 1988 Act. See *R.* v. *Secretary of State for the Environment, Ex parte Knowsley MBC* (1991), in the *Independent*, 25 September 1991.

26 See the comments of the Audit Commission, above, n. 18.

27 [1991] 1 All ER 454 (House of Lords); [1990] 3 All ER 33 (Court of Appeal).

28 See, for example, *A-G* v. *Manchester Corporation* [1906] 1 Ch 643; *A-G* v. *Fulham Corporation* [1921] 1 Ch 440; *Prescott* v. *Birmingham Corporation* [1954] 3 All ER 698; also, the recent House of Lords decision in *R.* v. *Richmond upon Thames London Borough Council, Ex parte McCarthy & Stone (Developments) Limited* (1991), in the *Times*, 15 November 1991.

29 That said, other threats to the viability of transactions remain, albeit in modified form, for example, as regards the implications of directors and others acting in breach of their authority, under section 109 of the 1989 Act.

30 See s. 16 of the 1980 Act and s. 10 of the 1988 Act.

31 'See, respectively, Department of Environment Circulars 19/83 and 19/88.

32 s. 101.

33 s. 111, as to the construction of which the Court of Appeal and House of Lords took a very different view in the *Hazell* case, above, n. 27.

34 On occasions, developments are overtaken by statute, for example, the provisions with regard to discretionary spending and companies in which local authorities have interests, contained in the Local Government Act 1989, parts III and V.

35 Under s. 222 Local Government Act 1972.

36 See s. 81(5).

37 (1990) 1 All ER 129.

38 (1990) 1 WLR 1237.

39 See s. 5(1) of the 1989 Act; also, s. 4.

40 Department of the Environment, *Competing for Quality. Competition in the Provision of Local Services: A Consultation Paper* (1991). The paper also suggests a revised framework for competition, for example, as regards the Secretary of State's sanction powers, at pp. 11–12. See also the Local Government Bill 1991, clauses 8–11.

41 See, above, n. 18.

42 id.

43 See Local Government Act 1988 s. 7. Clearly, different criteria will be applied – see, above, n. 40, and, in particular, the proposed enabling provision contained in clauses 8 and 9 of the Local Government Bill 1991.

44 For example, by Lord Justice Parker in *R.* v. *Islington LBC, Ex parte Building Employers Confederation* (1989), in the *Times*, 29 March 1989.

45 Above, n. 18.

46 id., at para. 84.
47 See the *Independent*, 26 June 1990.
48 Guidelines, produced in January 1990.
49 See *Law Society's Gazette*, 5 December 1990, at p. 10; and 12 June 1991, at p. 12.
50 See the *Times*, 9 April 1991.
51 The government's new Citizens Charter has seen partial restatement in the provisions of part I of the Local Government Bill with regard to publicity as well as competition in local government activities.

A Future for Legal Aid?

OLE HANSEN*

The Legal Aid scheme was originally erected on twin pillars. On one side was the wartime consensus on the need for a welfare state and on the other the pre-existing economic and social organization of the legal profession. That structure lasted for thirty years. In the last ten years, however, under the pressure of government expenditure restrictions and free market ideology, it has been seriously eroded. The result, at first sight paradoxical, has been to prepare the basis for a radical restructuring of legal services of the kind for which progressive public service professionals have been campaigning since the late sixties.

The origins of the present scheme lie with the Rushcliffe Committee which reported in May 1945. Civil legal aid, it recommended, unlike the Poor Persons Procedure it would replace, should be available not only to the poor but also to those of moderate means.[1] Those who could not afford to pay anything should get it free and the rest pay a contribution. In criminal cases, legal aid should be made available where necessary in the interests of justice, and any doubts should be resolved in favour of the applicant. That much was all of a piece with social and economic policies of the time which also included full employment and the creation of the welfare state and the National Health Service, and sprang out of the principles on which the Beveridge Report of 1942 had been based.[2]

Professor Peter Townsend has described the principle behind the Beveridge reforms as that of 'minimum rights for the many'.[3] The way in which 'the many' were included in the legal aid scheme was explicitly stated in the long title of the Legal Aid Act 1949. It was 'An Act to make legal aid and advice . . . more readily available for persons of small and moderate means'.

However, other aspects of the Rushcliffe proposals were more in keeping with what Townsend has described as the principle underlying the nineteenth century Poor Laws: 'the conditional welfare of the few'.[4] Social policy derived from that principle has as its characteristics 'the maximisation of relief through charity and voluntary effort, and public expenditure kept low by the barrier of means tests'.[5] Legal aid, unlike, for instance, help from the National Health Service, was to be means-tested and history would show that the extent to which it approximated towards the welfare rather than the Poor Law ideal

* *Department of Law and Government, South Bank Polytechnic, Borough Road, London SE 1, England*

varied with those means tests over the years – with a clear tendency towards the Poor Laws after 1979.

When it came to delivery of the new service, the Rushcliffe committee relied entirely on the existing private practice structure of the legal profession. In the main, the committee simply rubber-stamped a plan put forward by the Law Society, the trade association and professional body representing solicitors. Civil legal aid would be dispensed through solicitors and barristers in private practice who would be paid 'reasonable remuneration' on a case-by-case basis out of a legal aid fund provided by the government and administered by the Law Society: thus, not only preserving the existing, nineteenth century, economic and social structure of the legal profession, but further enhancing the status of the Law Society which, with its Scottish and Northern Irish siblings, became the only private body to dispense public money to its own members. Legal aid, as implemented on the Rushcliffe model, was not so much a public service as a private service paid for out of public funds. The proposals for criminal legal aid were similar except that most of the administration would be done by the courts.

In only one major respect did the Rushcliffe committee propose a new way to deliver legal services: the Law Society should employ solicitors to give legal advice to those who could not afford to pay for it. That, along with all its other recommendations, was incorporated in the 1949 Act but became the only one which was not brought into effect.

Thus, the legal aid scheme was created without in any way interfering with the existing professional order. It could be said that this was entirely in keeping with the intentions of the man credited with the blue print for the welfare state:

> In his plan Beveridge gave expression to a broad section of hardheaded opinion in the ruling class of his period. He was for social reform, so long as the existing structure of society remained fundamentally the same. In fact he was for social reform precisely *because* it would allow the existing order to continue essentially unchanged.[6]

However, the protection given to lawyers under the legal aid scheme exceeded that given to any other profession involved in the welfare state. Individual solicitors and barristers had no obligations, for instance, to accept cases within their locality or area of expertise or to keep their offices open for certain hours. Their duties only arose in respect of the individual cases and clients which they happened to accept. Furthermore, there was little public accountability for the running of the scheme. Although the Law Society had to deliver an annual report and accounts to the Lord Chancellor, he, in turn, has never been answerable to Parliament for the administration of the scheme. In any event, the Lord Chancellor is, of course, a semi-detached member of the government who combines the role of cabinet minister with that of judge and, sitting as he does in the House of Lords, he is outside the mainstream political process.

Contrast the position of the medical profession under the National Health Service. From the beginning, all doctors had to agree to contracts which required them to deliver a minimum quantity and quality of service if they were to be part of the new set-up. And it was not the British Medical

Association, long regarded as one of the most powerful interest groups in the country, which was entrusted with the running of the NHS. Instead, after protracted and often bitter political argument, the management responsibility for the NHS was handed to a tri-partite structure of hospitals, local health authorities and executive councils all of whom were answerable to the Secretary of State who, in turn, was answerable to the House of Commons.[7]

THE FINANCIAL CRISIS

Fundamental changes in the legal aid scheme during the eighties were brought about by what has been generally perceived as a financial crisis.[8] Overall legal aid expenditure in the Lord Chancellor's vote increased from a net £191.8 million in 1981/82 to an estimated £698 million in 1991/2, and £857 million for 1992/3.[9] Throughout the decade it rose at well above the rate of inflation or of public expenditure in most other areas.[10] The 1991 report from the Legal Aid Board calculates that, for the previous ten years, the scheme had been growing at nearly 17 per cent per annum compound or, with inflation excluded, 10 per cent per annum. At the same time national income was rising at about 2 per cent. Roughly three-fifths of the increase was said to be due to increases in the numbers of cases and two-fifths due to increases in the average cost of providing assistance under the scheme.[11]

The increase in the number of cases is not difficult to explain. Rising crime and more police are reflected in more cases in the criminal courts and, hence, more criminal legal aid. Duty solicitor schemes, responsible for expenditure of £44.1 million in 1990–91 (or 19.4 per cent of the criminal legal aid budget)[12] were introduced to 'balance' increased police powers of detention and interrogation in the Police and Criminal Evidence Act 1984. The increases would have mattered less if criminal legal aid had stayed in the Home Office budget where it had been since the inception of the scheme. Compared to the Home Office's many other responsibilities – the cost of many of which also rose steeply – legal aid expenditure would have been a minor item and might not have drawn much attention. However, in 1980, responsibility was transferred to the much smaller budget of the Lord Chancellor's department where its growing size was much more obvious. On the civil side, a rising divorce rate and increased home ownership have led not only to more cases but also to more complicated and protracted property disputes.

The causes, however, are less important than the fact that the increased expenditure drew the attention of the Treasury. The Treasury's concern was sharpened by the failure of the Lord Chancellor's department in the early eighties to devise a strategy to deal with the clearly foreseeable rise in expenditure and avoidable errors in estimating future costs.[13] As a result, in order to gain Treasury acceptance of its estimates, the Lord Chancellor's department was forced to make a number of concessions. One of these, in 1986, led to the first deliberate cut in legal aid eligibility since the inception of the legal aid scheme. Others have involved a series of enquiries and measures designed to strengthen government control over the scheme and reduce the extent to which legal aid expenditure is demand-led. In the short term, the effect has been to reduce coverage and delivery of legal aid to what one could fairly describe as Poor Law levels. At the same time, however, in an effort to achieve greater efficiency and tighter control over expenditure, the administration of the scheme was upgraded so that it became more comparable with that found in other areas of the welfare state.

THE EROSION OF ELIGIBILITY

Eligibility for legal aid depends on the applicant's financial circumstances.[14] There are separate income and capital limits to decide whether applicants qualify and, if so, whether they should make a financial contribution and how much that should be. In order to apply the limits it is necessary to calculate 'disposable' income and capital which involves deducting certain expenses and fixed 'allowances' for dependants. Therefore, the level of allowances as well as that of the limits themselves determines the proportion of the population which is eligible at any given time.

The poor have always been eligible for free legal aid. It is in relation to the other people contemplated by Rushcliffe and the 1949 Act, those of 'moderate means', that there has been considerable fluctuation and where the line may be said to lie between a scheme which is intended to form part of the welfare state and one which is only for the deserving poor.

From 1949, and until very recently, all governments accepted that measuring the proportion of the population which was eligible was a valid test of the effectiveness of the legal aid scheme.[15] In 1950, when the scheme was introduced, it covered over 80 per cent of the population on income alone.[16] However, by 1973, only 40 per cent of the population was eligible. The reason was that, while the eligibility limits had kept pace with inflation, earnings had risen faster and more wives had begun to earn money.

At the same time, the position of people outside the scheme had become worse than it was in 1950 because the cost of civil litigation had risen faster than earnings.[17] In 1974 the legal aid limits and allowances were pegged to supplementary benefit levels and as a result were increased annually in line with average earnings. That stopped the decline and in April 1979, it was substantially reversed during the last throes of the Callaghan government. The lower income limit was lifted from 21 per cent below the long-term supplementary benefit level to 50 per cent above it. Dependants' allowances were raised to 50 per cent above the supplementary benefit allowances. The upper income limit was set at 240 per cent above the lower limit. Those measures restored eligibility to something like the 1950 level.

But that was only maintained during the first year of the Conservative government. Michael Murphy has calculated that eleven million adults lost eligibility for civil legal aid between 1979 and 1990.[18] In personal injury cases, because of higher income limits introduced in 1990, nine million had lost eligibility. In percentage terms 79 per cent of the population was eligible in 1979. By 1990 that had dropped to 47 per cent generally and 52 per cent in personal injury cases.

The main reason was a failure to uprate the limits in 1980 and 1981. Betwen April 1979 and November 1981 the lower income limit fell from 50 per cent to 11 per cent above the long term supplementary benefit rate. By April 1987, the last year for which the comparison can be made (because of the abolition that year of supplementary benefit), the lower limit was only 16 per cent above the long term rate.

Compared to earnings, the income limits showed an even bigger fall. Between January 1980 and January 1988, average earnings rose by 107 per cent but the legal aid limits increased by only 37 per cent.[19] In April 1986, as a result of the crisis that year over the legal aid estimates, Lord Hailsham became the first Lord Chancellor to actively reduce eligibility: dependants' allowances were cut from 50 per cent to 25 per cent above supplementary rates.[20] This had the greatest effect on families with children.

The cumulative effect of limits which fell in real terms and the deliberate cuts in allowances is illustrated as follows. In November 1979 a married couple with three children aged four, eight, and thirteen would have remained eligible for legal aid until their total earnings were 52 per cent higher than average male earnings. By April 1988 they would have remained eligible only until the point when their earnings were 17 per cent above average male earnings.[21] For a married couple with two children aged four and eight, the point at which they ceased to be eligible was 37 per cent above the average male earnings in November 1979. By April 1988 that had fallen to 6 per cent above average male earnings.[22] At the same time, the effects of falling outside legal aid coverage had become worse because, again, legal costs were rising faster than earnings. For instance, in the five years between 1985–86 and 1989–90, average earnings rose by 38 per cent while the average legal aid bill rose by 60 per cent. It can safely be assumed that legal costs paid privately would have risen by at least as much as legal aid bills.[23]

In 1991, when it became impossible to argue that coverage had been maintained, the government took the goalposts away.[24] Thus, in the consultation paper, *Review of Financial Conditions for Legal Aid,* the Lord Chancellor's department says:

> It has been suggested that effectiveness of cover should be judged by the maintenance of a particular percentage of the population within the scheme. This approach is unsatisfactory for the following reasons:
> (a) It does not target need, because it does not relate means to costs.
> (b) It presupposes that the distribution and level of means in the population remains constant relative to the cost of litigation.
> (c) It sees legal aid as the only means of funding the litigation of those who cannot afford to fund it themselves. However, the volume of general litigation has increased, despite the perceived 'eligibility gap' . . . .[25]

Points (a) and (b) might have had some validity if earnings had risen faster than the cost of litigation but amount to disingenuous sophistry at a time when, demonstrably, on the government's own figures, legal costs have been rising more quickly than earnings. As to point (c), it cannot be argued that a general increase in the number of proceedings initiated in the courts disproves, or shows a narrowing of, the eligibility gap. For instance, increased commercial litigation or more possession actions by landlords, both of which appear to be factors in the figures quoted by the Lord Chancellor's Department, would not be an indication of the effectiveness of legal aid.

However, the consultation paper uses the argument in (c) as the launch pad for a series of proposals aimed at changing legal aid into a benefit which will be available only to the very poor. People of moderate means – in effect those who at present pay contributions towards their legal aid – are consigned to the private sector where, it is suggested, they will pay for litigation through legal expenses insurance, or a contingency fund, or the so-called 'safety net', where they would only be funded by legal aid once they had spent a certain amount of their own money (how much would depend on their income). All this is done in the name of what the review calls 'private client realism'. Thus:

> Litigants prove that they are serious by putting down their own money. A similar measure of importance does not exist for free legal aid.[26]

Leave aside the disregard this document displays for the pressures on all individual litigants, including the legally aided,[27] and its ignorance of the checks against abuse of legal aid.[28] It is clear that, whatever the specific changes enacted later as a result of the 1991 eligibility review, the Conservative government has explicitly abandoned welfare state principles in relation to legal aid.

THE ATTACK ON LAWYERS' REMUNERATION

In practice, the fees paid to lawyers on legal aid have never been as high as those which could be charged to privately paying clients for the same type of work.[29] To that extent, legal aid has always been a second class service with a Poor Law, or charitable, element.

However, it is only in the last ten years that a government has sought explicitly to abandon the principle that remuneration should be the same as for private work. In March 1986 the Lord Chancellor tried to impose fees for criminal work which both the Bar and the Law Society claimed were in breach of the statutory obligation to provide fair and reasonable remuneration. Both branches of the profession started proceedings for judicial review which were settled on terms which included the government paying the legal costs.[30]

The following year, in the legal aid White Paper the government made clear that legal aid was now officially a second class service:

> The Government does not consider that the rates for legally aided work should necessarily be the same as those for privately funded work.[31]

It proposed a wider introduction of 'standard' fees – paying lawyers for particular items of work rather than, as in the private sector, according how long the work has taken.

The government sought against the legal profession's opposition to implement the policy set out in the White Paper and to limit increases in standard fees and hourly rates to less than the rate of inflation.[32] That, in turn, led to claims from the profession that lawyers were giving up legal aid work because it is becoming inceasingly uneconomic.[33] It is difficult to say whether that is true. In 1986, few of the 206 solicitors who responded to a questionnaire in *Legal Action* were about to give up legal aid work. Only 1.5 per cent were thinking of cutting down 'completely', 7 per cent of cutting down 'considerably' and 21 per cent 'moderately'. However, 68 per cent indicated that they were not thinking of cutting down at all.[34]

A more recent, and fuller, survey conducted by the Law Society Research and Policy Plannning Unit in 1989 found that legal aid work was generally seen as the least profitable work or even as loss-making by a majority of solicitors.[35] 42 per cent of firms indicated that legal aid work just broke even and 18 per cent said that the work made a loss. 35 per cent said that the work was fairly profitable and just under 2 per cent of firms found the work very profitable. The study concluded:

> The contrast between the perceived profitability of legal aid work and both fee-paying client work and company client work is striking. Ninety per cent of firms considered both individual non-legally aided client work and company client work to be profitable, but only 37 per cent of legally aided client work was thought to be profitable. It is clear that legally aided client work is being subsidised by other categories of work such as residential conveyancing and probate work.[36]

The study found that solicitors were expecting an overall reduction in legal aid work but they were not planning the mass exodus one might have expected from the profit figures. 39 per cent expected legally-aided clients to be a less important source of fees five years later (that is, in 1994). But 21 per cent expected them to be a more important source of fees and one-third expected them to remain of the same importance.[37]

Anecdotal evidence supports the view that individual lawyers and firms have, in fact, given up legal aid work. However, whether moves away from legal aid work have intensified during the eighties is another matter. The same kind of anecdotal evidence, and my own twenty-year experience as a legal aid practitioner and commentator, also suggest that, as lawyers become older, they have always tended to move away from legal aid and into more lucrative areas of work. It is doubtful whether any trend away from legal aid over the past ten years amounts to more than that. As Roger Smith has shown, the numbers of solicitors' offices and individual barristers doing legal aid work actually went up between 1979–80 and 1989–90, although there was also evidence of increased specialization in legal aid.[38]

It should be added that by the beginning of 1992, the planned introduction of standard fees for legal aid criminal work in magistrates' courts had brought solicitors nearer to a collective withdrawal of labour than at any previous time in their history. At the time of writing (January 1992), despite a strong condemnation from the president of the Law Society, solicitors in Southampton (Hants) and Crawley (Sussex) had withdrawn indefinitely from

91

their duty solicitor schemes,[39] solicitors in Carlisle (Cumbria) had withdrawn for a week,[40] and colleagues in Devon and Exeter were planning to follow suit.[41] In Bristol, a meeting organized by the local law society and the Legal Aid Practitioners Group collected well over the 100 signatures needed to convene an extraordinary meeting of the Law Society nationally to discuss the issue.[42]

THE NEW STRUCTURES

Simultaneously with the attacks on legal aid eligibility and remuneration, and with the same aim of controlling expenditure, governments in the 1980s also began to chisel at the other pillar of the legal aid scheme, the reliance on the Law Society for the administration and traditional private practice for the delivery of the service. Paradoxically however, in view of what the same governments were doing to eligibility and remuneration and of their general ideological commitment to privatization, the effect was to move the administration and service delivery of legal aid closer to the welfare state model and to establish on a more secure institutional base a public service sector which had been emerging within the legal profession since the late sixties. Harold Perkin has distinguished two types of professionals.[43] On one side are those in the public sector such as teachers, social workers and public administrators who are committed to social justice, public expenditure and social management. They also 'benefit directly from public expenditure'. On the other side is the private sector: private corporation managers, and the professionals – such as lawyers, accountants and surveyors – who service private corporations and property. The private sector professionals are committed to low public expenditure, the protection of private property and the free market. They 'see themselves as the source' of public expenditure.

The public and private sectors are engaged, says Perkin, in the main struggle for society's resources.

> As the struggle between lord and peasant was the master conflict in feudal society and the struggle between capitalist and wage earner the master conflict in industrial society, so the struggle between the public and the private sector professions is the master conflict of professional society.[44]

Before legal aid, the legal profession's work had been entirely privately funded. The introduction of the legal aid scheme did little to alter that. The profession remained in the private sector, it continued to derive the overwhelming part of its income from private corporate and individual clients and, as already noted, legal aid did not alter in any way the economic structure in which solicitors were organized in private partnerships and barristers in private sole practice. Not surprisingly, therefore, with few exceptions, the Law Society was also primarily concerned with defending private sector interests. While this did not affect its day-to-day administration of the legal aid scheme, it did hinder policy initiatives which would have helped the legally-aided consumer of legal services (and the dedicated legal aid practitioner) but might not have been in the interests of the solicitors' profession generally.

To give just one example: advertising. Advertising could lead to price competition and was seen by the Law Society as unprofessional. Yet many potential legal aid clients needed to be told by means of advertising what a solicitor could do for them and where they could find a solicitor. However, until conveyancing was threatened by non-solicitors, the Law Society refused to allow individual advertising by solicitors.[45] That was the Law Society acting as a trade association and professional body. Not surprisingly it followed the same policy in its capacity of administrator of the legal aid scheme and it took years of pressure to induce the Society to publish lists of legal aid practitioners which contained enough information to be useful.[46]

Lawyers imbued with a public sector ideology began to emerge noticeably after the arrival of a Labour government in 1964 and the publication in 1967 of *Lawyers and the Courts*.[47] Those two events, together with the example of the legal services movement in the United States, led to the creation of the first law centres in this country and, more importantly from the point of view of legal aid, to the formation of the Legal Action Group (LAG) in 1971 by lawyers committed to the expansion and improvement of publicly funded legal services.[48]

From the start, LAG's interest in public administration made it the natural ally of those in the Lord Chancellor's department who wanted to bring the administration of the legal aid scheme under greater public control. Of the four lawyers who initiated LAG, two were drafted into the civil service in 1974: one as special consultant to the Lord Chancellor's legal aid advisory committee and the other to research and write a report on legal services needs and, in the same year, the group's vice-chair was appointed to the legal aid advisory committee.[49]

The cordial relationship between LAG and the Lord Chancellor's department cooled after the report of the Royal Commission on Legal Services was published in October 1979 but the two most important institutional reforms introduced by government in the late eighties may be clearly traced to proposals made by LAG some ten years earlier. Early in its life it had called for a Legal Services Commission to take over administration of the legal aid scheme from the Law Society and to co-ordinate all other legal services activities.[50] When the government decided in 1987 to take away the administration of legal aid from the Law Society and give it to a newly created Legal Aid Board it was clearly based on the same ideas as those which had inspired LAG's proposals. Even the title of the White Paper, *Legal Aid in England and Wales: A New Framework* and the lay out and presentation seemed to echo LAG's earlier papers.

The other major change, franchising, instituted by the Legal Aid Board itself in 1990 also has its origins in LAG. In 1978 LAG recommended to the Royal Commission that a select group of legal aid practitioners should be given contracts which, on the one hand, would require them to provide services of a defined quality – and quantity – and on the other, entitle them to special privileges such as grants and special payments on account.[51] The LAG proposals were closely modelled on the contracts which doctors in general practice had with the National Health Service.

That the franchising experiment is drawn on the LAG proposals should come as no surprise. The board's official directly in charge of it in the head office was a member of the LAG committee and was closely involved in formulating the recommendations to the Royal Commission.[52]

THE FUTURE

The franchising experiment, like the earlier LAG proposal, is based on the premise that some firms – a small minority compared to the profession as a whole – are committed to legal aid whereas others – the vast majority – do little or no legal aid work.

For instance, in 1978–79, 48.75 per cent of the payments from the legal aid fund went to only 9.75 per cent of the solicitors on the legal aid list. 72 per cent went to 22.51 per cent of the offices. Many of those received more than £100,000 a year – the equivalent of the total gross fees of a small solicitors' firm. At the other end of the scale, less than £5,000 a year was paid to 60.81 per cent of the solicitors on the list.[53] In other words, nearly two-thirds of the solicitors on the legal aid list received less than would have been needed to pay for one full-time assistant solicitor at the time. The figures, which are similar in any other year, show that legal aid work was concentrated within a small number of law firms. Indeed, the figures understated the concentration since they only show proportions of the firms on the legal aid list and therefore excluded those – such as most of the City of London firms – that undertook no legal aid work.

The most recent trend appears to be towards even greater concentration. In 1979–80 only 113 solicitors' offices received more than £60,000; in 1984–5, 195 offices received more than £120,000 and by 1989–90, 841 offices received more than £120,000.[54] The Law Society's research and planning unit made similar findings. In 1989 only 11 per cent of firms doing legal aid work obtained 50 per cent or more of their total fees from that client group.[55] Asked to predict what they would be doing in 1994, it was those firms deriving a higher volume of fees from legal aid that expected to be doing more of it in the future.[56]

The further concentration of legal aid work is likely to be aided by other developments in the profession and, in particular, the loss of conveyancing and probate work following the Courts and Legal Services Act 1990. As noted above, in most firms unprofitable legal aid work has been sustained by the fees from conveyancing and probate. Further, seven out of ten firms derived more than a quarter of their business from residential conveyancing.[57] Among the smaller firms, which are also the most likely to be doing legal aid work, residential conveyancing generated 38 per cent of the business.[58] Therefore, as conveyancing profits are squeezed, the network of general practices through which legal aid is dispensed is likely to contract and the work will become more concentrated.

94

Taken together with what is happening in other areas – such as corporate work and in relation to rights of audience – what we are witnessing is the breakdown of the homogenous legal profession noted by Rick Abel.[59] But as the old-style legal profession with its hegemonic private sector ideology starts to break up, the outlines of the public sector legal profession are likely to become even clearer. At the same time, the costs of providing public legal services, especially in the criminal justice system, are likely to continue to rise at a similar rate to that which we have experienced in the past decade.

Those factors are likely to cause continuing crises but they could also be the opportunity to carry out fundamental reform of public legal services. I mentioned, in opening, two of the principles for dealing with large-scale deprivation identified by Peter Townsend: the 'conditional welfare for the few' associated with the nineteenth-century Poor Laws and the 'minimum rights for the many' associated with the post-war welfare state. Legal aid, I suggested, had features of both.

But there is also a third principle: 'distributional justice for all'. Townsend does not fully define this but instead says:

> Characteristic of a policy worked out according to such a principle could be the de-stratification of society through economic, political and social reorganisation and the equal distribution and wider diffusion of all kinds of power and material resources.[60]

In legal services terms, that would mean not only an extension of public legal help to, for instance, tribunals and the establishment of non-means tested legal aid for the types of cases – such as protection of one's home or bodily safety – which are essential to a minimum standard of living in a developed society with pretensions to civilization,[61] but also the public funding of agencies to undertake education and publicity work and bring test cases in the higher courts.

It is unlikely that such functions could be undertaken by private practice, particularly since private practice has, in any event, shown itself particularly slow and collectively lacking in ingenuity in making use of the legal aid scheme. For instance, the geographical distribution of solicitors has never matched the needs of legally-aided clients. A study in 1973 showed that while there was one solicitors' office for every 4,700 people in England and Wales, the distribution varied enormously and the solicitors were more likely to be found in the more prosperous owner-occupier areas.[62] Thus, there was one office for every 2,000 people in Guildford and Bournemouth but only one for every 66,000 in Huyton in Liverpool. The position has not improved. In 1985 there was one solicitor for every 924 people in London and south-east England, and one for every 2,120 in the north of England.[63]

Similarly, private practice solicitors have not, on the whole, used the potential of the advice and assistance scheme to take on work outside the traditional areas of family work and crime. The Law Society was constitutionally unable to deal with the shortcomings of legal aid caused by its dependence on private practice. The Legal Aid Board suffers from no such inhibitions but, nonetheless, questions must be asked about its composition and terms of reference.

If the creation of the board by the Conservative government in 1987 appeared in some respects paradoxical, there was nothing paradoxical about its composition. Indeed the membership, appointed by the Lord Chancellor (under the Legal Aid Act 1988 s. 3(5)), reflected the government's aim of controlling public expenditure. All the non-specialist members of the Board – half the total members – were private-sector corporate managers. The other half was made up of two solicitors, two barristers, a legal academic, and an advice worker.[64]

The board's staff, of course, are another matter. Apart from a new chief executive drawn from the Lord Chancellor's department, the Legal Aid Board simply took over the existing employees of the Law Society's legal aid department who, freed from the Society's control, have been able to administer the legal aid scheme as the public service most of them by then wanted it to be.[65] The beneficial effects have been seen during the first years of the Board's existence in terms, for instance, of improved official forms and the more efficient handling of applications.

Nonetheless, if the Legal Aid Board is to be a vehicle for extending public legal services, it must be an immediate priority for a future Lord Chancellor to widen the range of its membership. In the slightly longer term, the method of appointment should be changed so as to allow organizations repesenting both providers and consumers of legal services the right to nominate members.[66]

That would require primary legislation to amend the Legal Aid Act 1988. But, in any event, the terms of reference of the Board would need to be changed by legislation since it is, in general terms, restricted to the running of the present legal aid scheme.[67] Nonetheless, within its present powers, the Board will, over the next few years, be engaged in a fundamental restructuring of the means by which legal aid is delivered.

The franchising pilot experiment began in July 1990 in Birmingham and is to test whether an improved and more efficient service could be achieved by contracting with firms of solicitors and others. It is due to be completed in late 1992. It is noteworthy that the scheme, unlike the rest of the legal aid scheme, is not confined to solicicitors firms or, at least, organizations such as law centres who employ solicitors to represent and advise the general public.[68] Applicants are monitored by the Board, both before a contract is awarded and during its currency, to see if they meet minimum standards of competence and quality. In return, they can work under the advice and assistance scheme without financial limit and make their own decisions about whether to grant emergency legal aid. In addition, they receive more generous payments on account than are generally available under the legal aid scheme.

Franchising has been criticized because it is seen as the beginning of a money-saving attempt to restrict the number of solicitors' offices able to dispense legal aid. Some support is lent to that view by the fact that it is mainly concerned with the advice and assistance scheme and appears to be the direct outcome of a deal struck between the Lord Chancellor and the Treasury in 1985.[69] The pilot experiment had teething problems – particularly in finding enough solicitors willing to participate – but there is little doubt that a scheme will go ahead. The chair of the Legal Aid Board, John Pitts, told the Bar Conference in 1989 that:

> Whether the franchising proposals for Green Form [advice and assistance] prove practicable in the form we have proposed or not, somewhat similar arrangements are likely to be developed.[70]

The Board has made similar proposals in relation to multi-party actions such as disaster or drug claims[71] and there can be little doubt that franchising offers greater protential for quality assurance in legal aid than anything which has been officially introduced previously.[72]

Franchising is only the first step towards changing the delivery of legal aid. The Legal Aid Board has already announced that it wants to invite tenders for duty representation schemes in housing possession cases.[73] More radical steps cannot be far behind: first on the agenda is likely to be the contracting out of criminal work. Although it is not, so far, the Board's policy to contract out duty solicitor schemes, it has been prepared to do so where the local scheme has collapsed.[74] The squeeze on criminal legal aid expenditure is likely to lead to more schemes collapsing and therefore to the Board stepping in to award a contract.

Other forms of salaried and contracted services cannot be ruled out. For the first time since the early seventies, the law centres' movemement has made a claim to deliver mainstream legal services better than private practice. The Law Centres Federation response to the Lord Chancellor's review of eligibility for legal aid envisages law centres as the hub of local networks of advice agencies and solicitors' offices which would be block-funded to give front-line advice. The law centres would provide back-up and undertake strategic work.[75]

Such an ambitious scheme is likely to founder on the suspicion that the law centres have not sorted out their own problems of accountability and internal management. But other bodies are arguing for developments in the same direction. The government-appointed National Consumer Council, for instance, in its response to the eligibility review stated:

> There should be an increased role for the salaried sector in providing legal services. There are certain areas of law where salaried services might provide a better service for consumers. We consider that there must be a basic provision of general advice services and in addition provision for specialist legal advice and assistance. We recommend that the Lord Chancellor should begin to plan for a strategic mixed model of provision. He should set up research to analyse the cost, cost-effectiveness, quality and consumer satisfaction of providing certain legal services currently provided by private practice through salaried services instead.[76]

In the area of criminal defence work, a salaried service has been considered at the Lord Chancellor's department for many years and could undoubtedly operate more cheaply than the present system of case by case legal aid. With a Lord Chancellor less committed to protecting the interests of the Bar than his predecessors – and with the Bar possibly due to shrink as a result of the Courts and Legal Services Act reforms – a salaried criminal defence service of some sort is a distinct possibility. Whether that will result in any improvement for the public is, of course, another matter and would depend on how the service was set up and, in particular, the level of its funding.

Finally, the question is not whether the next few years will see fundamental changes in the way public legal services are provided. The question is about the nature of those changes: whether cost-cutting or improving the quality of the service will be the main aim; whether legal aid is to become a service restricted to the deserving poor or, instead, be securely fixed as part of the welfare state or even serve as a means of distributive justice. The answers to those questions will, in turn, depend on the answers to the larger political questions which lie outside the legal services field.

NOTES AND REFERENCES

1 *Report of the Committee on Legal Aid and Legal Advice in England and Wales* (1945; Cmd. 6642) 2.

2 *Social Insurance and Allied Services* (1942; Cmd. 6404).

3 P. Townsend, *Poverty in the United Kingdom* (1979) 63.

4 id., p. 62.

5 id., p. 63.

6 J.C. Kincaid, *Poverty and Equality in Britain* (1973) 44–7. See, also, Michael Foot, *Aneurin Bevan 1945– 1960* (1975) chs. 3 and 4.

8 For example, Cyril Glasser, 'Legal Aid – Decline and Fall' *Law Society's Gazette*, 19 March 1986, 839.

9 *Times*, 7 November 1991.

10 See, for example, the Lord Chancellor, Lord Mackay, 491 *H.L. Debs.*, col. 606 (15 December 1987).

11 Legal Aid Board, *Report to the Lord Chancellor on the Operation and Finance of the Legal Aid Act 1988 for the year 1990–91, Session 1990–91* (1991; H.C. 513) Chairman's introduction.

12 id., p. 2.

13 Glasser, op. cit., n. 8.

14 For civil legal aid, the current rules, which have changed little since 1949, are set out in the Civil Legal Aid (Assessment of Resources) Regulations 1989. For criminal legal aid, the rules are set out in schedules 3 and 4 to the Legal Aid in Criminal and Care Proceedings (General) Regulations 1989. For advice and assistance, see schedule 2 to the Legal Advice and Assistance Regulations 1989.

15 National Consumer Council, *Eligibility for Civil Legal Aid – A Response to the Lord Chancellor's Review of the Financial Conditions for Legal Aid* (1991).

16 Insufficient information is available about individual capital holdings to include them in the calculations. Applying the capital limits would disqualify more people. Therefore, all estimates overstate the proportion of the population which is eligible.

17 The Law Society and the Lord Chancellor's Advisory Committee, Twenty-sixth Annual Report, *Legal Aid 1975–76* (1977; H.C. 12).

18 Michael Murphy, *Civil Legal Aid Eligibility Estimates 1979–90* (1990).

19 National Consumer Council, *Ordinary Justice* (1989) 85.

20 Glasser, op. cit., n. 8.

21 National Consumer Council, op. cit., n. 19, p. 86.

22 id.

23 id.

24 For example, Sir Ian Percival, Solicitor-General, 35 *H.C. Debs.* col. 428 (26 January 1983); Lord Hailsham L.C., 472 *H.L. Debs.*, col. 921 (18 March 1986).
25 Lord Chancellor's Department, *Review of Financial Conditions for Legal Aid* (1991) 11.
26 id.
27 See D. Harris et al., *Compensation and Support for Illness and Injury* (1984).
28 These are contained in the Legal Aid Act 1988 and the Legal Aid (General) Regulations 1989.
29 A Solicitor, 'Is a Legal Aid Practice Possible?' *LAG Bulletin*, [month?] 1978, 205; G. Bindman, 'Solicitors' costs, or virtue unrewarded' *LAG Bulletin*, [month?] 1978, 253.
30 'Criminal Legal Aid Fees – Law Society settles terms with Lord Chancellor' *Law Society Gazette*, 9 April 1986, 1022.
31 Lord Chancellor's Department, *Legal Aid in England and Wales: A New Framework* (1987; Cm. 118) para. 48.
32 See, for example, *Law Society Gazette*, 22 March 1989, 38.
33 *Law Society's Gazette*, 18 February 1987, 454; *Law Society's Gazette*, 22 March 1989, 2; *Times*, 13 December 1990; *New Law J.*, 22 February 1991, 226.
34 *Legal Action*, October 1986, 8.
35 G. Chambers and S. Harwood-Richardson, *Solicitors in England and Wales: Practice, Organisation and Perceptions. Second Report: The Private Practice Firm* (1991) 62.
36 id., p. 63.
37 id., p. 68.
38 R. Smith, 'The Market for Legal Services' *Legal Action*, December 1990, 9.
39 *Lawyer*, 10 December 1991.
40 *Newcastle Journal*, 9 December 1991.
41 *Lawyer*, op. cit., n. 39.
42 id. The Legal Aid Practitioners' Group, which represents the interests of legal aid solicitors, was set up in 1981 with the active support of the Legal Action Group.
43 H. Perkin, *The Rise of the Professional Society: England since 1800* (1990).
44 id., p. 10.
45 See, for example, *LAG Bulletin*, August 1978, 177.
46 See, for example, *LAG Bulletin*, June 1977, 122; August 1978, 174; August 1979, 175; March 1980, 53.
47 B. Abel-Smith and R. Stevens, *Lawyers and the Courts* (1967).
48 Cyril Glasser, 'LAG – the first ten years' *LAG Bulletin*, November 1981, 250.
49 Namely, Cyril Glasser, Richard White, and Peter Urquhart.
50 Legal Action Group, *Legal Services: a Blueprint for the Future* (1977); *Legal Services – A New Start* (1980).
51 *LAG Bulletin*, December 1978, 284.
52 Simon Hillyard.
53 Law Society and Legal Aid Advisory Committee, *29th Legal Aid Annual Report 1978–79* (1980) 43.
54 R. Smith, 'The Market for Legal Services', *Legal Action*, December 1990, 55, 68.
55 id., p. 63.
56 id., p. 68.
57 id., p. 44.
58 id., p. 46.
59 R. Abel, *The Legal Profession in England and Wales* (1988); R. Abel, 'The Decline of Professionalism' (1986) 49 *Modern Law Rev.* 1. See, also, C. Glasser, 'The Legal Profession in the 1990s – images of change' (1990) 10 *J. of Legal Studies* 1.
60 Townsend, op. cit., n. 3, p. 64.
61 LAG, op. cit., n. 50 (1980), p. 29.
62 K. Foster, 'The Location of Solicitors' (1973) 36 *Modern Law Rev.* 153.
63 Charles Watkins et al., *The Distribution of Solicitors in England and Wales* (1986) table 10.
64 'Management at the Helm' *Legal Action*, June 1988, 4.
65 The parallel changes within the Law Society proper which, since 1986, has seen public sector professionals take over its permanent administration, is an interesting phenomenon but does

not come within the remit of this article, and may be relatively short-lived. On the other hand, recent developments in the Lord Chancellor's department are turning it into a modern department of state with a minister in the House of Commons, see *New Law J.,* 17 January 1992, 50.

66 For instance, the National Association of Citizens Advice Bureaux, the Federation of Independent Advice Agencies, trades unions, the Law Society, and the Bar Council.

67 Legal Aid Board, *Report to the Lord Chancellor* (1989; Cm. 688).

68 Legal Aid Board, op. cit., n. 11, p. 23 and appendix 2.

69 'A limiting franchise on giving legal aid' *Guardian,* 22 September 1989.

70 Author's note of speech.

71 Legal Aid Board, op. cit. n. 11, appendix 4.

72 For a discussion of the issues, see National Consumer Council, *Professional Competence in Legal Services: What is it and how do you measure it?* (1990).

73 *Lawyer,* 24 September 1991.

74 Legal Aid Board, op. cit., n. 11, p. 22.

75 Law Centres Federation, *Response to the Lord Chancellor's Review of Eligibility for Legal Aid* (1991).

76 National Consumer Council, *Eligibility for Civil Legal Aid: A Response to the Lord Chancellor's Review of the Financial Conditions for Legal Aid* (1991) para. 2.4.1.

The Inner Cities: Law Centres and Legal Services

RUSSELL CAMPBELL*

When Mrs Thatcher came to power in 1979, the law centres movement in the United Kingdom was almost a decade old. The 1970s had seen the establishment of local agencies sited in inner cities, committed to providing legal services outside the mainstream legal establishment to clients and client groups ill-served by lawyers and advisers. The early participants in the movement were ambitious and radical, seeking a distinctive identity for law centres which would guarantee them a place in the future development of legal services and a pivotal role in improving access to justice for the members of their local communities.

The establishment of North Kensington law centre in 1970 had been followed by Adamsdown, in Cardiff, in 1972 and by law centres in Brent and Camden, both in London, and other similar communities in the following years. Thirty-two existed in 1979. The loose co-ordination of law centres in the 1970s led to the creation of the Law Centres Federation, dedicated to continuing the growth of the movement. When Mrs. Thatcher left office, the number of law centres had increased to sixty: a sure sign of success? Certainly, but the *politics* of legal services had developed at an ever swifter pace in the 1980s, and by 1989 the government had confidently set out its radical agenda for the new decade. Key measures included a White Paper on the structure of the legal profession and related matters;[1] the Courts and Legal Services Act 1990, the key 'enabling' measure of the reforms, followed soon after. Reform of civil procedure itself[2] to achieve 'a cheaper and speedier service'[3] had been under consideration since 1986, with many proposals impacting on law centres' substantive work in areas such as debt, welfare benefits, and housing. The administration of the legal aid scheme had been transferred to the Legal Aid Board, which, having been established by the Legal Aid Act 1988, had turned its attention to ensuring 'quality' and 'value for money' in the legal aid scheme. How should the law centres movement respond to these issues? If the movement had successfully achieved a distinctive identity at the start of the 1980s, what shape was it in by the end of that decade, and how should it develop in the 1990s?

In 1979, defining a 'law centre' was no easy task. The movement itself made no attempt to identify the features of a 'model' law centre, recognizing that the

*National Housing Law Service, Woolwich House, 43 George St., Croydon CR9 1EY, England

thirty-two centres then in existence provided services to their clients and client groups in response to local needs, the views of funding bodies, and in accordance with the particular founding ideologies. Nonetheless, all the law centres associated with the Law Centres Federation (which emerged from the law centres working group and which provided a focus for interests and concerns shared by local law centres) had a number of things in common which set them apart from all other providers of legal services. The appearance of a 'market' challenge to existing provision of legal services during the 1980s, incorporating a number of 'Thatcherite' themes has put under renewed pressure each of these distinctive features of law centres.

1. *Innovative Methods of Working and Organization*

Advice, assistance, representation and other services were almost without exception provided free of charge, although arrangements were made to act for individuals under the legal advice and assistance and legal aid schemes and to ensure that in appropriate circumstances costs were recovered from opponents in litigation or from third parties.

Salaried lawyers – solicitors and barristers – were employed by law centres to provide services to members of the public and groups of people. Many of the first participants in the movement brought with them a critique of conventional legal practice with its emphasis on the dispensing of advice, assistance, and representation in accordance with a professional ethic which was seen as having failed to provide adequate legal services to inner city comunities (notwithstanding the development of the legal aid scheme since the Legal Aid Act 1949). The employment of salaried lawyers was a break from this ethic. For some it was a development consistent with the concept of a 'national legal service' which might emerge in the future (broadly analagous in scope to the National Health Service). Special arrangements were needed to ensure that these salaried lawyers were able to practice within the scope of the professional codes of the Law Society and the Bar Council, and waivers of particular practice rules were negotiated as each law centre was established (soon evolving into a 'standard' form of waiver).

Lay advisers and others were employed to provide services to clients and client groups alongside lawyers. This recognition by law centres that expertise in the areas of law with which their clients were concerned was not confined to lawyers was years ahead of its time. During the 1980s, the Citizens Advice Bureau service demonstrated effectively that its lay advisers were able to provide advice on some matters to clients more cheaply (and to larger numbers) than conventional legal practice. In some areas of law, such as social security, debt, and consumer problems, the separate case was also made by the same agency that the advice itself was generally of at least the quality provided by solicitors in private pratcice. Towards the end of the 1980s, the government and the Legal Aid Board also expressed interest in lay advisers, although most commentators are agreed that it is the 'efficiency' demonstrated by their relatively low cost that lies at the heart of the attraction.

'Collective working' ensured that day-to-day management of law centres was achieved democratically, without regard to a hierarchy locating power with particular members of staff or with a director. Lawyers, lay advisers, administrative, and financial staff were to have an equal say. The early law centres did not always adopt this approach. For example, Camden, founded in 1973, began life with a director, salaried lawyers, and support staff in a conventional hierarchy of power. It was only in 1977 that the post of director was abolished and a collective established. In nearly all cases, collective working was accompanied by the abolition of the division of labour between advisers and support staff (such as secretaries and clerks) with typing, filing of documents, and other tasks being distributed amongst advisers. No large-scale analysis has been undertaken of the effects of this method of working on the quality of law centres' work, nor its impact on the numbers of clients seen or projects undertaken, nor on the effect of stemming the employment in law centres of skilled clerical and support workers with experience and expertise in the preparation of legal documents and materials. Nor has there been a sustained examination within the movement of the ideological assumption underlying and justifying the abolition of separate support staff, namely that the nature of such work lends itself to exploitative relations between lawyer/adviser and support worker.

Management committees of local people or representatives of community groups such as tenants associations or trades councils were personally responsible for the centres and for the employment of staff (most law centres are companies limited by guarantee with the management committee consisting of or drawn from the directors of the company). This remains a key feature of law centres. Management committees are intended to ensure that real control of a law centre lies in the community in which it is situated and to achieve accountability to the community and responsiveness to its needs and demands for legal services. As we shall see, law centres continue to argue for central funding (disimbursed through local authorities) to enable the establishment and secure running of law centres in all inner city communities and wherever demand for a law centre arises. Although this policy has been carried into the 1990s, it finds no welcoming response from the government or the Legal Aid Board. How funding arrangements of this type may be reconciled with an insistence on local control needs further thought.

Law centres aimed to provide services to clients and client groups and deploy supporting skills beyond legal advice, assistance, and representation. From the very earliest days of the movement, one aspect of the critique of conventional legal practice has been that lawyers often see a particular problem in too narrow a context and seek to achieve its resolution by relying on 'legal means' to the exclusion of other approaches, and perhaps to the disadvantage of the client. In their casework, law centres would explore the use of administrative procedures, lobbying, campaigning, and other techniques in addition to legal advice and litigation, or perhaps as an alternative to it, where this was felt to be in the client's best interests and in accordance with his or her instructions. For example, in housing cases, this might mean making representations to a local-authority landlord or enlisting help from or providing support to tenants' associations.

An emphasis on 'strategic' work has always been present in law centres, although the application of this term to prioritize cases or projects has varied from law centre to law centre. The early participants in the movement brought with them a number of left/liberal ideologies but an early publication by the law centres working group drew heavily on American experience in describing this aspect of law centres' work:

> Effective solution of (the legal problems of the poor) may require the lawyer to direct his attention away from the particular claim or grievance to the broader interests and policies at stake, and away from the individual client to a class of clients, in order to challenge more directly and with greater impact certain structural sources of injustice.[4]

2. *Areas of Work*

Law centres were set apart from conventional lawyers by the types of cases they accepted. In the 1970s, experience and expertise were quickly built up in welfare benefits and social security, immmigration, family work, crime, employment, and housing. During that decade and in the 1980s, as lawyers left law centres and set up their own firms, taking their experience and expertise with them, this broad scope of work narrowed somewhat, leaving a 'core' of immigration, employment, housing, and social security work remaining in law centres, with some variation to reflect local needs.

Leaving aside for the moment the difference between individual law centres and varying emphases on 'closed' and 'open door' law centres, the major weakness of the movement, which impeded the development of law centres during the 1980s and remains a source of vulnerability today, was the lack of a uniform funding scheme. By the end of the 1970s, there were three main sources of funding. The largest source, and one which funded all but a handful of law centres, was local government, which provided grants to cover establishment and running costs. The Lord Chancellor's department had taken over most of the funding of seven law centres including North Kensington.[5] The third source of funding, which became ever more important during the 1980s, was the legal aid fund, which paid for the costs of advice, assistance, and representation to those clients who fell within the scope of legal advice and legal aid schemes. Although this source provided short- and medium-term security to many law centres as local authority funding came under pressure (as a result of central government policies from the early 1980s onwards), it has had the unintended consequence of tying law centres to the fortunes of the legal aid scheme, which has itself come under pressure from the government and, since 1989, the Legal Aid Board.

Current arguments about restrictions in eligibility (with some analyses indicating that roughly a quarter of those eligible for legal aid in 1979 had ceased to be eligible by 1990), the possible exclusion of areas of work at the heart of law centres' practice (housing and welfare benefits have been considered as candidates for exclusion from the legal advice and assistance scheme; immigration came under scrutiny in 1991 with the Home Secretary's plans (now withdrawn) to remove this work from the scheme and provide increased funding instead to the United Kingdom Immigration Advisory service), and 'franchising' (with a pilot/research study nearing completion at the time of writing) are bad news for law centres such as Camden, North Kensington, and some other large ones, which now rely on the fund for 15–30 per cent of their income. Without a reliable central source of funding, each new law centre had to argue for its existence in the face of local circumstances unrelated to the community's need for legal services, with favourable outcomes depending on the political party in power locally, the views of particular councillors on the key committees, the effect of central government policies on the local authority's resources, and any number of other factors. In some cases, this had the effect of delaying for years the establishment of a new centre.[6]

In other cases, law centres have had to rely on a number of sources of funding, with all the insecurity and painstaking lobbying to maintain grants that this entails. The best illustration is Central London Community Law Centre, a small, high-quality law centre providing legal services in the heart of the capital. When founded in 1980, its funding was provided by three different authorities; the London Borough of Camden, the City of Westminster and the Greater London Council. Because the catchment area of the law centre was not confined within the boundaries of a single local authority this arrangement may have been inevitable, but many hours of staff and management time were needed to ensure that each funder continued to provide what was felt to be a fair amount, year after year. In 1983 the City of Westminster decided – at short notice – to withdraw its grant, which threatened the law centre with substantial cutbacks. The other funders then agreed to make up the shortfall to almost the previous level of funding. On the abolition of the Greater London Council in 1985, the London Boroughs Grant Scheme agreed to continue to take over and pay that authority's grant, but more uncertainty was built into the law centre's work as the funding body took a subtantial amount of time each year to agree to maintain its commitment. Finally, in 1989, a private firm of solicitors, the City firm of Titmuss Sainer and Webb, agreed to make a substantial donation which restored the funding of the law centre to its previous level. The firm is presently committed to funding but only from year to year.

The rate of expansion of the movement during the Thatcher years was impressive; in 1979 there were thirty-two law centres, by 1984 this number had grown to fifty-six and by the end of the decade, to sixty. But what state was the movement in at the start of this period, and what ambition did it carry forward through the 1980s and into the 1990s? Was its undeniably success in *surviving* and expanding during the Thatcher years unalloyed, or did growth in numbers mask a sidelining of law centres as providers of legal services? The Thatcher decade divides conveniently into sections, with the period 1979 to 1985 presenting challenges to law centres arising from political developments and legislative changes *other than* government-led changes to legal services, and the period 1986 to 1990 (beginning with the 'legal aid scrutiny' by the Lord Chancellor's department)[7] containing the government's reforms, intended to provide a framework of procedures and providers into the 1990s and beyond.

Set against the legal establishment in 1979 was the movement's proposal that a legal services commission be created which would, among other things, research into the public's needs for legal services, consider whether such needs were being met, and make proposals to meet them in the future. The commission would include representatives from the legal profession and government but a majority of its members would be drawn from community organizations providing legal services (such as law centres!). During the 1970s the call was for several hundred law centres, to be funded by central government via grants made by the proposed commission. In its submission to the Royal Commission on Legal Services, the Law Centres Working Group, on behalf of the law centres, proposed that the development of law centres take place 'in conjunction with a maximum use of the potential of other resources.'[8] This meant the development of working relationships locally between law centres, private practice and other agencies (principally Citizens' Advice Bureaux) which 'would allow law centres to concentrate on test cases, group work and educational work.'[9] The Royal Commission, in its final report, declined to place law centres at the heart of a programme of reform, but did nonetheless confirm that the movement had achieved a significant presence in only a few years of existence:

> The impact of law centres has been out of all proportion to their size, to the number of lawyers who work in them, and to the amount of work it is possible for them to undertake. The volume of work they have attracted shows how deep is the need which they are attempting to meet.[10]

Two obvious points may be made here; the emphasis is on *local* work undertaken by law centres, arising from local need; 'networking' or co-ordinating and directing resources held by a number of agencies is seen as an efficient means of providing legal services. There is no attempt on the part of the movement to move from a 'micro' to a 'macro' scale and develop law centres as providers of legal services *nationally*. Nor is there much emphasis on presenting the work of law centres – casework, 'groupwork' or whatever – as an 'oppositional ' critique of existing provision on a national scale. From time to time there is reliance on anecdotal evidence of particular cases or projects undertaken by individual law centres – an approach found early on, in the 1974 document, '*Towards Equal Justice*', which offered a number of fine examples of law centres' work but which failed to pin down the existing system or to marshall the evidence to best effect.[11] Given that throughout the movement's life *no other provider* has had a similar experience of undertaking large numbers of cases and projects in housing, immigration, social security, duty schemes in county courts, and so on, it is astonishing that no central records have been kept of clients seen, cases won and lost, strategies used, groups advised, and so on. The weakness of focusing on local work and experience emerges when *everyone else* moves from the 'micro' to the 'macro', as happened between 1986 and 1990 in response to government initiatives, particularly when the 'macro' theme for much of this period is how legal services are to be *funded* and when the future development of legal services is seen by the present government and the Legal Aid Board as inextricably linked to 'value for money', which draws the spotlight uncomfortably onto 'groupwork' and educational work. Making a case for this work, and for strategic casework – low in numbers but big in impact – requires a national profile and the effective presentation of all those local projects and cases.

The work of law centres in their communities during these years continued to be concentrated in areas in which private practitioners had, on the whole, little experience or expertise, such as housing, social security, immigration, and employment. Much of it involved advising and representing clients in tribunals for which no legal aid is available. The determined drive to increase access to justice was maintained. Perhaps the best example was the establishment and consolidation of county court duty schemes to provide advice and representation to tenants and other occupiers on possession days. This work does not fall within the legal aid or legal advice and assistance schemes (although for some years payment was recovered in some areas in particular circumstances under former regulations) and cannot easily be undertaken by private practitioners. Once established, these schemes have attracted support from judges and court staff and have played a key role in preventing evictions and homelessness and have contributed to a more consistent application of the law and procedure in possession actions. A decade or more after the first few were fully established in London, the Legal Aid Board is now considering ways of funding such schemes, although it is very likely, in view of the board's ideological approach, that a straightforward system of grants will be eschewed in favour of invitations to bid for a 'franchise' to run a particular scheme. Another example has been the involvement of law centres in inquests, acting on behalf of relatives of the deceased without charge, outside the scope of the legal aid scheme. With the support and encouragement of the clients, this work has attempted to highlight the very low standards in many houses in multiple occupation, often used by local authorities temporarily to house the homeless, and the substantial risks of fire fatalities.[12]

Local networks were consolidated in these years in a number of cities, with law centres, other advice agencies, and local firms of solicitors coming to informal agreements on the types of work each would undertake and the circumstances in which clients or enquirers would be referred from one agency to another. The 1979–82 recession and the impact on local government services – principally housing – of central government policies such as rate-capping meant an ever-increasing demand for legal and advice services, and networking was a practical response to difficult circumstances. It also found its way into the ideology of the movement, with calls for law centres to prepare, with others, 'local development plans' which would map out the need for legal and advice services in the locality and create strategies to meet the needs identified in the plan.

At the start of the decade, with pay parity a feature of nearly all law centres, the salary generally available to a solicitor was reasonably attractive to an individual without dependents and with two or three years post-qualification experience. It compared favourably with the salary available to a similarly experienced solicitor in a small-to-medium sized legal aid firm (say, £8,500 per annum in 1980, or £10,000 per annum in 1984). The Law Society treated law centres as solicitors' offices and required the presence each day of at least one solicitor with three practising certificates (generally showing three years post-qualification experience). Attracting such solicitors into law centres became increasingly difficult during the decade, as a gap emerged between law centre salaries and those available in private practice. Vacant posts for solicitors were often re-advertised. The longer a solicitor worked in a law centre the greater the gap, as increases in his or her pay were linked to inflation only, with most law centres awarding little to reflect experience or long service (and with even these increments falling far short of increases available in the private sector). By the end of the decade the movement was seeking to persuade the Law Society that the requirement be lessened from three to only one practising certificate to deal with the shortage of solicitors willing to work in law centres. A few centres gave up parity in the late 1980s, offering solicitors £2,000 or £3,000 a year more than other staff to attract applications.

In 1984 the Law Centres Federation (as the working group had become) published a 'design brief' calling for a hundred new law centres to be established through central government funding by 1989, with a long-term goal of attracting to the movement 10 per cent of the total legal services budget. There was no immediate government response. A debate on law centres was heard in the House of Lords a year later with absolutely nothing new promised to the movement.[13]

In the second half of the decade Thatcherism began to make its mark directly on legal services, with attention given to the legal aid scheme, the civil justice system, and the structure of the legal profession in rapid succession. By the end of this process a new paradigm was in place, presenting law centres with new threats to their existence and, of course, new opportunities.

In June 1986 the Lord Chancellor's department published *Legal Aid: Efficiency Scrutiny*. This report contained proposals for reform of the legal aid scheme and identified a number of concerns which have subsequently provided the major themes for action. The scrutiny was prompted largely by government concern at the increasing cost of the legal aid scheme – a demand-led public service whose costs appeared to be increasing without control. The report described the scheme as 'a big and thriving business' and noted that the legal aid bill had risen from £49 million in 1975–76 to £257 million in 1985–6. It noted that 'there is little in the system that ensures the *quality* of the activity paid for as legal aid.' The reforms proposed – such as a new 'Legal Services Board' to manage the scheme (which became the Legal Aid Board) were intended to achieve 'the best and most effective way of providing help to clients and value for money for the taxpayers.' For the first time, the role of advice agencies was to be made central to the scheme, in the proposals for the reform of 'legal advice under the Green Form scheme' which accounts for about 10 per cent of the entire legal aid budget. The scrutiny team noted that Citizens' Advice Bureuax dealt with 5.7 million enquiries in 1984–85 in areas such as social security, employment, housing, and consumer affairs, through 900 bureaux. Most of this work could have been done under the Green Form scheme by private practitioners or law-centre solicitors. However, the central government grant to the National Association of Citizens' Advice Bureaux was a mere £6.4 million in 1984–85. A useful connection had been made! *Making the assumption that a satisfactory quality threshold existed outside law centres and other specialists in welfare law*, the report recommended that the Green Form scheme in its existing form be abolished, with advice in 'family cases . . . and other civil cases' being provided 'by agencies such as CABx, rather than by private practitioners.' Law Centres would, of course, be included as 'other agencies' (with only fifty centres in existence at this time, 'macro' planning would have overlooked them if they had not been successful in their work) but the loss of income would be fatal to most of the large law centres who opened their doors to clients and enquirers in numbers as large as any CAB. Legal advice from private practitioners would be available from public funds only in criminal matters and for detailed family work or cases referred from 'the first-tier agency'. The report had failed to establish that very many referrals under these arrangements would be from the specialists (the law centre or other agency advisers) to the generalists (the private practitioners) with a loss of quality on the way up the High Street.

Not surprisingly, the proposal to abolish the Green Form scheme was rejected at the time, but other recommendations were acted upon, with certain areas of work taken out of scope of the scheme, such as advice concerning wills and conveyancing (with some exceptions). More importantly, the reports considered ways of ensuring that legal advice and tribunal representation were provided in a co-ordinated way. A promising idea at the time was to invite applications for contracts to provide services, which 'would . . . ensure flexibility to meet local need. . . (and) enable the legal aid administration to directly and explicitly buy the best service that could be obtained for the money available.' The report observed that: 'NACAB would be likely to seek the contracts in most areas, and other advice agencies or consortia of local solicitors might also compete.' In the five years since then, we have moved from applications for contracts to applications for 'franchises', with the Legal Aid Board soon to publish its proposals on completion of a pilot study in the Midlands. The board's stated views include the proposal that once a franchise is successfully established in a locality, the particular area of work – social security, housing or whatever – contained in the franchise would be withdrawn from the legal aid scheme. Existing providers of advice not included in the franchise would no longer be able to claim on a case-by-case basis. They would be able to apply for additional franchises, as would new providers setting up a new service.

The Law Centres Federation launched a successful initiative in the summer of 1985 to unify the main providers of public salaried advice and legal services, culminating in conferences in March and September 1986 under the auspices of the Advice Services Alliance and resulting in agreement on many parts of a funding strategy for legal and advice services. However, this display of unity was not enough to stall the development of the government's market approach to funding, nor did it banish the tension between the CABx and other participants (law centres and the small, independent advice agencies), with the former being the only providers with sufficient outlets to matter as a *national* provider of first-tier advice, and with the extra advantage of ready access to impressive statistics to show large numbers of clients seen and enquiries logged.

The approach to funding – and through funding, to *access* to advice – developed by the government following the scrutiny report and by the Legal Aid Board amounts to a rejection of the Law Centres Federation's strategy. Worse still, when fully implemented, the franchising scheme will put local law centres under still more pressure, with local authorities almost certain to require an application by the law centre for a franchise to provide advice in, say, housing or immigration or social security law as a condition of grant aid to fund administration of the centre or other areas of work. Why should local authorities fund advice of this kind when the board will pay for it through a franchise? Of course, law centres recover costs at present under the Green Form scheme, and local authorities know this and take it into account, but their hands will be forced by the proposed withdrawal of the scheme from the locality once a franchise is established. Once this happens, services by non-franchisees will either be funded by grant aid or they will not be funded at all. Work that does not fit easily into the traditional casework model to be funded through the franchise (which has to date been premised on the need to find new ways of funding individual cases) is most vulnerable to withdrawal of funding: work described by law centres as 'educational' or 'campaigning' work in which large numbers of people are advised about issues outside the traditional adviser/client relationships. Although the Legal Aid Board has not ruled out applications for grants to pay for work of this type, it would be surprising if they were not met by the argument that local campaigns for local people should be paid for locally, by the charge-capped local authority – a long-winded way of making this method of working extinct. On the other hand, law centres' vulnerability to this pressure flows directly from the reluctance of the movement to break out of local catchment areas and the failure to achieve a visible, dynamic, national presence (and drawing national attention from time to time to examples of local work, however forcefully done, does not count as an effective national presence!).

In the absence of an effective strategy to oppose it in the 1990s, the present government's programme of legal reform will stifle law centres and exclude them from any effective role in the development of legal services. Funding is, of course, a priority. Franchising and other measures to contain eligibility may well have capped legal aid expenditure by mid decade. Arguments about 'safety nets' and other means of redirecting resources will limit the income law centres derive from the legal aid scheme. Many of the larger centres now rely on this income and will not be able to maintain current levels of service without it. Calls to extend the legal aid scheme to cover representation before tribunals are unlikely to be met in the next few years and representation will have to be paid from other resources within law centres. If grant aid from local authorities is compromised by local franchises to do welfare work, there will be less opportunity for law centres to provide the full range of services currently available. Where grant aid from local authorities remains, the conflict between their roles as funders and defendants in proceedings (in housing cases, for example) will subvert any long term security in the relationship. Inevitably, unless funding is provided on a different basis, there will be pressure on law centres to look to other sources, notably private funders, as Central London and Tower Hamlets law centres have done in recent years. Though this may provide for local needs in the short term, it diverts attention from the need for a rational, secure funding policy. It is also consistent with an ascendant ideology which places legal services to the working class and poor *inside* traditional adviser/client relationships but *outside* state-funded services which would establish access to lawyers and advisers as a tangible right. Any substantial increase in funding from private sources would be a political disaster for law centres.

A change of government following the general election in 1992 will provide an opportunity for a change of direction. The current reforms, including the franchise proposals, may be pursued as appropriate. But law centres should not be forced to fit in to a new scheme if this involves abandoning effective local methods of working. Any new programme of funding must therefore guarantee that reliance on the legal aid scheme in individual cases and work with local client groups outside the scheme are not mutually exclusive. This would require formal recognition of the value of this type of work and the allocation of funds – in the form of grants – to ensure its survival. There can be no objection by law centres to continuing assessment of the quality of this kind of work and of the local need for it to satisfy a funder that grant aid is being well spent, but clearly local authorities cannot undertake this role. Even if new arrangements make central funds available to be disbursed by local authorities, 'quality control' should be carried out by an independent body. There is no early prospect of an incoming Labour government agreeing to fund new law centres in every inner city borough but steps should be taken soon in the life of a new parliament to ensure the security of the centres currently funded by the Lord Chancellor's department and then to remove the threats to the other existing centres, threats that arise from charge-capping and volatile local politics (as in Bradford, Brent, and Haringey, and in the case of those centres in London that rely on funding from the London Boroughs Grants Scheme). Restoring law centres recently cut, such as those in Wandsworth and Dudley, could then follow, with new centres being opened in other areas as soon as resources permit. There is no shortage of need, and provision is still haphazard. For example, there is an obvious and chronic shortage of law centres in the south London outer boroughs – none currently exist although one is planned in Merton. There are six in outer London north of the Thames.

There are currently no rural law centres, although research conducted by the Law Centres Federation in 1990 has shown the need for them and steering groups have been established in parts of the country.[14]

Funding apart, there is much that law centres can do for themselves to enhance their effectiveness and profile in the 1990s. It is now time to break with the limited aim of merely meeting needs in the locality. In 1979, in evidence to the Royal Commission, '. . . the purpose of law centres is to tackle the most pressing problems in their localities'[15] may have been an adequate statement of the ambition of the movement. But it is not adequate now. There is a real danger that legal services may in future be planned on the basis that access to the best lawyers and courts is reserved to corporate litigators and individuals with a few, particular types of problem, with vast numbers of disputes and conflicts affecting welfare rights referred to advice agencies and small claims procedures in the county courts, with no legal aid to fund representation. Some advice agencies with effective national presence, such as the Citizens' Advice Bureaux, may be seen by a Conservative government as playing a key role in such a scheme. Law centres, with their unique experience as employers of salaried lawyers providing advice and representation to the public, are well placed to continue to demonstrate how such a two-tier system would fail to provide adequate access to justice and to show how complex and difficult it can be to express and enforce welfare rights without access to lawyers (and skilled advisers). But this opposition to current provision and apparent new trends will only be fully effective if law centres make an impact nationally as well as locally. This means addressing the needs of clients and client groups *outside* local catchment areas and achieving greater visibility to other agencies, lawyers, funders, and the government.[16] This, in turn, requires greater co-ordination of work between law centres and greater mobility of skills and resources, with the establishment of a 'second-tier' of law centres being a natural development arising from this new orientation of the movement. Achieving these goals would bring profound success: the establishment of a salaried legal service providing advice, assistance, and representation locally (in individual cases and on behalf of groups, in a balance to be determined by local needs, funding and the availability of representation elsewhere) *which is also able to intervene nationally* to pursue issues through test or lead cases – wherever these arise geographically – and to participate in and influence the development of legal services.

Improving the visibility of law centres depends largely on making better use of a resource that has as yet barely been tapped – the accumulated casework experience of law centres. This asset is beyond the scope of other advice agencies and all but a few private practitioners. The very best practice in law centres should be available in each of them, so that the most up-to-date strategies and procedures can be brought to bear in every catchment area. Available technology should enable skills and resources to be made mobile to achieve greatest impact. Co-ordination between law centres would similarly improve the quality of service provided. Local networks involving law centres, other agencies, and private practice are in place in many areas; regional networks should be encouraged where there is a need arising from particular issues of law or social policy. There is no reason why the strategic reach of law centres should not be extended by developing long-distance legal services, including representation. These new services would be of enormous value in pursuing test or lead cases in homelessness or social security law over very large areas where there are no large conurbations – but plenty of inner cities – and only a few advice agencies, no expert private practitioners, and no law centres. Some of the few national agencies employing lawyers and advisers have pioneered new methods of working to provide advice and resources to local agencies tens or hundreds of miles away and then to provide representation in any ensuing litigation. Law centres should learn from these experiences. Probably the cheapest and most effective means of improving the movement's effectiveness and visibility is the establishment of several national law centres with expertise in the main areas of law centres' work, such as housing, employment, immigration, education, and social security. For relatively small sums, these organizations would increase the vitality of existing law centres, increase their impact and begin to provide a critique of legal services nationally. This critique would go beyond anecdotal evidence, to show the damage the Thatcher years have done to employment rights, housing rights, benefits, and to access to advice and lawyers. The idea is appealing. The Society of Labour Lawyers has called for '. . . funding national specialist agencies in the various areas of welfare law whose task would be to encourage coverage and good practice, to provide information and specialist backup and to take the "lead" and "test" cases.'[17] One million pounds per annum would fund about *five* of these second-tier bodies.

There is, then, an opportunity for law centres in the 1990s to realize many of the goals set in the early years of the 1970s, in spite of the hardships of the 1980s, when the lack of secure funding diverted energy away from providing services to clients and client groups. However, a failure to break out, figuratively, from the neighbourhoods and local communities in which all law centres start their lives will result in stagnation and only a nominal role in the provision of legal services. Law centres have grown up. Now they must leave home.

NOTES AND REFERENCES

1 *Legal Services: A Framework for the Future* (1989; Cm. 740).
2 See *The Civil Justice Review* (1988; Cm. 394).
3 op. cit., n. 1, p. 3, introductory remarks by Lord Mackay.
4 J. Carlin, J. Howard, and S. Messinger, *Civil Justice and the Poor* (1967).
5 The decision, taken by Lord Elwyn-Jones, was not related to any long-term policy regarding law centres; it was an emergency measure to prevent the total loss of the centres.
6 As with Luton law centre, which finally came into being in 1988 in spite of a change in power locally; fortunately, the incoming Conservative administration had been persuaded of the need for the law centre).
7 Lord Chancellor's Department, *Legal Aid: Efficiency Scrutiny* (1986).
8 Law Centres Working Group, *A Report on Law Centres,* (1979).

9   id.
10 The Royal Commission on Legal Services in England and Wales, *Final Report* (1979; Cmnd. 7648).
11 The Law Centres Working Group, *Towards Equal Justice* (1974).
12 As with the involvement in North Kensington law centre following the substantial loss of life in a fire in Clanricarde Gardens, London W2 in December 1982, and the involvement of Camden law centre in similar circumstances following a fire in Gloucester Place, London W1 in October 1984.
13 *H.L. Debs.*, (8 May 1985).
14 Law Centres Federation, *Coming of Age* (1991) 14.
15 op. cit., n. 10.
16 R. Campbell, 'The role of law centres', *Legal Action*, February 1989, 7.
17 The Society of Labour Lawyers, *Equal Rights for All* (1991).

The Country Lawyer: Iconography, Iconoclasm, and the Restoration of the Professional Image

KIM ECONOMIDES*

INTRODUCTION

The behaviour of contemporary lawyers, and the way we think about them, is dominated by the market and reference to the enterprise culture surrounding it.[1] The theory of 'market control' which asks how lawyers seek and attain competitive advantage within a free market has displaced most other perspectives on the modern legal profession.[2] This theory which developed alongside the rise of Thatcherism during the 1980s became increasingly influential while more and more practitioners also began to ask themselves the key question of how to compete in the commercial business arena. Even those criticizing the theory do not say the market is unimportant: rather, they argue it does not take the market seriously enough,[3] a criticism which could also be made of those firms unable to see their way through the recession. Tomorrow's lawyers, so it seems, will be those tough enough to survive today's market for legal services.

Here I consider a segment of this market – country lawyers – in order to gain insight into the new entrepreneurial ideology which may provide what Glasser has termed 'professional coherence' in a market which looks as if it will become increasingly fragmented and specialized.[4] I focus on three questions: first, perceptions of the distinctive nature and values of country practice and the extent to which they are compatible with the emergent ideology (iconography); second, rural practitioners' views about their capacity to survive changes in the legal market initiated by the radical conservatism of the 1980s (iconoclasm); and third, a vision of what kind of programme an incoming government might adopt if it wished to intervene in order to impose

* Faculty of Law, University of Exeter, Amory Building, Rennes Drive, Exeter EX4 4RJ, England

This article is based on a paper first presented at the Socio-Legal Studies Association Annual Conference, University of Bristol, 9–11 April 1990 and the findings of the *Access to Justice in Rural Britain Project* (ESRC Grant EOO 232 054), now published in M. Blacksell, K. Economides, and C. Watkins, *Justice Outside the City. Access to Legal Services in Rural Britain* (1991).

discipline and restructuring on the market for rural legal services (restoration). In emphasizing *behavioural* factors determining future legal services policy I aim to avoid some of the cruder forms of economic determinism associated with market analyses of the legal profession.

ICONOGRAPHY

Homo Economicus would not at first sight appear to be an apt description of the country lawyer. Traditionally, the country lawyer is cast in a paternalistic role which emphasizes status in the community rather than the pursuit of profit or legal expertise.[5] Hardman, writing in the *Law Society's Gazette* in 1961, provides a good example of the traditional view:

> The country practitioner is certainly no great lawyer; if he were he would be of less value to the community. It is not merely brains that earn a competent living in the country; it is rather a humanity grafted to a will to help people in their troubles without regard to reward. In spite of state aid in its various forms, he still does, as he always has done, an immense amount of work that carries little or no financial payment. He undertakes tasks which require a moderate knowledge of law, coupled with common sense and a kindly and courteous manner, and is a valuable member of the community in which he lives. As part of his service he acts for innumerable charities, bodies of trustees, church councils, and takes an interest in such varied activities as regattas and rowing clubs, youth clubs and moral welfare and other similar associations.[6]

More recent studies of country lawyers in Britain and the United States of America confirm that this image persists even today.[7] However, this characterization needs to be interpreted with caution for it does not follow that country lawyers are always poor entrepreneurs; in fact they may be very well attuned to their markets and, by taking a rather longer-term and broader view of their relationships with their clients and community, they may actually prove to be shrewd businesspeople. Free diagnostic interviews, voluntary public service, and the cultivation of business networks with other professional services might create an impression of time-wasting inefficiency but in reality prove to be an effective strategy for securing and retaining a niche in the local market. In other words, the casual style of country practitioners could be seen as a rather sophisticated and subtle response to the markets they serve. Country solicitors, more so than their urban counterparts, are vulnerable to community pressure and must therefore adopt a more sensitive attitude towards their clientele.[8] Evidence from the *Access to Justice in Rural Britain Project* suggests that images of rurality influence solicitors' decisions to practice in the country and the extent to which they find their work satisfying. Rural areas have tended to attract male solicitors in mid-career or nearing retirement rather than the newly qualified for whom opportunities have been somewhat restricted.[9] As a result, the average age of solicitors in the more remote rural areas tends to be higher than in urban areas and their views about the kinds of work they should undertake rather more conservative. Similarly, until recently, firms were also occupying a secure place in rural communities which meant they were reluctant to react to developments in new technology or advertise their services. This security was to a large extent based on the monopoly over residential conveyancing, much of which was and remains linked to areas where title remained unregistered. One consequence of this stability was widespread complacency concerning the service on offer: country solicitors believed that rural legal services were adequate and displayed little sympathy for those suffering from problems of access. As one respondent commented, 'Country people may be inhibited from going to a solicitor by the remoteness of their homes, but not prevented'.[10] The problems of female practitioners in small country practices were also not seen as an urgent priority.[11]

These research findings which, on the whole, reveal deeply entrenched conservative attitudes amongst both clients and practitioners, might insulate rural firms from external competition and enable the majority of them to survive. If this happens, a style of practice may be kept alive which would contrast strongly with the new entrepreneurial professional ideology generated by 'mega-lawyering' in the city.[12] However, if traditional country practice does survive, this may not be for very long, given the age profile of these firms and the fact that senior partners approaching retirement may prefer to wind-up their practices rather than confront the new challenges of the 1990s.

ICONOCLASM

I now address the difficult question of how rural practitioners perceive the changes and challenges which now lie before them. We know that country practice has a broad-based dependence on residential conveyancing backed up by wills and trusts, family, and general litigation. There is also evidence of greater dependence among rural practices on legal aid work.[13] Interestingly, some felt in 1985 that this base would enable them to survive while others took a very different view and believed that government policy would eventually lead to their demise. By the late 1980s the whole legal profession had started to move rapidly into a highly competitive, client-led, open market within which many thought only the better organized and effectively managed practices stood even a chance of survival. For the country lawyer it must have seemed as if the gales that had laid waste much of the countryside had found their parallel in the winds of change culminating in the Courts and Legal Services Act 1990.

In order to see how country lawyers might cope with change, it may be helpful to look more closely at their reactions to the future in 1985 when they were asked to contemplate life without conveyancing. While circumstances have clearly changed since that date it may be that basic attitudes have not and that the kinds of response found then are still valid today. The four categories of country lawyer identified in our 1985 study were: (i) 'pessimists'; (ii) 'entrepreneurs'; (iii) 'specialists'; and (iv) 'fatalists'.[14]

117

1. 'Pessimists'

This group consisted of older solicitors in more remote rural locations who had few ideas about how best to cope with change. They felt threatened by the loss of conveyancing and the narrowing scope of legal aid. They voiced complaints about the introduction of the Crown Prosecution Service, the concentration of specialist work in rural areas and the erosion of professional standards. This category felt particularly vulnerable to mergers, closures, and staff reductions.

2. 'Entrepreneurs'

While this category was not in any sense optimistic about the future, they were prepared to think about the long term, and a strategic response to new circumstances. These lawyers were based in more urban or suburban locations and tended to be younger. They were more flexible in their outlook and more open to applications of new technology. The size of firms in this category varied; some were 'one-man bands' who specialized in order to retain a 'competitive edge' while others were larger firms able to diversify and take advantage of economies of scale.

3. 'Specialists'

This was a very small group for whom conveyancing was never very important. These lawyers were based in urban settings (Plymouth, Exeter or within a five-mile radius of these cities) and concentrated on litigation, family work or business affairs.

4. 'Fatalists'

Although the largest group, the 'fatalists' did not focus on a single view of the future. They were not as anxious as the 'pessimists' but were not so confident as the 'entrepreneurs'. They adopted an essentially cautious attitude to the future but did not question their own survival. In the short term, many felt that client loyalty, land registration, and the complexities of conveying rural properties and agricultural land would shield them from competition from banks and building societies, the competitors they most feared in the long term.

More recent evidence, conducted at a national level, broadly confirms trends brought out in these findings: despite the recession, nine out of ten solicitors expected in 1989 that they would still be in practice in five years' time although there would be a major shift from generalist work to specialist work.[15] Moreover, firms have not actually changed a great deal in terms of their structure and size despite a lot of media hype about 'merger-mania'; solicitors' firms remain essentially small businesses with eight out of ten having less than five partners.[16] Perceptions of future growth over the same five-year period (1989–1994) reveal, however, significant regional variations. The growth in the size of firms was estimated at a national average of 48 per cent, yet growth in the south-west of England was expected to be as low as 23 per cent. This stands in stark contrast to a growth rate of 102 per cent predicted by the City firms.[17]

To a large extent, the future of country lawyers is beyond their immediate control. Residential conveyancing and probate, wills and trusts cases continue to dominate the work of the private practitioner. On average, residential conveyancing represents 36 per cent of firms' cases making the profession extremely vulnerable to changes in the property market.[18] As Chambers and Harwood-Richardson point out:

> The prolonged property market recession of 1989 to 1991 has brought about the closure of many estate agents' offices; the large network of offices operated by the big insurance companies and building societies have been particularly badly affected. The effect on solicitors' firms may not be so clearly marked, although the Law Society has begun to record some redundancies within the profession. There will be scope for some firms to divert resources temporarily to other areas of legal business during the property market slump, but if the banks and building societies take on wholesale provision of conveyancing services, many small firms might face closure. The consequence of this would be that the public would lose their access to the whole range of legal services which those firms currently provide in addition to conveyancing.[19]

Apart from the downturn in the property market, country lawyers also feel themselves threatened by several proposals to close down rural magistrates' courts, to reform legal aid (franchising, the 'safety net scheme' and fixed fees) as well as current proposals for a licensing scheme governing firms taking on trainee solicitors.[20] The cumulative effect of these developments may force the country lawyer to withdraw from rural areas into larger urban-based units of production and abandon legal aid work and the training of the next generation of lawyers. In the short term, it seems likely that many country lawyers will struggle hard to ride out the recession and hold on to the attractions of living in pleasant surroundings and enjoying the unique professional status and autonomy afforded by small-scale practice within loyal client communities. While the prospect of new technology may hold out some hope for sustaining these centripetal tendencies in the future, for example, by allowing access to remote data bases,[21] it is also apparent that many country lawyers are fully aware of powerful centrifugal market forces which could eventually overwhelm them.

RESTORATION

The above analysis suggests that even if the majority of country lawyers survive the recession, a heavy price will be exacted in terms of forcing them to adopt a more aggressive approach towards marketing their services. The 'pessimists' will probably retire while the remainder will no longer be able to cross-subsidize uneconomic categories of work. Some new branch offices might be opened in a desperate attempt to bring in new work but the safer option of consolidation in larger, more urban-based units is likely to be the favoured option.[22] This will increase existing gaps in the market – perceived both in terms of areas of legal work as well as geographical areas – which para-legal and generalist advice agencies will find hard to cover, given their own restraints of finite financial resources, limited legal expertise, and pre-dominantly urban locations.[23] Any incoming government will therefore have to face the question of whether it wishes to intervene in the market for rural legal services or else ignore it.

To ignore the problem could be costly in terms of undermining the overall legitimacy of the legal system as well as professional status. Free-market and new entrepreneurial ideologies are unlikely to supplant traditional professional values totally and, in any event, all the major political parties have subscribed to a 'mixed delivery system' combining private practice with 'public sector' legal services, at least since the 1983 general election.[24] It therefore seems unlikely that any incoming government would completely ignore the problem, and indeed the Conservatives, supposedly the least interventionist of the political parties, have subsequently proven themselves capable of producing the most radical reforms of the organization and work of the legal profession of any government this century, culminating in the Legal Aid Act 1988 and the Courts and Legal Services Act 1990.[25] On the other hand, it should not be assumed either that an incoming Labour government would place a high priority on rural legal services, given that rural constituencies traditionally provide minimum support for Labour. If government has a difficulty with legal services policy it will concern not whether it can intervene, but how.

Faced with the prospect of country lawyers withdrawing from uneconomic work in rural communities, the government has the option of trying to bolster the existing service or else creating a new one, either as a complement or substitute. The first option might take the form of granting country solicitors special tax concessions, rates of remuneration, subsidies, and other induce-ments to encourage them to continue working in rural areas.[26] The second option might involve developing a salaried service by creating a national network of legal-aid lawyers or law centres.[27] This would in effect reduce the dependency of rural communities on the private profession and bring them into the 'mixed delivery' system.

The escalating cost of legal aid administered through the private profession, coupled with the need to focus more precisely on the legal needs of rural communities, may encourage the incoming government, and the Legal Aid Board, to explore seriously the possibilities of the second option. Foreign experience, sporadic as it is, is encouraging and if linked to geographical analyses of where to locate public sector services, it should be possible to develop a comprehensive legal service delivery system at reasonable expense.[28] There is an urgent need for 'action research' on public legal services in rural areas in order to determine their cost-effectiveness in relation to the services provided by the private profession. At present, we simply lack enough reliable information on which to make an informed judgement about the respective merits of these options.

The Birmingham franchising experiment should provide some new and interesting data on the meaning of 'quality' in legal aid work while also opening up the possibility of imposing some discipline on the private market. As part of their franchise contracts with the Legal Aid Board private firms could be directed to serve areas of unmet need.[29] The fact that country lawyers are more dependent on their legal aid income than their urban counterparts, particularly at a time of recession, may provide the Legal Aid Board with the leverage it needs to explore the full potential of the franchising concept as a mechanism to deliver legal services to rural areas. In any event, the Legal Aid Board, together with government, the legal professions, and other providers of legal services, need to consider planning a comprehensive legal services policy capable of defining, implementing, and monitoring standards of provision which include and are responsive to rural communities.[30] Furthermore, consumers are unlikely to be the sole beneficiaries of such a policy which, if implemented, should go some distance towards restoring the confidence and professional status of the country lawyer.

CONCLUSION

If the destiny of country lawyers is to be determined by the future market for their services, we should not ignore the shifting political and ideological foundations of that market. This market is susceptible to restructuring as well as manipulation and could change dramatically should the electorate choose a government more committed to the welfare state. At a local level, country lawyers must seek their salvation not simply in terms of defending traditional markets but also in their capacity to create and enter new ones, a quest which could be greatly assisted by planning and investment in legal education, research, and new technology.

NOTES AND REFERENCES

1 R. Abel, *The Legal Profession in England and Wales* (1988); R. Abel, 'Between Market and State: The Legal Profession in Turmoil' (1989) 53 *Modern Law Rev.* 285–325; C. Stanley, 'Justice Enters the Marketplace: Enterprise Culture and the Provision of Legal Services' in *Enterprise Culture*, ed. R. Keat and N. Abercrombie (1991); C. Stanley, 'Enterprising Lawyers: Changes in the Market for Legal Services' (1991) 25 *The Law Teacher* 44–51.

2 See, generally, R. Dingwall and P. Lewis (eds.), *The Sociology of the Professions* (1983); see also the different approach taken by C. Glasser, 'The Legal Profession in the 1990s – Images of Change' (1990) 10 *Legal Studies* 1–11.

3 See, for example, A. Paterson, 'Changing Perceptions of Professionalism' (1987) 32 *J. of the Law Society of Scotland* 368–73; A. Paterson, 'The Legal Profession in Scotland. An Endangered Species or a Problem Case for Market Theory?' in *Lawyers in Society: The Common Law World*, eds. R. Abel and P. Lewis (1988).

4 Glasser, op. cit., n. 2, p. 2.

5 See generally, M. Blacksell, K. Economides, and C. Watkins, *Justice Outside the City* (1991)

52–5; M. Blacksell, K. Economides, and C. Watkins, 'Country Solicitors: Their Professional Role in Rural Britain' (1987) 25 *Sociologica Ruralis* 181–96. For self-portraits of the country lawyer, see: T. W. Goad, *Just a Country Solicitor* (1989); J. Francis, *Gumboot Practice* (1989) and *Dales Law* (1991).

6 G. W. Hardman, 'The Qualities of the Country Practitioner' (1961) 58 *Law Society Gazette* 77.

7 Blacksell, Economides, and Watkins, op. cit., n. 5; D. Landon, *Country Lawyers. The Impact of Context on Professional Practice* (1990).

8 id., pp. 81–95; 119–146. T. D. Landon, 'Lawyers and Localities: The Interaction of Community Context and Professionalism' (1982) *Am. Bar Foundation Research J.* 459–85.

9 Blacksell, Economides, and Watkins (1991), op. cit., n. 5, pp. 57–62. According to the latest statistics prepared by the Law Society Research and Policy Planning Unit, 'Some 43 per cent of trainee solicitors commenced training in articles in central London . . . in the year 1st August 1990 to 31st July 1991. By comparison, in 1985–86, 30 per cent of articles were registered in central London.' S. Harwood-Richardson, *Annual Statistical Report 1991* (1991) 3. Local anecdotal evidence suggests that fewer provincial firms will be able to take on trainee solicitors in the future.

10 M. Blacksell, K. Economides, and C. Watkins, *Solicitors and Access to Legal Services in Ruaral Areas: Evidence from Devon and Cornwall* (1986) 29.

11 Blacksell, Economides, and Watkins (1991), op. cit., n. 5, pp. 71–3.

12 See R. Lee, pp. 31–48, and C. Whelan and D. McBarnet, pp. 49–68 in this volume.

13 See Blacksell, Economides, and Watkins (1991), op. cit., n. 5, pp. 80–5.

14 id., pp. 92–9. K. Economides, S. Blacksell, and M. Blacksell, *Referrals to Solicitors in Rural Areas with Particular Reference to Cornwall and Devon* (forthcoming). Compare classifications by Paterson (1987), op. cit., n. 3; Paterson, Farmer, Stephen, and Love, 'Competition and the Market for Legal Services' (1988) 15 *J. of Law and Society* 361–73; Glasser, op. cit., n. 2.

15 G. Chambers and S. Harwood, *Solicitors in England and Wales: Practice, Organisation and Perceptions. First Report: The Work of the Solicitor in Private Practice* (1990) 7–11.

16 G. Chambers and S. Harwood-Richardson *Solicitors in England and Wales: Practice, Organisation and Perceptions. Second Report: The Private Practise Firm* (1991) 9–17.

17 id., p. 14.

18 id., p. 48.

19 id.

20 A. Paterson, 'Legal Aid at the Crossroads' (1991) 10 *Civil Justice Q.* 124–37; Lord Mackay of Clashfern, 'Access to Justice – the Price' (1991) 25 *The Law Teacher* 96–108. The Devon and Exeter Law Society has led a rebellion against the impending standard fee system in the magistrates' courts by voting in favour of withdrawing from the twenty-four-hour duty solicitor scheme, a decision which could be followed by other local law societies. See E. Gilvarry, 'Fixed fee protest at SGM' *Law Society's Gazette* 5 February 1992, 4, 14–15. The legal aid franchising proposals have also drawn criticism from country lawyers, see K. Economides, 'Franchising and Rural Legal Services' in *European Yearbook in the Sociology of Law* (forthcoming). On the perceived impact of training licences on rural firms see K. Economides and J. Smallcombe, *Preparatory Skills Training for Trainee Solicitors* (1991) 19–20.

21 See A. Clark, pp. 15–30 in this volume.

22 Blacksell, Economides, and Watkins (1991), op. cit., n. 5, pp. 64–9.

23 id., pp. 102–31; M. Blacksell, A. Clark, K. Economides, and C. Watkins, 'Citizens Advice Bureaux: Problems of an Emerging Service in Rural Areas' (1990) 24 *Social Policy and Administration* 212–15.

24 See K. Economides and B. Garth, 'The Determination of Legal Services Policy in the United Kingdom and the United States of America' (1984) 2 *Environment and Planning C: Government and Policy* 445 at 447–50.

25 See, generally, Paterson, op. cit., n. 20; M. Partington, 'Change or no-change? Reflections on the Courts and Legal Services Act 1990' (1991) 54 *Modern Law Rev.* 702–12; F. Cownie, 'The Reform of the Legal Profession' in *The Changing Law*, eds. F. Patfield and R. White (1990).

26 See Royal Commission on Legal Services, *Final Report* (1979; Cmnd. 7648) para. 8.38, 16.23–9. Blacksell, Economides, and Watkins (1991), op. cit., n. 5, pp. 7–8.

27 id., pp. 179–82. K. Economides, 'Legal Services and Rural Deprivation' (1982) 15 *Bracton Law J.* 41–78; M. McKeone, 'Salary Scheme Mooted to Trim Legal Aid Bill' *Law Society Gazette* 27 November 1991, 6.

28 Blacksell, Economides, and Watkins (1991), op. cit., n. 5, pp. 191–93; M. Blacksell, A. Clark, K. Economides, and C. Watkins, 'Legal Services in Rural Areas: Problems of Access and Local Need' 12 *Progress in Human Geography* 47–65.

29 See Economides, op. cit., n. 20; paper by D. Beale, 'Access to legal services and the Legal Aid Board', *Institute of British Geographers Annual Conference* (1992) 7–10 January, University of Swansea.

30 See further, Blacksell, Economides, and Watkins (1991), op. cit., n. 5, pp. 193–200.

Lawyers in a Divided Society: Legal Culture and Legal Services in Northern Ireland

MARIE FOX* AND JOHN MORISON*

We start from the premise that the operation of law in Northern Ireland is different in significant respects from that elsewhere in the United Kingdom and seek to explore the implications of this for the development of legal services in the 1990s. We maintain that the differences stem from the political and economic situation pertaining in Northern Ireland which results in persons experiencing the legal system here in significantly different ways from how it is experienced in the rest of the United Kingdom – a factor which has obvious implications not only for the provision and consumption of legal services but for the environment in which they are offered.

THE LEGAL CULTURE IN NORTHERN IRELAND

In many respects Northern Ireland has an almost pre-Thatcherite character having been insulated from many of the changes that occurred in Great Britain during the 1980s. Indeed, one commentator has referred to the 'the independent Keynesian Republic of Northern Ireland, where monetarism remains unknown'.[1] Although the Thatcher revolution did not bypass the province, it is certainly true that its impact there was reduced and uneven.[2] Northern Ireland remains a region with a declining economic base of manufacturing industry which is increasingly incapable of supporting a growing population which depends more and more upon the state intervening as a source of welfare and employment. Rather than pursuing the radical programme of cutting public spending and reconstituting the role of the state which marked the Thatcher years in Great Britain, successive Conservative governments largely adopted the policies that have characterized all British government action since the inception of this most recent bout of 'troubles'. This has, in the main, centred around applying the band-aid of financial support to the economic and political wounds of the province, which have been exacerbated by more than twenty years of civil disorder. Whilst public spending was being pruned elsewhere in Britain, Northern Ireland remained relatively protected from the chill wind of financial stringency.[3]

* School of Law, Queen's University, Belfast BT7 1NN, Northern Ireland

In an area of relative poverty, where unemployment runs at just under 20 per cent, there remains a degree of dependence on the state for basic provision which is politically inexpedient to shake off. For example, public sector tenants still comprise just over one-third of all households compared to just over one quarter in Britain. Overall, Northern Ireland must be seen as a region where pragmatism has often prevailed over Thatcherite principle. In key areas, the Northern Ireland administration has operated highly interventionist strategies reminiscent of an essentially pre-Thatcherite programme to underwrite a failing economy and guarantee basic social standards.

As a result, the client base for legal services in Northern Ireland retains a profile similar to that in many disadvantaged regions of Britain in the 1960s and 1970s. The 1.5 million population has the lowest average household income per individual in the United Kingdom.[4] Despite its long industrial history, the withering of traditional employment areas is advanced. Industry accounts for only 28 per cent of the workforce while agriculture employs only a further 7.3 per cent. Service industry has expanded to accommodate a remarkable 64.8 per cent of the workforce.[5] Nevertheless, its unemployment rate remains substantially higher than in any other region while gross domestic product is low. Although there is a small entrepreneurial class, the vast majority of citizens are either employed in the declining activities of industry and agriculture or dependent on the state either indirectly, as one of the 40 per cent of the workforce who are currently employed in the public sector or directly, as a recipient of benefit. In their survey of economic and social change since 1979, Gaffikin and Morrissey report that:

> [t]he proportion of average household income made up of social security benefits increased by two per cent from 1979 to 1987. In 1986–87, payments of sickness and invalidity benefits per head in Northern Ireland were fifty-eight per cent higher than the UK average, unemployment benefit ten per cent and supplementary benefit forty-eight per cent higher.[6]

There is thus a dependency on the state, as employer or provider, which is reminiscent of the pre-Thatcher era.

However, the impact of the 1980s has not been negligible. Reductions in social security payment levels that are general to the United Kingdom have, in some senses, had more effect in Northern Ireland. The higher level of dependency upon social security in the region means that, although everywhere claimants suffer, Northern Ireland suffers that much more. In general, whilst the state remains central to life in Northern Ireland, it is unlikely to be able to perform at the level that is required. For example, the average cost of creating a single job is estimated by the Local Development Enterprise Unit to be around £4,000 and the cost of eliminating unemployment in West Belfast would exceed £44 million.[7] There is, inevitably, a gap between need and the satisfaction of that need and this provides the focus for one aspect of the problems facing potential users of legal services in the province.

Another focus of problems that may be amenable to lawyers' intervention arises from the relationship between citizens and the state. The security situation of the last twenty years provides in itself a range of problems facing particular individuals as well as ushering in some of the factors which, we argue, prefigure directions to be taken more generally in the United Kingdom. The scale and longevity of what is known euphemistically as 'the troubles' in Northern Ireland is unique within the context of western Europe. It is undeniable that the conflict has touched the lives of everyone in the province. More than two decades of violence have claimed the lives of nearly 3,000 persons. It has produced a garrison state which requires more than twice as many full-time police officers per head of population than in the rest of the United Kingdom. Within the protestant population, one in ten of the workforce are employed in security. Meanwhile, certain sectors of the catholic population, particularly in disadvantaged urban areas, perceive themselves to be the target of a massive policing operation.[8]

Strategies to counter the terrorist offensive have varied as the conflict has evolved.[9] However, they have all involved the deployment of significant additional legal powers to augment the ordinary criminal law. Enhanced powers to stop and search, wider powers of arrest and detention, single judge courts operating with more relaxed rules of evidence, and even powers to issue exclusion orders, are all familiar aspects of the British government's medium-term strategy to contain violence within 'acceptable levels' whilst the increasingly vain search for a political accommodation continues. The deployment of this formidable armoury of state power clearly has a dramatic impact, but the extent of its effect in the legal process is limited to a numerically relatively small section of the population. This in itself may contribute significantly to the marginalization of that population, as we shall argue below. However, the courts and legal profession have not, since the mid 1970s, been overstretched by processing large numbers of legally-aided terrorist suspects.[10] Whilst the operation of emergency powers has considerably exercised the European Court of Human Rights,[11] the legal strategy for the containment of terrorism has not resulted in much litigation additional to the immediate trial process.[12] Indeed, it is an interesting feature that historically the civil rights movement in Northern Ireland, in contrast to that in the United States of America from which it took inspiration, did not rely much on the courts.[13] It still remains the case that political, social, and military strategies are more significant than legal ones. In the absence of a legal instrument such as a bill of rights and a developed civil liberties culture among lawyers in the province, legal action is generally of a defensive character and limited in its use.[14]

If the security situation does not produce the level of demand for lawyer's services that might be anticipated, then this is not compensated for by regular criminal work. Non-terrorist crime, or 'ordinary decent crime' as the security forces term it, is, it seems, relatively uncommon in the province. Although some doubt can be cast on the official crime figures and the interpretation given to them,[15] it does seem as if Northern Ireland may be remarkably crime-free. The most striking evidence of this comes from an international victim survey which found that the province had the lowest overall crime rate of fourteen European and non-European countries examined over a five-year period.[16]

Whilst this cannot be taken as conclusive, it does seem to reinforce the view of Northern Ireland offered in some official circles as normal, decent, and law-abiding with strong church and family ties, under a veneer of terrorism provided by the 'men of violence'. The consequences for the legal profession can be seen in the declining rate of defendants proceeded against in the magistrates courts (43,221 in 1989) and the figure of 911 persons prosecuted for non-scheduled offences in the Crown courts – the lowest since 1973. The numbers of fine defaulters, while declining after a fourfold increase in the first half of the 1980s, still constitute a larger figure (at 1,669) than the numbers of those admitted to immediate custody (1,451).[17]

So far, the context for legal services that we have been describing sets Northern Ireland apart from the rest of the United Kingdom. What we have outlined resembles more closely a pre-Thatcherite Britain from perhaps the 1960s or 1970s – overlaid with a special political crisis and associated security problem – than it does the rest of the United Kingdom in the 1990s. There is, however, another feature which distinguishes Northern Ireland from Great Britain and this, we argue, is rather more post-Thatcherite in character. There is a sense in which Northern Ireland provides a more advanced version of trends that are nascent in Great Britain. These relate to the way in which public power is distributed and used in the province and the levels at which law is used as a control mechanism in the absence of a stable, self-regulating political culture.[18] This is an important factor in understanding the legal culture which predominates in Northern Ireland.

It is conventional wisdom to hold that what is required in Northern Ireland is a political solution – a constitutional compromise that will end the alienation of the minority and marginalize the terrorists. Each successive Secretary of State is given the opportunity to find a formula that will satisfy the conflicting demands of the parties involved. Despite fairly obvious evidence that the various parties hold positions that are fundamentally irreconcilable, the search for that elusive will-o'-the-wisp – a political deal that can be rendered into viable constitutional form – remains the chief strategy. It is not, however, the only one. There is some evidence of a realization that orthodox constitutionalism will inevitably fail in the wake of the failure of ordinary politics. At one level this has meant simply ensuring that the province is effectively governed by the direct rule mechanism. At another it has involved taking a few, very tentative, steps towards developing another form of constitutionalism – one aimed at individuals and introducing values rather than simply seeking to create structures for party politics. Both of these have implications for the climate in which the resources of the legal profession are deployed.

First there is the matter of how the province is governed. The formal direct rule mechanism, whereby law is generally made by order in council and a Secretary of State discharges the executive function, hides the reality of government by civil servant experts. With the political parties deemed to be incapable of anything but the most lowly functions of local government (literally burying the dead, collecting rubbish and administering leisure centres) the sole democratic imput comes from that small group selected to serve on the 147 quangos that effectively oversee all the key functions of housing, education, health, industrial investment and planning, and so on.[19] As Livingstone remarks:

> the advantages of such an *ad hoc* constitutional structure are seen mainly as being that it allows the business of government to get done, rather than be paralysed by political disagreement, and that it produces more impartial decisions and policies.'[20]

However, the disadvantages are that a large number of persons are excluded from any democratic imput into public decision-making across a whole range of basic matters. Given the relationship with the state that pertains in Northern Ireland (outlined above) this has very significant repercussions for how individuals relate to public power in key areas of their lives. The accountability mechanisms for this exercise of power are largely based in Parliament – as is suitable for a 'Westminster system' of which this is seen to be only a 'temporary' version. There is widespread criticism of the adequacy of this system of accountability[21] but a seeming inability to devise alternatives coupled with an unwillingness to improve it as this might reflect on its 'temporary' nature.

This removal of power from the lives of people, coupled with the inadequacy of the political accountability mechanism, might seem to suggest a fertile ground for the growth of judicial review. However, as in the United Kingdom generally,[22] while the judicial doctrine of review might be well developed, and the academic specialism that it has spawned may be a buoyant one,[23] there must remain some doubt as to the real, quantitative effect of the doctrine on the actual exercise of public power. Although recent indications suggest that the doctrine will remain a remedy for aggrieved individuals rather than a tool to improve the performance of administration generally,[24] there is clearly potential for this area to be used more frequently – at least on an individual basis and by those whose income will permit it. However, at present, informal contacts and strategic influence remain more potent tools for anyone able to employ them.

We have argued that government has a greater role in a larger number of aspects of everyday life in Northern Ireland than elsewhere in the United Kingdom. That there are problems with administrative procedures within the various bureaucracies that affect the small concerns of ordinary people is undoubted, as the experience of the Northern Ireland Ombudsman reveals. The offices of the Parliamentary Commissioner for Complaints and Commissioner for Administration (held in Northern Ireland by the single person of one ombudsman) handle a number of complaints proportionally as much as four times greater per annum than in Great Britain – even allowing for the discrepancies in jurisdiction between the two systems.[25] The ombudsman as a source of remedy may have disappointed many in the province.[26] However, the level of complaints, particularly about matters such as planning which are centrally controlled in a department rather than by local authority, is perhaps suggestive of a larger iceberg of dissatisfaction beneath the tip of the workload of the ombudsman's office. The direct-rule mechanism, with its lack of accountability and participation, may well be producing a whole range of small-scale problems which currently are not being fully seen.

Another significant aspect of the legal culture in Northern Ireland is one which again prefigures trends in post-Thatcherite Britain. This involves the use of law in a general disciplinary sense to change society by reconstituting and redesignating certain basic conditions and categories.[27] Whilst direct rule and anti-terrorist law remains as a short- or medium-term solution to the political problems of Northern Ireland, there is the beginning of a project to reconstitute the society through the deployment and manipulation of classifications underwritten by law. In many ways this is a new approach to constitutional issues within the British context. Instead of focusing exclusively on structures and institutions, it has become necessary to think in terms of using values and procedures.[28] In the main, this is concentrated around the creation and regulation of two identities within the province. As early as 1981, the British authorities were talking in terms of there being two, equally legitimate, groupings within Northern Ireland which it was the task of law to sustain and protect.[29] It was of course the Anglo-Irish Agreement of 1985 that gave full voice to the notion of two cultural traditions: a protestant, unionist one defined in relation to Great Britain and a catholic, nationalist one which is orientated towards the Republic of Ireland. The general political aim behind this relates to the failure to reach a political accomodation at the institutional level. The idea of making each mutually hostile faction equally valid – so long as they eschew violence – goes some way towards legitimizing and demarginalizing the minority community and thus bringing them into the political fold. This, however, is achieved at the expense of entrenching and perpetuating the catholic/protestant dichotomy, which we suggest is too simplistic and reductionist to reflect the fragmented nature of political identity in Northern Ireland.[30]

However, beyond this, the creation of two groupings based on perceived religous affiliation is important in so far as relations between the two groups can be regulated. Basic ground rules for the public expression of opinion have been set.[31] In addition, there has been a much larger process whereby the law has recognized and reinforced the existence of two identities and sought to protect each one in the more everyday situations where they encounter one another. This involves ensuring that individuals and groups as they combine and meet as fellow citizens, employers and employees, providers and receivers of goods and services, and so on, are restrained from discriminating against one another. Government too, in preparation for its eventual resumption by local political parties, is restrained from discriminating. Overall, the relative distribution of basic social goods – jobs, houses, and so on – is subject to control by law along the lines of endorsing this idea of identity. Thus there is far reaching legislation via the Fair Employment (Northern Ireland) Act 1989 which requires monitoring of the workforce as part of a process to ensure a balance between those who are perceived to be protestants and those who are perceived to be catholics. This is the legislative centrepiece of what might be described an anti-discrimination industry in Northern Ireland. It is much tougher than corresponding United Kingdom provisions on race and sex discrimination, empowering the Fair Employment Commission (FEC) to launch investigations on its own initiative rather than waiting for complaints. The legislation also instituted a special Fair Employment Tribunal which may impose more stringent penalties than industrial tribunals may for other forms of discrimination. Both the FEC (formerly the Fair Employment Agency) with its staff of sixty, and the Equal Opportunities Commission (EOC) who employ twenty-five people, deal directly with discrimination issues. Although not all those working for such bodies are lawyers, they do contribute to the legalization of this basic political issue in the province. The two bodies receive substantial funding from the Department of Economic Development[32], and are active not just in encouraging better practice, but in using the legislation to try to ensure it.[33]

In addition, there are a number of other bodies which use the state's economic power within a legislative framework to define, restructure, and facilitate the community's basic political problem along the lines of the Identikit plan of the two identities. For example, the Community Relations Council has been created to encourage and fund various projects and organizations where, a cynic might maintain, they appear worthy and safe to official eyes. It has a cultural traditions programme to encourage awareness of what the same cynic might regard as as an officially sanctioned past. Integrated education is now being encouraged and funded. In ordinary schooling there is a complusory programme entitled 'Education for Mutual Understanding' which reinforces ideas about there being two communities along the lines that the government authorizes. More generally, there also exists a Standing Advisory Committee on Human Rights (SACHR) which was set up under the Northern Ireland Constitution Act 1973 to advise the Secretary of State on the adequacy and effectiveness of the law in prohibiting discrimination based on religious belief or political opinion. (In practice though, SACHR has always had a broader remit, and it reviews many other areas of law, monitoring for example discrimination against homosexuals, changes in family law, and laws such as those on public order and prevention of terrorism which affect civil liberties and human rights in general.)

Whilst such initiatives may generate some work directly for lawyers in individual cases, their main significance lies in their contribution to the legal culture of the province. To a much greater extent than elsewhere, politics has become legalized. Two identities are created and officially sanctioned so as to isolate and police other identities as being aberrant. Meanwhile, the relationship between the two legitimate identities is being controlled and shaped. The limits and possibilities of using law in this way are begining to be fully explored. This contributes to an environment or culture where the scope and impact of law is greater than elsewhere. It is significant, however, that law is being aimed at a particular analysis of a problem rather than being available to empower the citizen. It is not so much that it is an undemocratic use of the state's power but that the legal framework thus created leaves the citizen as a passive being to be shaped and regulated rather than as an agent capable of

130

using the law, alongside ordinary political activity, to solve problems and achieve goals in an empowering and self-determining way.

THE STRUCTURE OF THE LEGAL PROFESSION IN NORTHERN IRELAND

Structurally, the organization of the profession is also very different in Northern Ireland from England and Wales – a fact which we suggest reflects its separate legal culture. The legal profession in Northern Ireland has remained largely unreconstructed by wider economic change, and lacks a strong commercial base. There is a preponderance of small firms – only about twenty firms employ more than twenty-five employees – and they tend to be less specialized than their counterparts in England and Wales. They are heavily dependent upon maintaining a variety of work – legal aid, matrimonial, conveyancing and probate.[34] This perhaps results from the fact that the demand for legal services reflects Northern Irish society which is largely rural in character with a small and scattered population. Perhaps it is also justified (on the assumption that the community in Northern Ireland actually *needs* legal services) on the grounds that they will be best provided by a number of small, broadly-based practices. The differences which already existed between the legal profession here and that in England and Wales at the beginning of the 1980s were heightened by profound legal reforms which occurred in Britain during the 1980s after years of stagnation.[35] Traditionally Northern Ireland has lagged behind the rest of the United Kingdom in government-led reforms of the legal profession. Thus, for example legal aid was not introduced until 1965. Similarly the two major legislative iniatives affecting legal services in the 1980s – the Legal Aid Act 1988 and the Courts and Legal Services Act 1990 have not applied to Northern Ireland. Now, belatedly, a policy paper has been published by the Northern Ireland Court Service setting out the government's proposals on the provision of legal services.[36] This document clearly envisages the reforms effected by the Courts and Legal Services Act being transplanted wholesale to this jurisdiction, but we would contend that this fails to recognize the separate legal culture as outlined above.

In practice, it may be questioned whether such reforms will have the radical effect that they are expected to produce in the rest of Britain. For example, the proposal to open up rights of audience, and the right to conduct litigation along the lines enacted in the Courts and Legal Services Act is unlikely to have much impact, given that solicitors already possess more extensive rights of audience in Northern Ireland but that these are little used.[37] Similarly, it is unlikely that the removal of statutory barriers to multi-disciplinary or multi-national practices will be significant, given the limited opportunities for expansion into new legal markets within the Northern Irish profession. The lack of such opportunities may be significant in view of the proposal to abolish the conveyancing monopoly and reform probate practices,[38] the most fiercely contested of the proposed changes. There are fears that this, combined with

131

less discretion in welfare benefit entitlement and the absence of new legal markets to diversify into (as happened in England and Wales in the 1980s with fields such as banking, environmental, and medical law affording new markets) may push smaller firms to the wall. The Law Society of Northern Ireland has claimed that up to 50 per cent of solicitors' firms could be forced out of business if the proposals were implemented. It dissented from the opinion expressed in the Northern Ireland Supplement to the Green Papers on Reform of the Legal Profession that the potential for specialization in Northern Ireland was more limited than in England and Wales 'due to the preponderance of small general legal practices in the province'. Rather, in their view, it was 'the limited size of the market' which effectively discourages such specialization.[39] Thus, for example, given that there are only some 2,500 divorces per year in Northern Ireland, there is little opportunity for a specialization in matrimonial law. Indeed, in many areas of law, in order to specialize, a firm of solicitors would require a market share so large as to be effectively anti-competitive. The homogeneity of law firms in terms of size, type of work undertaken, and so on, has enabled the Northern Irish profession to present a more united front in its opposition to the government's proposals than was the case in England and Wales, where, as Dickson points out, the larger firms were much less hostile to the proposals in view of the opportunities they presented to enter new markets, set up multi-disciplinary practices, and so on.[40] This united opposition has proved fairly successful, in the short term at least, forcing the Lord Chancellor to agree to postpone the introduction of legislation until after a general election, and to set up a legal services liason group to provide a forum for discussion between the Law Society and the government.[41]

For similar reasons the Bar is also less specialized in comparison with the rest of the United Kingdom. The only significant specialism is in terms of criminal law. A fairly small group of practitioners work regularly in the Crown court at Crumlin Road, and from accounts of other barristers, jealously guard their own patch, especially given that the amount of criminal work seems to be contracting.[42] The general nature of practice is also dictated by the Bar Library system, which may lead to a greater willingness on the part of young barristers to take whatever work is available, and foster a lack of specialization in their subsequent careers. The advantage of such a system for young barristers is that they are spared the obstacle of having to find a tenancy in a set of chambers. However, at a later stage in their careers, they may lack the advantages of junior barristers in successful chambers who benefit from work free-falling from those higher in chambers, although informal groupings do operate and many masters will pass work on to former pupils. A further disadvantage is that barristers operating out of a Bar Library system must plan their careers without any of the feedback that may be obtained from solicitors' offices via the services of a brokerage clerk.[43]

The fact that, unlike with the Courts and Legal Services legislation, there are no plans to introduce to Northern Ireland the reforms contained in the Legal Aid Act 1988, despite the heavy reliance of many practices here on legal aid work, can probably be explained by the fact that the administration of legal aid here has always been much more streamlined than was the case in Britain prior to the passage of the 1988 legislation. Because it is dealing with a much smaller jurisdiction, the legal aid system is administered by the Law Society of Northern Ireland under the general guidance of the Lord Chancellor acting through the Northern Ireland Court Service, rather than by a variety of separate bodies as was the case in Britain prior to the setting up of the Legal Aid Board. Given that the client base for legal services in Northern Ireland is composed of poor people to a much greater extent than elsewhere in the United Kingdom, we contend that it would have been better in considering demand-led reforms to devote more consideration to the types of legal services which are needed in Northern Ireland: namely, not large-scale multi-disciplinary practices but better access to basic legal services. Given the relatively higher levels of poverty in Northern Ireland,[44] one would expect that the demand for legal help targeted specifically at poorer people and their problems would be greater. Yet this type of service is very inadequately provided for. It would seem that less is generally paid per head to applicants in Northern Ireland, despite the fact that fewer claimants here are liable to make contributions.[45]

Northern Ireland's only law centre is located in middle-class South Belfast. It serves a larger geographical area than any other law centre in the United Kingdom, and fewer than 10 per cent of British law centres serve comparable populations. The bulk of its cases are concerned with social security, housing, debt, and employment problems, although it does also specialize in immigration law. The demands on this centre necessarily dictate that it operates on a referral-only basis and concentrates on test cases, rather than the provision of legal services to the public. Indeed, 50 per cent of its work and budget are allocated to the provision of training and information services. Given the strain on its resources, only four of its full-time permanent staff are actually employed in case-work. This effectively means that the law centre, which by its constitution is designed to serve the whole of Northern Ireland, is limited to doing case-work in the Greater Belfast area alone, although a pilot scheme under which a part-time solicitor is employed is currently operating in Derry. This position is clearly unsatisfactory.

However, calling for greater resourcing for or provision of law centres in Northern Ireland, and an expansion of legal aid[46] does raise the issue of whether it is desirable to transform individuals or groups with social problems into legal clients, and how far law should be constituted as central in solving socio-political problems.[47] Bankowski and Mungham argue that:

> The basic function of the law centre is to help the under-privileged to assert their rights by using the law to obtain redress and protection. In this view a lack of respect for law is derived from a lack of participation in the legal system.[48]

However, the establishment of law centres need not be motivated by such considerations, and we would question whether they do always function to increase respect for the law. Certainly, some of the iniatives taken by Belfast Law Centre do seem to have empowered people without necessarily increasing respect for the law or the state. The 'take-up' campaigns of government benefits organized by the centre in the early 1980s are probably the best example. Also, in practice, it is unclear to what extent Belfast Law Centre actually does generate new legal clients and channel them into the local legal profession. This does undoubtedly happen to a limited extent, but the majority of clients are referred instead to non-legal agencies. Moreover, given the non-specialized nature of the local profession, it has been left to the Law Centre to develop an expertise in immigration (a statistically small, but complex and expensive area of work, in which the Law Centre does provide legal advice and representation), mental health, and housing law. None of these were likely to be sufficiently lucrative for the private profession to become interested in them. Perhaps, therefore, it is particularly important in a jurisdiction where law firms tend to be small and non-specialist to provide public funds for the provision of legal services which would otherwise not exist.

Whilst we would not wish to suggest that legal solutions to the problems of the poor are necessarily the most suitable or satisfactory, it must be questioned whether, particularly in the short-term, there are extra-legal means of dispute resolution available. Even in terms of the provision of what may be broadly termed 'legal' advice by other advice agencies, Northern Ireland fares badly in comparison with other regions of the United Kingdom. What has emerged from research over the past few years is that advice provision throughout the region is very patchy. Craigavon is the only area with an adequate advice service. Even the relatively large numbers of advice centres which operate in the urban areas of Belfast and Derry are inadequate in view of the high density of population and index of deprivation in those areas. There are problems in terms of staffing, particularly the lack of permanent, full-time, experienced staff; of access, especially in rural areas; and in the range of services offered. In particular, there is concern over the inability of advice centres to provide representation at tribunals and in small claims courts.[49] From a study by Belfast Law Centre, it emerged that advice workers felt the need, not only for better resources, but for more specifically 'legal' back-up, training in tribunal representation, and in specialized areas of law, such as employment law. It also became apparent that there was a lack of materials dealing specifically with the law in Northern Ireland.[50]

The problem of lack of trained advice workers has been exacerbated by the heavy dependence of most advice centres on volunteers and the funding of workers through the Action for Community Employment (ACE) Scheme. Under this scheme, workers may only be employed for one year, and it consequently has a disruptive effect upon the work of advice centres. Even more disruption has been occasioned by the withdrawal of funding from some groups after the vetting of ACE employees.[51] Such vetting, and consequent withdrawal of funding on the grounds of alleged paramilitary involvement, has affected many groups offering advice services. These include the Conway Education Centre, Twinbrook Tenants and Community Association, and Shantallow Tenants Association. The effect of such allegations and loss of

134

funding has been to de-legitimize many such groups, and allow church groups in both nationalist and loyalist areas to monopolize government funding. Whilst, in the short-term, such tactics have, ironically, politicized many of the groups concerned, the long-term effect may be debilitating, and work to stifle local political iniatives of the type Bankowski and Mungham believe should be encouraged, without the compensatory channelling of funds into more 'professional' and legal means of problem-solving. Regardless of whether such developments should be welcomed or not, the government's reluctance to provide the funding which would transform these social problems into legal ones may be contrasted with its strategy of 'legalizing' political problems. It readily funds the work of quangos which also provide legal services in a different (more acceptable?) context, which has very little 'grass-roots' input.[52] The difference in approach may also fuel allegations that much of the impetus for such funding results from pressure from the United States of America.

In addition to the inadequacy of funding for law centres and legal aid, a further significant gap in the provision of legal services in Northern Ireland, as contrasted with England and Wales, is the absence of a network of duty solicitor schemes. It is notable that whereas the Police and Criminal Evidence Act 1984 (the PACE Act) makes statutory provision for duty solicitor schemes, and for legal advice and assistance to be extended to cover any other scheme aimed at encouraging the presence of solicitors to advise and assist persons detained under the Act at police stations or courts,[53] there are no such provisions in the equivalent Northern Irish legislation – the Police and Criminal Evidence Order 1989 (the PACE Order). Such an omission is particularly significant in view of the effective abolition of the 'right to silence' by the Criminal Evidence Order 1988. Currently, the only duty solicitor scheme operating in Northern Ireland is the Belfast scheme, following the winding up of the Craigavon scheme owing to what was designated a 'lack of demand'. The scheme in Belfast is also under strain following the withdrawal of assistance by Belfast Citizens Advice Bureaux in 1989, and the absence of resources to appoint a full-time assistant to the duty solicitor scheme. There has been a dramatic decline in use of the Belfast scheme over the past few years.[54] However, it seems unlikely, given the number of terrorist investigations and interrogations still carried out in Northern Ireland, that there is a lack of demand in real terms for duty solicitors. This must be especially questionable in view of the concerns raised by Amnesty International, the Helsinki Watch and the Committee on the Administration of Justice (CAJ – the Northern Ireland Civil Liberties Council) over the increasing numbers of complaints of ill-treatment and denial of access to a lawyer by the Royal Ulster Constabulary (RUC) during interrogations.[55] Under the Legal Advice and Assistance (Amendment no. 2) Regulations (Northern Ireland) 1989, the Law Society has circulated to the RUC lists of solicitors willing to attend upon persons detained at police stations. However, it is unlikely that such a service will prove adequate. It means the police are faced with the problem of telephoning solicitors to find one willing to come to the police station, as there is no 24-hour air-call scheme, such as the one operating in England and Wales, to ensure a direct line between the person requesting legal advice and the duty solicitor. Further, under the PACE Order there is no provision for a solicitor to be paid to *represent* a person who is brought before a magistrate where the RUC apply for a further detention under the legislation. As an editorial in the CAJ newsletter stated:

> ... the differences between the [English and Northern Irish legislation] are so fundamental as to suggest that the origins of these [omissions] were not a study of how the provisions of the Act could apply to Northern Ireland, but a completely separate agenda: an agenda set by the requirements of the security lobby as opposed to a debate about the criminal justice system.[56]

Bankowski and Mungham take the view that the duty solicitor scheme has the effect of increasing the domination of law over people's lives,[57] and is concerned less with 'helping' or providing a social service than with resolving conflict in local legal communities over the carving up of criminal legal work – breaking the monopoly on criminal legal aid work enjoyed by a minority of firms and providing solicitors 'with a base from which [they] can begin infiltrating into the structure of informal social relations that characterise all magistrates' courts in process.'[58] In contrast, Bevan and Lidstone comment that:

> It can be argued that the right of a detained person to secure legal advice is his most important protection. The pressures of police interrogation and the technicality of the criminal law mean that the interests of a suspect can only be properly secured after he has obtained legal advice.[59]

Whilst we would dissent from the view that 'legal' advice is the only useful protection for an accused, and have some sympathy for Bankowski and Munghams' opinion that 'multiplying such superficial options [as help in finding a solicitor] may actually obscure significant alternatives',[60] the reality is that options such as self-representation or representation by friends are often not practical alternatives.

Moreover, notwithstanding Bankowski and Mungham's scepticism about the value of lay participation in the legal process, we would contend that the fact that, in comparison to the rest of the United Kingdom, there are many fewer opportunities for members of the public to have any input into the legal system here may contribute to its perceived lack of legitimacy, and further discourage attempts at self-representation. For example, no lay magistrates try criminal cases in Northern Ireland. (Historically all resident magistrates are full-time and legally qualified.) Powers of part-time lay magistrates are much more limited than in Britain.[61] More controversially, the abolition of trial by jury for 'scheduled' offences has removed the element of lay participation in some of the most visible and 'political' trials in Northern Ireland. For those who already feel disaffected with the legal system, the fact that 'terrorist' trials are presided over by a single judge without any community involvement may heighten their disaffection.[62] Furthermore, as Doran points out, it is virtually impossibe for a judge sitting without a jury in a Diplock trial to fulfil the symbolic function of the summing up at the end of the trial. He argues that the interaction between the judge's summing up at the end of the 'ordinary' criminal trial and the jury's final decision on the facts represents a vehicle for the expression of values such as fairness to the accused, and the integrity of the legal system. In the absence of the jury, it is virtually impossible for the trial to represent such values.[63] Hence the absence of a jury not only denies the public the right to participate in the administration of criminal justice, but may symbolically undermine the legitimacy of the criminal process.

In addition to the fact that legislative initiatives on legal services have either by-passed the region, contained signficant omissions, or misunderstood the legal culture in Northern Ireland, the legal profession has also remained insulated from other changes which have occurred in the past decade which were not prompted solely by legislative initiatives. For instance, the fact that the profession here is relatively over-crowded meant that it did not experience the recruitment crisis which characterized the late 1980s in the United Kingdom. Consequently the positive side of that recruitment crisis – the efforts which it prompted to attract female solicitors to return to employment after career breaks for families,[64] – have totally by-passed Northern Ireland. The only systematic research into the status of women in the profession here was carried out by the Northern Ireland Young Solicitors Group, and unfortunately had a disappointingly low response rate.[65] The survey did however seem to bear out impressions that despite the high numbers of female entrants to the profession in recent years,[66] they remain concentrated at the lower reaches of the profession. Virtually no firms provide the flexibility that is needed in order to ensure that women who wish to have a family can compete with men, the excuse invariably being that firms are not large enough to provide crèches or cover for staff who wish to take extended maternity leave or work part-time. The Young Solicitors Group and Equal Opportunities Commission for Northern Ireland concluded:

> Outdated ideas concerning the status of males and females clearly remain in the profession; with the themes of perceived commitment, consistency and profits tending to marginalise women who wish to develop a career but who also want to have a family and/ or take time off for domestic reasons . . . Women are also more likely to be given certain types of work for example, matrimonial and conveyancing.[67]

The Bar is, if anything, male-dominated to an even greater extent – there is only one female senior counsel and there has never been a female judge in the Supreme Court of Northern Ireland.[68] The legal profession thus reflects the Northern Irish population – it is male-dominated, conservative, and the vast majority of lawyers are Northern Irish and therefore, to some extent, ethnically homogenous.

This may result from the system of legal education. A pre-requisite for entry to either branch of the legal profession in Northern Ireland is the completion of the Certificate in Professional Legal Studies at the Institue of Professional Legal Studies (IPLS) in Belfast which was inauguarated in 1977. Whilst it is constitutionally part of Queen's University, in practice the admission committee of its governing body – the Council of Legal Education – is dominated by the professions. There are ninety places available annually, of which only seventy are funded. These are allocated to the first seventy students on the basis of 'merit', which is assessed primarily by performance in a test set by the IPLS, but partly on the basis of degree result, academic references, and in some cases interviews.[69] The vast majority of applicants for admission to this course, and certainly most successful candidates, are graduates in law from Queen's University. In view of the fact that the overwhelming majority of successful applicants for the LL B course at Queens have conventional advanced-level qualifications (little effort is made to recruit a broader range of applicants with alternative qualifications) and are therefore likely to be middle-class,[70] the class composition of university education in Northern Ireland exerts a controlling influence on the class composition of the legal profession.[71] Consequently, most new entrants to the legal profession are in their early twenties, white, middle-class, have grown up in Northern Ireland and graduated with a law degree from Queens. This can only perpetuate the conservative ethos of the legal profession. No account is taken of financial need in the award of bursaries for places on the IPLS course, which may discriminate against those students who qualify for an unfunded place but cannot afford the fees. Most of the applications that do not originate from Queens graduates are from students originally from Northern Ireland who have obtained law degrees from English, Welsh, or Southern Irish universities. In terms of provision for non-law graduates, the School of Law at Queens University offers a two-year certificate in academic legal studies (CALS) course. There are ten places available annually on this course, aimed at mature students who have graduated in another discipline. The fact that no grants are available for the CALS course means it is open only to those with independent financial support, or those who are prepared to undertake the course over three years on a part-time basis. Persons from outside Northern Ireland are further discouraged from applying to the IPLS by the Council of Legal Education requirement that, for admission to the Institute, applicants should demonstrate a desire to practice in Northern Ireland and have passed examinations in evidence and company law.[72] The middle-class profile of the legal profession may well become more pronounced as a result of the recently imposed requirement that intending solicitors should spend a three-month period gaining practical experience in a solicitor's office. This is likely to mean that those applicants with contacts in the legal profession stand a better chance of being accepted on the course. As noted above, for junior barristers the Bar Library system which operates in Northern Ireland may make it easier to set up practice at the Bar without the advantage of contacts or family connections in the legal profession. However, Bar students, having successfully passed their Institute examinations, are unable to do fee-earning work for the first six months of pupillage, which is likely to prove an obstacle for those from poorer backgrounds.

No figures are available on the religious composition of the legal profession. With regard to the judiciary, it would be fair to say, however, that at the advent of the Civil Rights Movement twenty years ago, the judges, in common with the rest of the Ulster establishment, were perceived as predominantly protestant/unionist. In recent years this does not seem to have been an issue, and in practice representation of catholics amongst the Supreme Court judges does roughly reflect their proportion in the population as a whole. It is less clear that catholics are as well represented at the senior levels of branch of the profession. Certainly, an argument constantly used to refute suggestions that three-judge courts, on the model of the Republic of Ireland's Special Criminal Court, should be introduced to replace the Diplock system has been the lack of suitably qualified and experienced catholic senior counsel for judicial appointment.[73] However, it seems reasonable to suppose that catholics are well-represented in the lower reaches of the profession, given that the majority of new entrants to the legal profession are law graduates from Queens, and that since 1979/80 an overall majority of students enrolled in the School of Law have been catholic.[74] Greer may therefore be right in suggesting that 'the available evidence tends to suggest that the Roman Catholic minority in the province is adequately, if not disproportionately, represented in the membership of the legal profession' and that 'inequality of opportunity on grounds of religion has not been a major issue as regards admission to either branch of the legal profession'.[75] However, as with the position of women, there are grounds for concern in that catholics seem to remain concentrated in the lower reaches of the professions. What does seem to be true is that catholics as a group probably tend to fare better in the legal profession than women do. Generally, the religious composition of the legal profession does not therefore appear to be a significant political issue. However, the murder of a catholic solicitor, Pat Finucane, a leading criminal defence lawyer, in February 1989 did cause concern amongst lawyers involved in emergency law work. It raised worries about the possibilities of collusion between the RUC and loyalist paramilitaries to target prominent lawyers.[76]

CONCLUSION

Looking at the context of legal services in Northern Ireland, we have argued that there are both pre-Thatcherite and post-Thatcherite elements which together constitute a very particular legal culture and client base in Northern Ireland. The normal issues of resources and needs are present. Clients are poor – to a significantly greater extent than in the rest of the United Kingdom – and are dependent on the state in a higher proportion and to a greater extent. They are generally not, however, repressed (at least by the legal system). Nonetheless, the use of repressive laws against a small minority from each sectarian grouping may create a climate whereby that minority are increasingly marginalized and come to view law as an instrument of oppression and therefore alien to them. The majority of the community remain, if not actually repressed, at least subject to law in a way that we view as post-Thatcherite. As the other part of a general disciplinary project which has as one aspect the use of oppressive laws directed against a few, there is the use of enabling and facilitating law to define and categorize the majority in positive and legitimating terms. The use of law to create and underwrite two basic religious categories, and then arrange for the distribution of social benefits along the lines of officially sanctioned identities, is becoming highly developed in this jurisdiction. Law is being used instead of, or in place of, politics for the simple reason that participatory politics are not possible. Legal regulation of the two identities or communities (coupled with the policing of other identities as aberrant) is increasingly appearing as more viable than institutional-level, constitutional settlement. However, it should be remembered that this 'liberal' framework has not emerged from the community. It has been imposed by government legislating in a 'top down' project and it may not necessarily reflect the lived experience of many in the province.

The use of law in this way has implications for the rest of the United Kingdom: the idea of citizenship is central to the post-Thatcher political agenda in Britain. Whether the basis of that citizenship will be consumer rights – the social market or whatever – remains a matter for party political dispute. And there is always a chance that in Britain too, a concept of citizenship will be imposed through regulation at a micro-constitutional level. Self-government and 'bottom up' democracy cannot be taken as givens in Britain today. Of course, in Northern Ireland, such ideas are completely absent and 'citizens' there are left with only law.

At the prescriptive level, we would suggest that given the centrality of law in Northern Ireland and the likelihood that its importance in this regard will increase, citizens should be able to use the law to actually change lives in a self-determining way. However, it is difficult to envisage the legal profession in Northern Ireland changing significantly to assist in this. The small, closed nature of the profession here makes it unlikely that there will be significant changes in its composition. The nature of the community it serves in social and economic terms means that there are few opportunities for the legal profession to expand into new markets. Its relative geographical isolation limits opportunities for multi-national practices, and governmental initiatives to enforce/dictate changes from outside are likely to be unsuccessful given the failure to appreciate and take into account the different market conditions which pertain in Northern Ireland. Such tendencies are reinforced by the fact that the more homogeneous nature of the profession here makes it easier for it to present a united front against changes which it does not welcome. The role of legal education is unlikely to change matters significantly: more women and catholics are likely to continue to enter the legal profession, but it remains to be seen whether they will make an impact in its higher echelons.

This pessimism about the possibility of change is tinged with a sense of urgency about the need for change. Instead of government increasingly concentrating on using law to constitute and police identities, there is a need for the community to be able to use the law and make it more responsive to their real needs. The use of law as a substitute for politics can never be empowering for those at the grass roots who are the objects of such strategy. However, legal services for the community are essential to enable people to respond at the level where power is being exercised. Only if they can respond in

140

this way can they seek to mediate the effect of law and shape its impact across the range of matters that it controls.

The social, political and economic situation in Northern Ireland means that much attention is naturally focused upon the notion of justice. Currently we contend that there is insufficient access to legal mechanisms which would enable people to use the law in an empowering way to improve the quality of their lives. Without such access, talk of justice is legitimizing not legitimate.

NOTES AND REFERENCES

1 See Ian Aitken writing in the *Guardian*, 26 July 1989.
2 See, generally, F. Gaffikin and M. Morrissey, *Northern Ireland: The Thatcher Years* (1990).
3 For example, the Northern Ireland Economic Council reported in 1989 that public expenditure in the province (excluding social security) had grown in real terms by about 1.3 per cent per annum over the previous five years while it decreased nationally by approximately 0.5 per cent. (See Northern Ireland Economic Council, *Economic Strategy: Overall Review, Report 73* (1989)). Figures released in 1990 showed the level of public spending per head in the United Kingdom to be at an average of £2,275 while in Northern Ireland it was £3,626. This is subsidized to the level of 40 per cent by the Westminster Exchequer which provides an annual £1.6 billion subvention. (Figures quoted in Gaffikin and Morrissey, id., p. 49.)
4 id., p. 51.
5 Figures from Central Statistical Office, *Regional Trends 1989* (1989).
6 Gaffikin and Morrissey, op. cit., n. 2, p. 61.
7 See B. Rolston and M. Tomlinson, *Winding Up West Belfast* (1989).
8 Figures suggesting that in the ten-year period from 1975–1985 one in four of all catholic men between the ages of 16 and 44 years were arrested at least once tend to reinforce this. (See P. Hillyard, 'Political and Social Dimensions of Emergency Law in Northern Ireland' in *Justice Under Fire: The Abuse of Civil Liberties in Northern Ireland*, ed. A. Jennings (1990) 197.) Generally, surveys of attitudes towards law and legal institutions have displayed the unsurprising feature of catholics having significantly lower respect for the law as an institution than protestants. Whilst protestants hold more conservative views, catholics are significantly less punitive in outlook. Although there are problems with such surveys, (see, for example, E. Cairns, 'Is Northern Ireland a Conservative Society?' in *Social Attitudes in Northern Ireland 1990–1991*, eds. P. Stringer and G. Robinson (1991) 142, reporting the findings of the survey carried out in 1989), the findings of the latest Social Attitudes survey do perhaps suggest, as Moxon-Browne points out, that whilst in Britain political conflicts are mediated by rules and institutions which command widespread consensus, in Northern Ireland the conflict is rooted in legal rules and institutions themselves. (See, further, E. Moxon-Browne, 'National Identity in Northern Ireland' in Stringer and Robinson, above, p. 23.) Of course, such perceptions of the legal system as a whole (which may be tied in with an identification of it solely with the criminal, anti-terrorist law) do not translate directly into attitudes towards legal services. However, factors such as the murder of catholic lawyers (see p. 139 above) may well influence the attitudes of catholics as consumers of legal services.
9 See, further, for example, T. Hadden, K. Boyle, and C. Campbell, 'Emergency Law in Northern Ireland: The Context', in Jennings, id., p. 1.
10 Indeed, the most recent Northern Ireland Office *Commentary on Northern Ireland Crime Statistics 1989* (1990) notes the number of persons proceeded against for scheduled offences to be steadily declining to a figure of 456 for 1989 – the lowest since 1978 (p. 29). The same source also reveals that the prison population, once a source of significant post-trial litigation, has declined by one-third since a peak in 1978 (p. 50).

11 See, for example, C. Warbrick, 'The European Convention and the Prevention of Terrorism' (1983) 32 *International and Comparative Law Q.* 82; S. Livingstone, 'A week is a long time in detention: Brogan and Others v. the UK' (1989) 40 *N. Ire. Legal Q.* 280.

12 Even compensation for criminal injuries which, at its height in the mid 1970s, was 90 per cent related to terrorism and which in the words of one academic commentator retains 'the Irish tradition of a court-based scheme', (D. Greer, *Compensation for Criminal Injury* (1990)) no longer yields as much work as it once did. In the 1980s compensation still averaged over £10 million per annum (with the level of compensation paid more than nine times as high per 1,000 of the population than in Great Britain) but it is estimated that more recently only 25 to 30 per cent of claims related to terrorism (Greer, id., p. 36). Current levels of compensation (and the demand for legal advice that may attend such claims) have declined significantly from the record year of 1975–76 when the relative rate of compensation per 1,000 of the population exceeded that in Great Britain by a factor of 44 (Greer, id., p. 32).

13 See, further, K. Boyle, T. Hadden, and P. Hillyard, *Law and State: The Case of Northern Ireland* (1977) 22–3.

14 See further S. Livingstone, 'Using law to Change a Society: The Case of Northern Ireland' in *Law, Society and Change*, eds. S. Livingstone and J. Morison (1990) 51.

15 See, further, J. Morison and R. Geary, 'Crime, Conflict and Counting: Another Commentary on Northern Ireland Crime Statistics' (1989) 28 *The Howard J. of Criminal Justice* 9.

16 See J. Van Dijk, P. Mayhew, and M. Killias, *Experiences of Crime Across the World: Key Findings from the 1989 International Crime Survey* (1990). See also R. Geary and J. Morison, 'Fear of Crime in Northern Ireland' in *Social Attitudes in Northern Ireland 1991–92 Edition*, eds. P. Stringer and G. Robinson (forthcoming in 1992).

17 Figures taken from Northern Ireland Office, op. cit., n. 10, chs. 4 and 6.

18 We term this trend 'post-Thatcherite' in so much as it prefigures aspects of political life in Great Britain as reconstituted during the Thatcher years. There, there has been simultaneously a strengthening of central power with the concomitant diminution in the effectiveness of parliamentary control mechanisms, combined with the hiving off of what were previously government functions to other bodies. Of course, the relative failure of constitutional democracy in each jurisdiction has not been prompted by the same forces. Nevertheless, the responses to the same basic problem share many similarities. Although the process of rendering public decisions into administrative ones, or of legalizing politics, is not yet so advanced in Great Britain, there is still a trend that produces remarkably similar, and equally undemocratic, consequences.

19 An investigation by the Ulster Unionist Party begun in July 1991 suggests that, whilst local government employs almost 9,000 personnel, the limited range of quangos that they have investigated so far employ in excess of 41,000. Local government controls some £155 million while quangos control at least £1.5 billion (*Ulster Newsletter*, 28 October 1991).

20 Livingstone, op. cit., n. 14, p. 64.

21 See, for example, B. Hadfield, 'Legislation for Northern Ireland at Westminster' in *Public Policy in Northern Ireland: Adoption or Adaption*, eds. M. Connelly and S. Loughlin (1990) 55. It is also perhaps significant that the Public Law Project, a pressure group committed to improving the quality of government, focused on this issue at their first conference held in Belfast in June 1991.

22 See, for example, T. Prosser, 'Judicial Review (1979) *Public Law* 59; A. Hutchinson, 'The Rise and Ruse of Administrative Law' (1985) 48 *Modern Law Rev.* 293; R. Rawlings, 'Judicial Review and the 'Control of Government'' (1986) 64 *Public Administration* 293.

23 See B. Hadfield, 'Judicial Review in Northern Ireland: A Primer' (1991) 42 *N. Ire. Legal Q.* 332–57.

24 See, further, P. P. Craig, 'English Administrative Law' (1990) 2 *European Rev. of Public Law* 423.

25 See M. Hayes, 'The Ombudsman' in *Lessons from Northern Ireland*, eds. J. Hayes and P. O'Higgins (1990) 37.

26 See, further, Hayes, id., 47–9.

27 For the use of law generally in such a project, and its deployment in this way in Britain during the 1980s, see, further, J. Morison, 'How to Change Things with Rules' in Livingstone and

Morison, op. cit., n. 14, p. 5. For the use of law in this way in the context of Northern Ireland specifically, see Livingstone, id., n. 14. See also J. Morison, 'Crisis and Control: A "New Constitutionalism" for the UK from Northern Ireland' in *Crisis and Control: Symposium of the Centre for Constitutional Law, Erasmus Universitat*, ed. P. Akkermas (forthcoming 1992).

28 See, further, C. McCrudden, 'Northern Ireland and the British Constitution' in *The Changing Constitution*, eds. J. Jowell and D. Oliver (2nd. ed. 1989) 297.

29 See, further, D. G. Boyce, 'The Irish Connection' in *The Thatcher Effect: A Decade of Change*, eds. D. Kavanagh and A. Seldon (1989) 226.

30 See J. Whyte, *Interpreting Northern Ireland* (1990) 67–93.

31 See, for example, the law about incitement to religious hatred, the ban from the broadcast media of certain organizations, and the requirement that some elected officials swear an oath of non-violence.

32 For the year ending March 1991, the FEC received a budget of £1,519,000 whilst the EOC received £934,000. For the same period the FEC received 1,011 enquiries from individuals about prospective or actual proceedings before the Fair Employment Tribunal. Of these, 728 were general enquiries with 238 requesting further advice and/or assistance. Complaints were subsequently withdrawn in 83 cases and two complaints were settled and withdrawn. Public demand for advice and assistance had exceeded that of the previous year. In the year 1989–90, 138 persons submitted complaints under the old 1976 Act procedure and 62 applied to the FEC for assistance to bring a case to the Fair Employment Tribunal under the 1989 Act making an overall total of 200. In 1990–91, eight persons submitted complaints under the 1976 Act procedure and 283 sought advice and/or assistance in connection with proceedinds before the Fair Employment Tribunal making an overall total of 291 – an increase of 46 per cent on the previous year, and the highest level of activity yet recorded. (Source – Fair Empoyment Commission, *Second Annual Report and Accounts 1990–91* (1991).) Figures are no longer broken down into complaints on the basis of religion, but it appears, unsurprisingly, that a greater number of catholics lodge complaints with the FEC. For example, in the year ending March 1989 a total of 126 complaints were made. Of these 30 per cent were lodged by protestants and 69 per cent by catholics. (Source – Fair Employment Agency for Northern Ireland, *Thirteenth Report and Statement of Accounts 1988–89* (1989.) In 1990–91, the EOC received a total of 1,040 legal complaints and enquiries – which represented a slight decrease from 1,055 in 1989–90. (Source – Equal Opportunities Commission for Northern Ireland, *Fifteenth Annual Report 1990–91* (1991).)

33 It is interesting to compare indications of attitudes to such legislative programmes among the two communities with their attitudes to the legal system generally. As we noted earlier (see n. 8 above), the major study in this area, the 1989 Social Attitudes Survey, suggests that attitudes to law generally vary as between the two communities. One commentator has concluded that there is a somewhat paradoxical attitude towards the role of law and the state on the part of catholics: on the one hand, it is argued, catholics are more likely than protestants to support 'liberal' governmental intervention to end inequality but, at the same time, are more likely to endorse 'violent resistence' when 'flaws in government become intolerable' and are less likely to support punitive measures to deal with such resistance (see A. Greely, 'Protestant and Catholic: Is the analogical imagination extinct?' (1989) 54 *Am. Sociological Rev.* 485). The Social Attitudes Survey seems to suggest that although people in Northern Ireland generally are conservative on issues such as censorship and authority, they do hold more radical views on the redistribution of wealth, welfare provisions, and political protest than people in Great Britain, and more catholics than protestants hold such views (see Cairns, op. cit., n. 9, pp. 149, 155–6). This translates into support for anti-discrimination law to give a picture of more catholics than protestants supporting (and, in the case of discrimination on the basis of religious/political belief) using (n. 32 above) such measures, and fewer opposing them (see R. D. Osbourne, 'Discrimination and Fair Employment' in Stringer and Robinson, op. cit., n. 8, p. 31).

34 See D. Greer, 'Access to legal education and the legal profession in Northern Ireland' in *Access to Legal Education and the Legal Profession*, eds. R. Dhavan et al. (1989) 190.

143

35 For details see B. Dickson, (1990) 'Legal Services and Legal Procedures in the 1990s' in Livingstone and Morison, op. cit., n. 14, p. 167.

36 Northern Ireland Court Service, *Legal Services in Northern Ireland: The Government's Proposals* (1991).

37 For details, see B. Dickson, *The Legal System of Northern Ireland* (2nd ed. 1989) 70–71.

38 Northern Ireland Court Service, op. cit., n. 36, paras 9.01–19.

39 The Law Society of Northern Ireland, *Working for Justice* (Response to the Green Papers on the Legal Profession and to the Northern Ireland Supplement published by the Secretary of State – undated).

40 See Dickson, op. cit., n. 35, p. 171. Such changes in England had been pre-figured in the Administration of Justice Act 1985 which permitted licensed conveyencers to carry out domestic (but not commercial) conveyances; and the Building Societies Act 1986 which provided the framework for such institutions to do conveyancing provided there was no conflict of interest with lending functions.

41 *Belfast Telegraph*, 28 October 1991.

42 See J. Morison and P. Leith, *The Barrister's World and the Nature of Law* (1992) 38–9.

43 id., pp. 23–38.

44 See n. 3 above.

45 Government grants to the Legal Aid Fund in 1989–90 totalled only £6,039,547, despite the fact that for civil legal aid a higher percentage of Northern Irish applicants are eligible for free legal aid – 86.32 per cent in 1989–90 and 86.76 per cent in 1988–9 as compared to 67.49 per cent in England and Wales in 1988–9. In 1988–9, the overall cost of civil legal aid actually fell by £475,000 compared to the previous year. Under the Legal Advice and Assistance Scheme the average claim to the Legal Aid fund in Northern Ireland was £38.44 in 1989–90, and £33.00 in 1988–9 as against £58.41 in England and Wales in 1988–9. For assistance by way of representation, the overall average of claims paid was £129.35 in 1989–90 and £124.32 in 1988–9 as against £242.57 in England and Wales in 1988–9.

46 For further details see Belfast Law Centre, *Development Plan* (1990).

47 See Z. Bankowski and G. Mungham, *Images of Law* (1976) 32–48, and P. Lewis, 'Unmet Legal Needs' in *Social Needs and Legal Action*, eds. P. Morris et al. (1973) 73.

48 id., p. 74.

49 General Consumer Council for Northern Ireland, *Good Advice – How Does Northern Ireland Measure Up?* (1991); L. Lundy, *Report on the Provision of Legal Advice Services in Northern Ireland* (1990).

50 Belfast Law Centre, *Advice Service in Northern Ireland* (1987)

51 See NIVCA, *The Political Vetting of Community Work in Northern Ireland* (1990).

52 For example, Belfast Law Centre which receives its funding from the Northern Ireland Office and the Department of Social Security, received only £134,000 and £133,841 respectively from these bodies for the year ending 30 March 1990 (see Belfast Law Centre, *Annual Review 1990–91* (1991). This may be compared with the amount spent by government on quangos dealing with anti-discrimination laws – see n. 32 above.

53 Section 59.

54 In 1986, 4,386 people were seen at the Duty Solicitor desk, and 713 cases presented, whereas in 1989 only 543 people were seen, and 426 cases presented. (Northern Ireland Court Service, *Legal Aid Annual Report 1989–90* (1991) 28–9.

55 See, for example, the *Independent*, 30 August 1991; *Guardian*, 13 November 1991; *Just News*, November 1991.

56 *Just News*, December 1989.

57 Bankowski and Mungham, op. cit., n. 47, p. 69.

58 id., pp. 49–64, 61.

59 V. Bevan and K. Lidstone, *Guide to the Police and Criminal Evidence Act* (1985) 248.

60 Bankowski and Mungham, op. cit., n. 47, p. 69, citing B. Barber, *Superman and Common Man* (1972) p. 75.

61 See Dickson, op. cit., n. 37, pp. 20–2 for more detail.

62 S. Greer and A. White, *Abolishing the Diplock Courts* (1986).

144

63 S. Doran, 'The Symbolic Function of the Summing-up in the Criminal Trial: Can the Diplock Judgement Compensate?' (1991) 42 *N. Ire. Legal Q*. 365–73.

64 See, for example, The Law Society, *Equal in the Law: Report of the Working Party on Women's Careers* (1988); Young Solicitors' Group, 'Equal in the Law: a Response' (1988) 132 *Solicitors J*. 918; J. Ahrends, 'Women Lawyers' Fight for Success', *Lawyer*, 4 October 1988, 16; E. Crawley, 'Keeping women solicitors in touch with the law' (1989) 133 *Solicitors J*. 374; J. Warburton, 'Women and working practices in the legal profession' (1989) 133 *Solicitors' J*. 986; Note, 'Recruitment crisis: women may offer a solution', *Law Society's Gazette*, 15 February 1989, 4.

65 Approximately 500 questionnaires were distributed, but only seventy-one replies received (a response rate of approximately 16 per cent).

66 In recent years, there have been approximately equal numbers of each gender graduating from the Institute of Professional Legal Studies (see below). In 1990, women were in a slight minority. Similarly, larger numbers of women have been graduating from Queen's University with law degrees. (Source – *Vice-Chancellor's Annual Reports 1987–90*.

67 This tendency to marginalize female lawyers, and push them into areas of law deemed appropriate to their gender, also emerged in an earlier survey by the EOC. See EOC for Northern Ireland, *Women in the Professions* 39–41.

68 In Northern Ireland, the Court of Appeal, High Court, and Crown Court together make up the Supreme Court of Judicature in Northern Ireland – a total of ten judges including the Lord Chief Justice and three other Court of Appeal judges. See Dickson, op. cit., n. 37, 14–16 for details.

69 For details, see Greer, op. cit., n. 34, pp. 205–9.

70 See R.D. Osbourne, *Education and Policy in Northern Ireland* (1987).

71 See R. Abel, *The Legal Profession in England and Wales* (1988) 79.

72 See Greer, op. cit., n. 34, p. 76.

73 Greer and White, op. cit., n. 62, p. 76, note the lack of senior counsel generally as a problem in this regard.

74. See Fair Employment Agency, *Report of an Investigation into the Queen's University of Belfast under section 12 of the Fair Employment (Northern Ireland) Act 1978*, Appendix II (1988). Currently the proportion of catholic students in the Law Faculty is almost 60 per cent.

75 Greer, op. cit., n. 34, p. 192.

76 See S. Lee, 'Northern Ireland: Where Angels Fear to Tread' in Hayes and O'Higgins, op. cit., n. 25, p. 261.

Tomorrow's Lawyers in Scotland

IAN D. WILLOCK

In the three general elections of 1979, 1983 and 1987, which gave authority to the government of Margaret Thatcher, the Scottish electorate voted for the Conservative party in diminishing numbers. In 1987 only 24 per cent of those voting supported it, giving the Conservatives only ten Scottish seats out of seventy-two in the House of Commons.[1] Yet the impact of the social revolution which she engineereed has been felt no less in Scotland than in the rest of Great Britain. Among many Scots this has led to a widespread disenchantment with Westminster rule; it would not be going too far to call it a crisis of legitimacy. Thus, resistance to some at least of the changes which the Thatcher government introduced has been prolonged and conducted with a sense of aggrieved justification, and, on the part of some, even with outrage.

I look briefly at the familiar characteristics of these changes, and then at the distinctive Scottish circumstances to which they were applied. Then, I consider how they are affecting the legal profession and the delivery of legal services. Finally, I project these trends and, applying some value judgements, examine what shape legal services might acquire before the end of this century.

THATCHERISM DEFINED

I consider the principal tenets of the political creed enunciated and put into practice by Margaret Thatcher to be as follows:

(i)   The ambitions and acquisitiveness of individuals should be given the fullest play, in the belief that, mediated through free markets, the creation of wealth will thereby be maximized and eventually redound to the good of everyone.

(ii) The role of the state should be confined to creating an environment favourable to such personal drives and the operation of markets.

(iii) Taxation should be reduced, so far as compatible with that limited role, and public expenditure should be subject to the test of giving value for money.

Faculty of Law, University of Dundee, Dundee DD1 4HN, Scotland

(iv) The role of local authorities should be confined to providing such services as can be supplied only by them, and they should contract with private organizations for the rest. In so doing, they should be accountable to the local electorate by a clear link between their expenditure and local taxation falling on individual residents.

(v) Collective bodies which impede the activities of individuals should be restrained. Chief among these are trades unions, but professional organizations also incur this censure to a lesser degree and must be able to justify their practices as being in the public interest.

SCOTLAND UNDER THATCHER

Scotland, as part of the United Kingdom, has not been exempt from the effect of these doctrines, despite the low level of Conservative support there. But in the local authorities, overwhelmingly Labour-controlled, the government has met an alternative source of power, which has offered, at most, reluctant collaboration and, at times, resistance. Thus, benefit take-up campaigns, led by regional council welfare rights teams, have brought into their areas millions of pounds of extra spending power at the expense of the Department of Social Security. The government has criticized district councils for delaying the completion of council-house sale transactions and, in consequence, linked capital expenditure on housing to receipts from sales. It has complained of excessive local government spending, particularly on pay-rolls, and began by capping the rates, and later replaced the domestic rates by the poll tax. Being notoriously difficult to collect and the only part of the councils' income within their control, the poll tax has seriously circumscribed their freedom of action. It compelled the disposal of council transport services and imposed tendering for services such as cleansing and housing repairs. There has been a long war of attrition, which has left local government seriously weakened and central government correspondingly more powerful, though this may have been unintentional. Even where new powers have been bestowed on local authorities, such as offender services, now 100 per cent centrally funded, and community care, it is under such detailed control that the councils are virtually reduced to agents of central government in carrying out its purposes.

THE SCOTTISH LEGAL PROFESSION

The legal profession in Scotland is divided between advocates and solicitors. The former, approximately equivalent to barristers, number about 280 in active practice. Hitherto, they have enjoyed a monopoly of representation in the superior courts and supply Opinions on points of law. Solicitors, numbering some 7,000, peform every other kind of legal task, a few of them also giving Opinions. Advocates form the Faculty of Advocates. Solicitors, by statute, must all be members of the Law Society of Scotland. The memberships of the two bodies have until now shared the monopoly of paid representation in the courts, and the solicitors have had a monopoly of the preparation of deeds for payment.

Both sectors of the legal profession have felt the impact of Thatcherism, initially in the form of pressure to change certain of their practices which seemed to inhibit competition, but culminating in the drastic changes to their *raison d'être* and relationship to each other contained in the prosaicly named Law Reform (Miscellaneous Provisions)(Scotland) Act 1990. Its very title, concealing as it did the most radical changes to the legal profession, was viewed by many of its members as a provocation.

The solicitors had submitted to government pressure in two ways to facilitate internal competition. From the start of 1985, the Law Society abolished scale and percentage fees which had been uniformly applied to conveyancing and executry work. Instead, it gives guidance on the factors to be taken into account in charging a fair and reasonable fee. In the same year it extended authorized advertising by solicitors, pressure for which from the Monopolies and Mergers Commission in 1976 antedated the first Thatcher government and was reiterated in 1980 in the report of the Hughes Royal Commission on Legal Services in Scotland.[2] Now solicitors may advertise on radio and television and by direct mailing as well as in the press. They may include a statement of proposed fees and of the services offered. But they may not draw comparisons between themselves and other solicitors.[3]

More threatening than any of these was the expansion of estate agencies in Scotland. Solicitors in Scotland had long enjoyed a *de facto* monopoly in bringing together seller and purchaser in the sale of domestic property. House factors and property agents confined themselves to tenanted accommodation. But in the 1970s a few estate agents, by skilled marketing methods which solicitors could not match, made large inroads into this side of their business. In the early 1980s this competition was greatly intensified when certain insurance companies and building societies began to offer this service on a nation-wide basis. The volume of business available grew along with the trend to owner-occupation in Scotland. The right given to public authority tenants to buy their homes at very favourable discounts was a further incentive. Solicitors used the competition from outside their number as a spur to close ranks and meet the estate agents on their own ground. In cities and towns all over Scotland, firms of solicitors banded together to set up attractive Solicitors' Property Centres where house-hunters could, without any sales pressure, browse among the particulars of all the local houses offered for sale by solicitors.

A symbolic set-back of some magnitude was suffered by solicitors when their Law Society was deprived of the management of the legal aid system. Since the introduction of civil legal aid in 1949, the Law Society, through a central legal aid committee and sixteen local committees, had administered the scheme on behalf of the state. Subsequently it took on the adminstration of criminal legal aid and legal advice and assistance. But, as the Hughes Royal Commission on Legal Services in Scotland pointed out, it was 'wrong in principle for the governing body of the legal profession to be responsible for servicing the payment of public funds to its own members'.[4] Moreover, the representation of the public interest on the central committee was minimal, only two of the five places for non-lawyers being filled. The Commission proposed that the administration of legal aid should be a main function of an independent Legal Services Commission.[5]

Spurred on by a desire to contain the spiralling cost to the Exchequer of this demand-led service, the government first, by means of the Divorce Jurisdiction, Court Fees and Legal Aid (Scotland) Act 1983, made the Secretary of State for Scotland responsible for fixing the rate of remuneration of advocates and solicitors. Then, as it expressed it in a consultation paper on legal aid, with the object of 'eliminating scope for abuse, . . . achieving greater consistency and obtaining value for money', it took the radical step of creating the Scottish Legal Aid Board to administer from April 1987 all forms of legal aid in place of the Law Society. The society did not oppose the transfer, which secretly it may have regarded as relieving it of an invidious burden, but with injured innocence its spokespersons complained that no evidence of abuse or inefficiency had been produced.

The board comprises fifteen members appointed by the Secretary of State, of whom only three are solicitors, two are advocates and one a sheriff. In the four full years since its creation, the board has been operating the forms of legal aid inherited from the Law Society with only minor changes (that is, criminal legal aid, civil legal aid, advice and assistance, and advice by way of representation). Solicitors in private practice are still used to advise the board on questions of probable cause and the courts continue to be responsible for the granting of legal aid in criminal cases under solemn procedure (that is, where a jury is to be used).

If the creation of the board was principally designed to introduce means of controlling legal aid expenditure, it has not yet succeeded. In 1987–88, its first year of operation, the Board paid out £47 million on all forms of legal aid. By 1990–91 that figure had risen to £67 million. Sums recovered, by way of contributions from assisted persons, recovery of expenses and from damages received actually dropped between these years from £4 million to £3 million. However, in July 1991, the Scottish Office issued the first of a series of consultation papers, entitled *Eligibility for Civil Legal Aid in Scotland* (other than matrimonial actions). This follows a similar general review initiated by the Lord Chancellor in England and Wales. A new test of 'affordability' for both the individual litigant and the taxpayer has been enunciated. That criterion and the exploration of alternative funding sources, such as insurance and contingency fees, clearly presage the ending of the state's open-ended commitment to financing the civil actions of qualified litigants, in accordance with the government's policy of reining in public expenditure.

Until the momentous legislation of 1990, the Faculty of Advocates was largely free of pressure to change its time- honoured practices. But in response

149

to criticism from the Monopolies and Mergers Commission,[6] it did abandon in 1977 the rule by which a senior advocate (or Queen's Counsel) must always be assisted by a junior. A senior may still so insist, but the client may then decline to instruct that senior. The restrictive practice that an advocate may be instructed only by a solicitor was also breached to a minor extent when advocates were permitted to receive instructions direct from well-informed clients, such as the chief executive of a local authority or a patent agent.

THE LAW REFORM BILL CONTROVERSY

Both branches of the Scottish legal profession were placed equally under threat by a consultation paper entitled *The Legal Profession in Scotland*, which the Secretary of State for Scotland, Malcolm Rifkind, himself an advocate, issued in March 1989. It followed in philosophy the much fuller Green Papers issued for the English legal profession, by the Scots Lord Chancellor, Lord Mackay, also a member of the Faculty of Advocates. The pretensions of professions, and in particular of 'the profession' as Scottish solicitors like to style themselves, were rent asunder in the opening paragraphs. Their Thatcherite inspiration was obvious as they stated:

> The Government is fully committed to the promotion of competition in the provision of goods and services in the interest of the community as a whole. It has encouraged a preference for the market mechanism as a means of allocating resources. Any restriction on the free supply of services is a distortion of the competitive market in that it restricts choice and may inhibit cost effectiveness.

It went on to affirm that professional practices would not be allowed to interfere with the market for legal services, unless justified in the public interest, and there would be no exemptions for the legal professions from a proposed competition authority.

The threats to the advocates and the solicitors were different. The advocates were faced with the loss of their monopoly, not only to competent solicitors but other unspecified persons who passed a test of competence in the work of the courts. Solicitors would become eligible to be appointed judges of the highest courts, the Court of Session and High Court of Justiciary. But the seriousness of the threat was uncertain. No-one could predict how many would take up an opportunity to parade in Parliament House in wig and gown. It was also proposed that advocates should be permitted to form partnerships, among themselves and with other professionals, such as solicitors.

For the solicitors, the challenge was more urgent and visible. The government proposed to deprive them of their practical monopoly in conveyancing and in the confirmation of executors. In place of the former, it proposed that a class of qualified conveyancer should be created, members of which would undergo study and training narrower than that of a solicitor and/or that institutions such as building societies should be allowed to perform conveyancing by means of employed solicitors. Building societies were already established in large numbers and attractive premises in every city and town, and were handling the mortgage requirements of house purchasers. Estate agencies, some of them run by building societies, were also well-established and in first touch with buyers and sellers of houses. Banks too, being also in the mortgage business, were acting for some of the better-off house purchasers. Executry practitioners presented less of a threat, for the only likely take-up was from the banks who were already doing executry work through their employed solicitors.

Both organizations were confronted with a sinister threat, as they saw it, in that the Secretary of State criticized them for failing 'to codify adequately the rules as to conduct and practice' and allowing anti-competitive restrictions to become established. He thus proposed to take powers to make regulations requiring the professional bodies to regulate their members in certain ways.

The Law Society in a dignified response[7] first replied to the government on its own ground, by rejecting its unqualified belief in the merits of competition. To make profitability the dominant motivation of lawyers would entail that the less profitable areas of law would be neglected. Unrestricted competition could be prejudicial to the public. Predictably, the society welcomed the suggestion that suitably qualified solicitors should have rights of audience in the superior courts. But on the major question of conveyancing services, it pointed out that there was already (though only since 1985) competition among over 1,000 firms of solicitors for business, and that opening up this market to powerful financial institutions – some of them English-based – could drive many solicitors out of business and deprive house purchasers of independent advice on the insurance and mortgage aspects of the transaction.

The Faculty of Advocates strenuously resisted the suggestion that solicitors should be given rights of audience in the superior courts. It saw this as undermining the independence of advocates and the efficiency of the courts and, ultimately, as likely to lead to the fusion of the two legal professions. It also rejected the provision of conveyancing services by banks, building societies, and so on, and accepted non-solicitor conveyancers only if they received a wide-ranging legal training.[8]

In October 1989 the government in turn responded in a terse White Paper entitled *The Scottish Legal Profession: the Way Forward*. The one major concession that was made by the Secretary of State was the withdrawal of his intention to create a general framework within which the legal professions might regulate themselves. However, the story did not end there, for the government ran into heavy opposition in both the House of Lords and, more crucially, the Commons on parts of the very variegated Law Reform (Miscellaneous Provisions) Bill, not least from their own handful of MPs from Scottish constituencies. The enactment of the bill was imperilled; on 4 July 1990, the Secretary of State announced, somewhat disingenuously, that he had reached an agreement with the Law Society whereby, in return for his withdrawing the clauses conferring on financial institutions the power to carry out conveyancing, the society would withdraw its opposition to the creation of the category of qualified or licensed conveyancers. The bill would restrict membership of that class to natural persons. Financial institutions would still be able to provide executry services, a role that was little contested, as banks were already engaging in executry and trust work.

The society's concession was a trivial one. A new class of conveyancers who would have to know all that solicitors know about property transactions, undergo a period of study and training, and be subject to the supervision of a board comparable in that respect to the Law Society, would be unlikely to attract many entrants. But the government's concession was a major one and at variance with their immoveable stance on the same issue in England and Wales.

The bill became the Law Reform (Miscellaneous Provisions) (Scotland) Act 1990 and its part II, dealing with legal services, is now in the process of implementation. A Scottish Conveyancing and Executry Services Board, chaired by a professor of conveyancing and former president of the Law Society, has been set up to regulate the activities of qualified conveyancers and executry practitioners, terms which exclude solicitors. The Law Society is consulting on draft rules, which will have to be approved by the Lord President of the Court of Session, and then by the Secretary of State, for the admission of solicitors to plead in criminal matters before the High Court and/ or in civil matters before the Court of Session, the House of Lords, and the Privy Council. The requirements will be completion of a course in evidence and pleading, knowledge of the practice, procedure, and professional conduct of the courts, and being a fit and proper person to have such a right of audience.

Solicitors obtaining a right of audience will, like advocates, have to give precedence to instructions to appear in court over any other professional obligation (unless confined by a contract of employment to working for one employer). An unusual sub-section seems to anticipate delaying tactics in that it states that, where any function is conferred on any person or body under section 24 on rights of audience in the superior courts, it shall be exercised as soon as is reasonably practicable.

Other provisions of the Act regarding the organization of legal services allow any professional or other body to apply to the Secretary of State and the Lord President for consent to conduct litigation and for the rights of audience; allow the Secretary of State, after consulting the Lord President, to prescribe circumstances and conditions for practice in Scottish courts by persons qualified in England and Wales or Northern Ireland; stipulate that rules prohibiting an advocate from jointly offering professional services to the public with another advocate or any other person shall have no effect unless they are approved by the Lord President and the Secretary of State after the latter has consulted the Director General of Fair Trading; and stipulate that rules prohibiting solicitors from forming multi-disciplinary practices shall be of no effect unless approved by the Secretary of State after consulting the

152

Director General. Multinational practices are allowed for in that solicitors may combine with foreign lawyers who have registered with the Law Society. Existing legislation applicable to solicitors may be applied to them by the Secretary of State after consulting the Law Society and subject to affirmative resolution by Parliament.

These provisions in their totality have the potential to transform the delivery of legal services in Scotland; and all in the name of competition, defined as the friend of the consumer. But will they do so? They create more opportunities, but how many will want to take advantage of them? That is one imponderable. A second is that their attractiveness will depend in large part on the attached conditions. These will be framed or approved by the Lord President and the Secretary of State for Scotland acting in various forms of concert or by the latter alone as regards the Conveyancing and Executry Services Board. The Council of the Law Society also has a significant role, for example, in restraining the creation of multi-disciplinary partnerships. As Dean of the Faculty of Advocates, the present Lord President, then David Hope QC, led the Faculty's opposition to most of the government's proposals. He did so in the name of the independence of the Bar and its role in securing the efficient administration of justice. Thus, while one would not expect him to impede the operation of an Act of Parliament, one might expect him to approve the sharing of the advocates' rights of audience with solicitors, and members of other professions and bodies only where their members were likely to observe equivalent standards of individual probity and compliance with the practices of the courts. It is the legal profession in its present guise that guards the gateways to these new forms of legal practice. It is unlikely to welcome new competitors in the interest of the virtue of competition, nor to accept those who might challenge or undercut established lucrative procedures.

The competition which has always existed among individual advocates and has already been achieved among solicitors, since the abolition of scale fees and percentage fees, is actual and genuine. But it is competition strictly according to the rules of the club and for members only.

That is the situation, with its known and uncertain elements, which awaits today's lawyers. What of those who are training to become tomorrow's lawyers?

LEGAL EDUCATION

Legal education in Scotland is overwhelmingly orientated towards the practice of the law in Scotland and, thus, to the support of the Scottish legal profession. Advocates and solicitors, whether or not currently in practice, occupy many of the positions of leadership in the Schools of Law. Of those who study for the Bachelor of Laws degree for three or four years, over 80 per cent proceed to the one-year diploma in legal practice. This is explicitly a comprehensive training for the practice of the law in Scotland and consists of simulated exercises in court and chamber practice, and lectures on the subjects which lawyers use most in practice. It is conducted almost entirely by practising lawyers, who teach part-time, often in the evenings. As the diploma purports to instruct in the application of principles already acquired, it dominates the structure of the first degree and, where degree students have a choice of courses, their exercise of that choice. The links between the schools of law and the legal profession are further strengthened by the provision by the former for the latter of brief courses on new developments in the law.

Four of the six compulsory subjects of the diploma in legal practice are concerned with the maintenance and transfer of property rights: accountancy; conveyancing; finance, taxation, and investment; and wills, trusts, and executries. Likewise, one of the optional subjects is formation and management of companies. The other, public administration, is solely for those intending to enter local government. The other two obligatory courses are in court practice and professional responsibility. The student will already have had to obtain passes in courses in conveyancing, taxation, mercantile or commercial law, and evidence, during the LL B degree, in preparation for these professional courses. There is nothing that addresses the legal needs of the under-privileged in relation to jobs, housing, family relationships, health, social security, and so on. There is nothing that prepares the new lawyer for appearances before tribunals. There is nothing that prepares him or her for encounters with professionals other than lawyers.

The dominant emphasis of the teaching is on the use of rules of law to maximize advantages for clients and minimize detriments. In such an adversarial context there is no room for the skills of interviewing, negotiation, and compromise. Yet this legal practice course, which began in 1980, was reviewed after five years, with minimal effect, producing only some re-arrangement of the courses.

The diploma in legal practice course casts a shadow over legal education in Scotland. It determines the composition of the LL B degree course in a way which makes it attractive, almost exclusively, to intending legal practitioners. The minority who do not wish to practice may discover that courses such as legal history, sociology of law, comparative law, international law, available on paper, are not running because of shortage of enrolments. Courses in arts subjects, such as foreign languages, history, economics, politics, and so on, which are open to law students are almost entirely ignored by them. Of the minority, some will reluctantly follow the diploma course as a safeguard or because they wish to take up a career for which the qualification of solicitor will be an advantage, despite the irrelevance of the diploma courses to them. For example, the diploma does not cater for posts with international organizations, child protection or social work generally. The effort that goes into supplying the needs of future professional lawyers in Scotland inhibits the provision of courses for other users of the law.

Thus, legal practice and legal education are in Scotland inextricably linked like Siamese twins, mutually dependent and supporting each other. Legal education gives training in what lawyers do. Legal practice recruits those who are trained in what lawyers do. Self-criticism and innovation are thus discouraged. Major changes have occurred but they have been the result of external pressure on the legal profession, from its competitors and from the state.

THE LEGAL PROFESSION IN THE 1990s

The legal profession these lawyers of tomorrow will enter is in a state of incipient flux. The opportunities for the formation of partnerships and incorporated practices with other professionals, and for solicitors to enjoy the same privileges as advocates exist. If they are widely taken, the very concept of a legal profesion will be diluted. But the specification of the terms of association remains with legal professionals. That and the *esprit de corps* among both advocates and lawyers makes it unlikely that the opportunities will turn out to be very attractive.

In respect of conditions of admission and of discipline, the indicators of professionalism remain. Indeed the powers of discipline have been intensified. The Law Society under the Solicitors (Scotland) Act 1988 (and also the Scottish Solicitors Discipline Tribunal) now has powers, where a solicitor provides inadequate professional services, to order a refund or waiver of fees or the rectification of the incompetent work at the solicitor's own expense. Under the Law Reform Act 1990 the Faculty of Advocates and the new Conveyancing and Executry Services Board, as well as the Law Society as before, have a duty to investigate complaints and all must make a written report to both the complainer and the practitioner. Their handling of complaints is, under the 1990 Act, subject to the scrutiny of the Scottish Legal Services Ombudsman.

The control of the legal profession over legal education remains powerful. It was demonstrated in 1989 when the legal education committee of the Law Society decreed that, with impending adoption of the Single European Act from 1st January 1992, all entrant solicitors from that date should have a pass in European Community law. Every Law School had, with only a few months' notice, to amend its LL B courses to make that provision, and students, even those in their final year of study, had to take on this extra subject. The Faculty of Advocates then imposed the same requirement from January 1991.

However, even before these statutory changes, the exposure of solicitors to competition from accountants, estate agents, building societies, banks, insurance companies, and so on, in some of the areas from which they derived a steady income, was making them much more conscious of efficiency and the pursuit of profit. A close watch was kept on the hourly earnings of fee- earners, aided by computer packages, and clients were targetted with offers of services to meet their special needs. Competitive advertising is engaged in, conspicuously in the telephone Yellow Pages, and firms individually and collectively set up financial services subsidiaries. Missives (the offer and acceptance for the

155

purchase of real property) and the dispositions conveying it, and wills, wherever possible, are reduced to standard documents which can be held on a word-processor. This de-skilling of legal tasks enables as much work as possible to be performed by unqualified and thus lower-paid staff. In this atmosphere of intense competition, the professional requirements administered by the Law Society, in particular the compulsory insurance against professional negligence, and subscriptions to the guarantee fund which compensates the victims of dishonest solicitors, have come to be resented as restraints on trade which do not apply to the solicitors' competitors.

Tomorrow's lawyers in Scotland will thus be entering an occupation in which aggressive marketing takes place within a framework of strict statutory restraints. What are the implications of the Thatcherite transformation of the solicitors' role for the users and potential users of legal services? The pursuit of profitable business directs the energies of solicitors. This has several manifestations. The smartest and most ambitious go where the rewards are perceived to be greatest: the affairs of companies and other corporate bodies. Within Scotland they are drawn to the largest firms in Edinburgh and Glasgow. In England, there are still greater inducements. Once a Scottish legal qualification would have been a bar to employment. But those with the right training in corporate law found a ready welcome in London and were soon numerous enough to form their own Society of Scots Lawyers in London in 1987. Now the English Law Society admits Scots-trained lawyers who have taken an additional course in property and equity. Strathclyde University has come forward to supply this new demand with a twenty-lecture conversion course, bearing the price tag of £500. Few Scots lawyers have yet made the leap into mainland Europe, but it seems likely that those who have the linguistic competence will in increasing numbers soon be pursuing the lucrative opportunities offered by the expanding economic unity of the European Community.

The pursuit of more profitable work also operates at lower levels. But another route to profit is to engage in similar high-volume transactions which can readily be reduced to routine operations, such as selling insurance, arranging mortgages and pensions, and the more straightforward con-veyances of domestic property. An unsought expansion of work, with low profitability and sometimes unforeseen pitfalls, but capable of routinization, is the transfer from tenancies to owner-occupation of large numbers of local authority housing under the right of purchase, which has been exercised over 100,000 times, and also of much tenement property, formerly owned by private landlords.

In theory, as the ability of individuals to pay for legal services declines, the deficit should be made up by the Legal Aid Fund. But it is predominantly those legal services for which some clients pay that are extended to those who can pay little or nothing. The distribution of subject-matter on which grants of advice and assistance were paid in 1990–91 suggests strongly that the utilization of this form of legal aid was determined primarily by lawyers' skills and only secondly by clients' needs. Of 240,937 grants, 108,389 were in respect of criminal advice and representation and 52,086 for family and matrimonial matters, making 60 per cent of the total. But help with state benefits was the subject of only 3,487 grants, with the presentation of cases to tribunals 166, with employment matters 4,416 and with housing, landlord, and tenant matters, 8,395. Often these criminal and family grants were a preliminary to full criminal and civil legal aid respectively. Of the total expenditure on legal aid of £67 million, criminal legal aid took £39 million, and advice and assistance on criminal matters a further £4.5 million.[9]

It might be thought that the steep rise in the number of Scottish lawyers in the 1980s would have led to an expansion of legal services into neglected areas. In 1981 there were 5,065 members of the Law Society holding practising certificates. By 1990 that number had risen to 7,087. The extra recruits – about 400 a year – had been effortlessly absorbed into traditional areas of legal business, performing more of the same. The most obvious example is the growth of owner-occupation, and thus of house purchase, loan and insurance transactions, coupled with the steep rise in property values in the 1980s. Unemployment among lawyers is virtually nil.

WOMEN IN THE LAW

The gender composition of the Scottish legal profession has changed sharply in the 1980s with minimal impact on what it does and how it is organized. For most of the last ten years the output of law graduates has been around 50 per cent male and 50 per cent female, followed by a similar proportion entering the profession of solicitor. In October 1990 there were 2,402 women on the Roll of Solicitors (which includes non-practising ones) out of a total of 8,510.[10] Yet there are only four out of forty-seven on the policy-making council of the Law Society. There are forty practising women advocates out of 280.[11] Twenty-six people were in training at the end of 1991 to become advocates: four were women. There are only five full-time women sheriffs out of ninety, and six out of ninety-three temporary sheriffs, from whom full-time ones are recruited. There are, of course, no women judges, yet women, though few in number, have been members of the Faculty of Advocates since 1923. Women seem to have been content to meet the growing demand for trained lawyers in domestic conveyancing and matrimonial breakdown, which are more easily reconciled with family commitments. But they are prominent within the full-time procurator-fiscal service, which also calls for mobility. Of 255 fiscals, 99 are women. Recruitment is under the stringent equal opportunity rules of the Civil Service and its maternity laws provisions. If they can flourish in that demanding and previously male-dominated occupation, it may be that there is a discrimination factor at work which prevents their advancement in other forms of legal employment.

A NEGLECTED NEED FOR LAW?

The concept of unmet legal need became familiar in the late 1960s and 70s in works such as *Justice for All* by the Society of Labour Lawyers (1968), *Legal Problems and the Citizen* by B. Abel-Smith, M. Zander and R. Brooke (1973) and M. Zander, *Legal Services for the Community* (1978). The Thatcher decade intensified the legal profession's propensity to follow wealth. Money talks. Those who have most wealth (now usually held in corporate form) have the strongest incentive to defend their positions through law and the greatest means to do so. Work for the poor is arduous, often unappreciated, and paid, if at all, through legal aid. The rates of pay determined by the Legal Aid Board, acting for the government, do not measure up to the standards of living which lawyers expect to enjoy and which they can enjoy by working for the affluent and corporate bodies. For the majority of the populace, the government's schemes to increase competition in the provision of legal services must be like a mysterious game of musical chairs played by strangers in fancy dress and glimpsed through the open windows of an exclusive ballroom. Only those who can afford to pay a professional for legal services, and find one who can supply the service they need, stand to benefit from these manoeuvres.

Some may say that it is an inescapable fact of social life that legal services can be bought and sold: the rich will always be able to buy more than their share; the poor should leave the law to those who can afford it and get on with their own lives without it. Who needs to go through the expensive trauma of divorce when married couples can simply part, make some arrangements for their off-spring and joint possessions, and get on with their lives with new partners? Who needs to add to the pains of bereavement by bringing in a lawyer on a death in the family? Far better just to divide the residual items. The Savings Bank and the insurance company will pay up with little formality. Why, when your partner dies, take an expensive and public action of declarator that you were really married by habit and repute when the Department of Social Security will pay a widow's pension without such formality after making its own inquiries? Some of the new generation of owner-occupiers, still thinking in terms of moon-lighting from rented homes, abandon their houses to the building society when finances are tight. Self-employment, doing little jobs for cash, without involving VAT or income tax, is appealing by comparison with a job, the protections of which, both collective and individual, have been much eroded since 1980.

The astute, who see past lawyers, and the simple, into whose purview they never come, already act thus. But when it comes to problems with the basic requirements of what to live on, whether it comes from benefits or a job, and how to keep a roof over one's head, it is increasingly difficult to do without the law. And when one is arraigned by the state through its criminal justice system, the only way to resist law is with some contrary law. The steady erosion of employment protection and tenancy protection laws under the Thatcher regime has skewed the law more against workers and tenants. Part of the social security system has been converted from a system of rights to one of discretion limited by available cash – the Social Fund. In these circumstances it is all the more important that those for whose benefit the remaining laws exist should have unimpeded access to them. The high-profile use of law in a repressive way can also create an attitude of alienation from the whole of law. There comes a point where laws or the way they are applied can seem so oppressive that people turn against them and try to block their operation. Examples were seen during the miners' strike in 1984–85 and, in 1991–92, in the physical resistance to attempts to collect the poll tax.

The inability or unwillingness of the legal profession in Scotland to respond to certain legal needs of the disadvantaged has been met with a variety of responses. Chief among these has been the employment of salaried welfare rights officers by the regional councils, which to varying degrees have led resistance to the policies of the Tory government. Strathclyde, the largest region, has led the way with the employment since 1976 of seventy-two officers who organize take-up campaigns, provide representation at tribunals, and advise and train social workers on developments in welfare law. Smaller welfare rights teams are to be found in Lothian, Grampian, Central, and Tayside regions. More recently, money advice centres, many funded jointly by central government through urban aid and local authorities, have spread rapidly and now number about fifty. They were a response to the problem of debt created by easy credit, but have taken as their remit all means of increasing incomes, including maximizing social security benefits. The Citizens Advice Bureaux are probably the largest suppliers of legal advice in Scotland. They estimate that about 40 per cent of their annual inquiries of over half a million have a legal content. They have struggled less successfully to provide representation at tribunals and small claims courts, but have been thwarted by cuts in funding for this purpose in Glasgow and Dundee. Sympathetic local solicitors act as honorary advisers to some bureaux.

Law centres on the English model have not caught on in Scotland, with the exception of the pioneering Castlemilk Law Centre in Glasgow. It had the advantage of a clearly-defined community in a peripheral estate of some 35,000 people, with one landlord, the district council, and used the law successfully against damp homes and for leases that did not disadvantage the tenants. A further law centre is about to open in Drumchapel, a similar scheme on the outskirts of Glasgow. The term has also been adopted by an ethnic minorities organization in Glasgow and by the Legal Services Agency, an organization in Glasgow, funded mainly by the European Community, which holds training sessions on the law and specializes in helping tenants' associations to make use of the law. However some organizations which have given free legal advice and representation over many years, notably the Edinburgh Citizens Rights Office and the Dundee Legal Advice Centre have run out of public funding, and continue on a limited scale with volunteer staffing.

Ironically, the Legal Advice and Assistance Act of 1972 has allowed the legal aid authorities to pay salaried solicitors through the Law Society to operate through 'local organizations' giving 'advice or guidance'. The government has steadfastly refused to implement this provision, despite having renewed it in part V of the Legal Aid (Scotland) Act 1986.[12]

The legal profession, having been encouraged in its natural propensity to follow the rich, is unlikely (with some honourable exceptions) to turn back to the unrewarding work of dealing with the problems of the poor. Markets are amoral and the more involved lawyers become in the market-place, the more threadbare become their moral pretensions.[13] For the government the paramount value, as implied in the introduction to the consultation paper *The Legal Profession in Scotland* is cheapness; law is a commodity like any other. To its credit, the Law Society roundly rejected these propositions in its response, but its corporate posture does not necessarily reflect what its conscript members do. At a more fundamental level, the notion that law is to be bought and sold in the market-place runs counter to the very function and justification of law; that it seeks, by general formulae, to equalize the chances of all who come within a defined category. Put another way, justice demands the equal treatment of equals. Barriers which impede access to these laws destroy their purpose. If access depends on handing over money then their equalizing purpose is negated.

Can anything be done to rectify this betrayal of law? Where there is entrenched power, the best policy is not to attack it head-on, but to go round it, as when confronted with a check-point on a road. That tactic might seem to lead to a wilderness of lawlessness, leaving the holders of power undisturbed. But here and there are examples of new growth germinating. What they require is to be drawn together and given impetus and direction. The people involved need a sense of what they are doing. We need a fresh picture of law, not as an instrument that forces people to do things that they do not want to do, but as one device for regulating human behaviour, one which can be used to help people sort out their disputes and problems, something that is enabling rather than crushing, a framework within which people can settle their controversies. It is not invariably something which declares winners and losers; it can also be used to adjust competing claims. At the first point of contact with the inquirer, the question to the adviser should be: is there any law that might help me here? If so, how would it apply to my situation? Resort to a court should be viewed as a remote and risky prospect, the very last resort.

The growth of the legal profession with an overwhelming financial interest in selling law has had several distorting effects. It has thrown the emphasis on the court: what a court would do overshadows all law as we know it, whereas going to court is a mercifully uncommon experience for most people and usually an unsatisfactory one. The vast majority of human discords are resolved without any resort to courts. Negotiations need not always take the form of guesses as to what a court might do. But when lawyers are conducting them, that is what they tend to be. For the parties, however, what may matter most is how each can emerge with honour satisfied, and resume their relationship without embarrassing publicity. Lawyers are not the best people to produce such a result. That aim is true not only of individuals. Insurance companies and their corporate clients may well prefer to settle a claim in a manner which will avoid adverse publicity and time-consuming attendance at court. Lawyers' monopoly of representation in the courts has given the legal profession a financial stake in selling legal remedies to the exclusion of all others, thus holding itself aloof from other professions that involve themselves in human problems, for example, medical practitioners, social workers, and psychiatrists.

What are some of these signs of new growth? A good example is conciliation in claims for compensation for unfair dismissal and certain claims of discrimination. Before the applications can proceed to an industrial tribunal, they must be referred to a conciliation officer of the Advisory, Conciliation, and Arbitration Service (ACAS). These officers are not legally-qualified, but have a detailed knowledge of the legislation and its application. They seek to make contact separately with the ex-employee and employer. Unfortunately they do not always get a hearing from the latter's solicitors. Nevertheless, over one-third of applications to tribunals in respect of unfair dismissal are settled in this way. When one includes direct complaints to ACAS which could have been made to the Central Office of Industrial Tribunals, well over two-thirds of the total claims are settled by conciliation.[14]

Another area being recaptured from arms-length negotiation between solicitors and court hearings, which can exacerbate disputes rather than resolve them, is conciliation over custody of and access to children in marital breakdown. Voluntary conciliators who have some legal knowledge, but no formal legal training, seek to replace the opposed positions of the parents with an awareness of common interests. Since 1990, sheriffs have had power to direct the parties to family conciliation services, though coverage is still patchy.[15] The possibility of conciliation being extended to property matters is being mooted and is meeting with hostility from the legal profession.

These are examples of delegation by law of functions to non-lawyers which lawyers could perform, though in a different way. The small-claims procedure allows suitable non-lawyers to represent parties and, of course, the parties may act for themselves. The participation of solicitors is discouraged by rules limiting awards of expenses and the absence of legal aid. Yet the formality and intimidating nature of the proceedings has been heavily criticized by the Citizens Advice Bureaux and other advisers, and small claims are likely to remain a continuing battle-ground between the legal profession (including judges) and their critics.[16]

Examples of substantial sources of advice on what the law says, whether to use it and if so, how, include the Citizens' Advice Bureaux network of over sixty bureaux, the welfare rights officers, and the money advice centres mentioned above. The funding of all of them is precarious as most rely on local authorities whose budgets are being squeezed. But they do demonstrate a determination on behalf of disadvantaged people to grasp the kind of law that they need and, if it seems the best thing to do, to use it to their advantage. In this still inchoate movement we may have the embryo of an alternative legal service, through which a different sort of lawyer is emerging. They are largely self-taught, but the polytechnics and colleges now grooming themselves for university status have an opportunity here to supply what could be a huge need for part-time courses in legal topics neglected by the present universities.

NOTES AND REFERENCES

1 Their parliamentary representation (nine seats at present) slightly understates Conservative party support in Scotland which, both at the 1987 election and in subsequent opinion polls, has fluctuated between 18 and 25 per cent.
2 Monopolies and Mergers Commission, *Services of Solicitors in Scotland* (1975–76; H.C. 558).
3 Solicitors (Scotland) (Advertising and Promotion) Practice Rules 1991.
4 *Report of the Royal Commission on Legal Services in Scotland* (1980; Cmnd. 7846, Chair: Lord Hughes) para. 8.68.
5 id., para. 8.73.
6 *Advocates' Services* (1975–76; H.C. 513). See, also, Faculty of Advocates, *Guide to the Professional Conduct of Advocates* (1988).
7 The Law Society, *Public Protection: Professional Independence* (1989).
8 Faculty of Advocates, *Response to the Consultation Paper* (1989).
9 Figures from the Scottish Legal Aid Board, *Annual Report for 1990–91* (1991).
10 Law Society of Scotland, *Annual Report for 1990* (1991).
11 See A. Paxton, 'A Study of Women at the Scottish Bar' (1984) *Scots Law Times (News)* 53.
12 *H.C. Debs.*, col. 633 (3 May 1990).
13 It is not only the legal market place that solicitors are involved in. A senior partner in an Edinburgh firm of solicitors was in 1991 imprisoned for ten years for defrauding banks and building societies of £4 million to finance nursing homes, bars, and restaurants which he unsuccessfully tried to run.
14 Figures for Great Britain from ACAS, *Annual Reports 1975–*.
15 Sheriff Courts (Scotland) Act 1907, Sch. 1, rule 132 F.
16 See Scottish Office Central Research Unit, *Small Claims in the Sheriff Court in Scotland* (1991).

Professional Legal Training

AVROM SHERR*

TRANSFORMATION

The legal profession, and solicitors' firms in particular, have undergone a major transformation in the past ten years, reflecting both changes within the culture and political economy of the United Kingdom, and those generated by the nature of the legal enterprise itself. The legal industry has become more responsive to economic trends and has thus been raised high on the swell of commercial opulence in the late 1980s only to be dashed onto the cobbles by the ebb tides of recession. A more 'oak-panelled' profession hiding behind sombre doors and small brass nameplates would not have been so buffeted by the winds of change.

Real market changes also had their effect on the nature of work carried out. The shadowy threat of competition was little understood by a profession which perceived the coming of licenced conveyancers as a real problem. But the cuts in conveyancing costs between 1983 and 1986[1] did not hurt the profession which was bolstered by rising house-price inflation which balanced cuts in conveyancing costs. These cuts only began to bite when the conveyancing market itself collapsed and lower fees became the norm. The profession that had relied on conveyancing for more than 60 per cent of its income found that proportion dropping markedly. Not even the staple kinds of work could be relied upon in a changing environment. Other areas which had been reliable began to be less remunerative. Legal aid did not pay quite as well, and firms began to move away from legally aided work. To cap it all, Lord Mackay and the government were pushing further down the line of competition with the Courts and Legal Services Act 1990, and the Single Ecomomic Market was bringing with it its own pressures to change the relevant law and legal approach to vast areas of commercial and other legal activities.

Lastly, the sudden needs of massive expansion caused by boom, immediately followed by the sudden dearth of vacancies in recession, caused the profession to reconsider its entrance policies. How could the professional bodies ensure that the correct number of new entrants were coming forward, both when the profession needed more, *and* when it needed fewer new lawyers?

* *Professor of Law, Director, Centre for Business and Professional Law, The University of Liverpool, P.O. Box 147, Liverpool L69 3BX, England*

It all began to look as if the system of training also needed to be changed in order to cope with the other changes that had occurred within the legal profession.

THE LEGAL PRACTICE COURSE – THE NEW LAW SOCIETY FINALS

The foundation for the most profound changes in terms of training for solicitor practitioners will be laid with the new Law Society finals course and examination which begins in September 1993.

The old course, which had been remodelled in 1980, was still the bastion of old-style legal education. It relied mainly, if not entirely, on memorizing large tracts of law and procedure, and regurgitating them in stylistic form at the end of a ten-month course through the medium of two- and three-hour examinations in some seven different papers. It was as much a physical as a mental travail, and recognized as such by the Law Society, which seemed to feel that its effectiveness as a rite of initiation would otherwise be dispelled.

The last attempt at a new course in 1980 had promised to be more practical and less tied to 'black-letter law'. In the event, it was more procedural as well as still needing the old black-letter stuff. Written around the hypothetical 'four-partner firm in Oldham', which the original drafters had visualized as their model of the typical solicitors' practice of the 1980s, the course still concentrated on the needs of the high-street firm. They were not to know in 1979 that by 1988, the largest number of entrants into solicitors firms would be going to the large city-type firms dealing almost entirely with commercial law. Neither could they know that by 1992, approximately 70 per cent of trainee solicitors would be working in such firms.

The old finals course was also the epitome of the 'this was the way we were taught and suffered, this is the way you'll be taught and suffer' approach. Enlightenment could not be let in to the crucial area of solicitors' training even though it was beginning to shine through in almost all other forms of education. Even the Bar, a much stronger bastion against change in almost every other aspect, was four years ahead of the Law Society with its new course based on the skills of practice which began in 1989. For the Bar, however, it was one thing to set up a good new course for nice British folk. The foreigners still had to do the old-style course and examinations. Anyone who was not intending to practice in the United Kingdom got stuck with the old-style course, a cause of considerable annoyance and discomfort to overseas students who had already paid dearly for their specially funded places at United Kingdom universities.[2]

The fundamental criticisms of the old Law Society course were many. It concentrated exclusively on the final examination: all teaching and learning was therefore approached with the examination in mind, rather than attempting to teach or learn the principles of good practice or good behaviour as a solicitor. Teaching, even at the best institutions, was largely by way of dictated notes. Seminars were introduced in the early 1980s but were not well taught or well attended in most institutions. The law which was learnt was in large part inapplicable to most of those who took the course. The life and work of a legal practitioner was different from that portrayed in the course, and beginning in articles was therefore a traumatic shock for most trainees.[3]

The law too was constantly changing. What was the purpose of memorizing laws which were neither relevant nor likely to be extant for more than five to ten years of practice – even if the practitioner could remember what had been learnt during finals? Most qualified lawyers would specialize, and needed the ability to assimilate new law, practice, and a 'commercial approach', rather than be able to learn by rote.

There was also pressure from other parts of the Commonwealth which had begun to follow the North American 'clinical' model in which the skills of practice rather than black-letter law were taught. A concentration on the behavioural techniques of interviewing, drafting, negotiating, and advocacy would bring aspiring practitioners much closer to the real necessities of life in a solicitor's office or at the Bar.

Experiments had already begun at a number of institutions. The University of Kent ran its 'praxis' course in 1974, the University of Warwick had operated its legal practice course from 1975 onwards, and polytechnics such as the South Bank, London, and Birmingham had begun to model part of their work on simulated cases or real cases. The beginnings of a literature on legal skills was also being created and teachers could face the thought that there might be – just might be – something more to law that notes and examinations.

And so, the new finals course, known as the 'Legal Practice Course', was conceived. After its lengthy gestation, undergraduate teaching institutions and others such as the College of Law were invited to tender for the possibility of teaching the new course. In theory, its application could be varied. It could be taken part-time, as an adjunct to an existing undergraduate degree, as an adjunct to a post-graduate degree, or by itself. In theory, it could take just over half a year or a whole year. In practice, most suggested courses have begun to look fairly similar in style and application: a ten-month, full- time, separate course.

Many law firms, especially those with large numbers of trainees entering each year, have begun to worry about the turnout of the new course. Will they buy places on courses organized to suit their own particular requirements? Will the Law Society allow them to do so? Will there be a two-tier arrangement whereby some courses cater for the big City firms and others for high-street and local government solicitors?

How will the teaching institutions choose the appropriate graduates? The Bar has already offended all by saying that it will not take anyone with less than a lower second-class degree. Strong charges of racism were levelled against the method of selection for places on the existing Law Society finals course which seemed to prefer university to polytechnic students, and those with good grades to those without. A clearing house seemed to exacerbate rather than solve major problems. Teaching institutions appeared to give priority to their own students, either from undergraduate law courses, or the common professional examination. It was, thus, difficult to break in if, as a student, you were not already part of the scene.

What will the legal practice course finally look like? It appears as if it will be based much more on the skills of practice but still have a fair degree of requisite law. There will be much more student participation in the learning experience, and testing will occur through continuous assessment as well as some examinations. Apart from a core element, there will be options which can be taken by lawyers intending to practice in different ways. It will not cater perfectly for all, but it might well turn out a better-equipped neophyte professional than the current system.

Although experience is probably the best teacher, unmonitored experience can be a very poor teacher. Laying firm foundations for legal skills at the Law Society finals stage seems to be an excellent basis on which to follow through such teaching while undergoing articles of training. It would be sad if all that was gained at the finals stage was lost as soon as the trainee entered the socializing world of the law office: 'Oh, you don't want to be bothered about all that skills stuff here.'

The new lawyers, fresh off the legal practice course, should be more ready for the real world of the trainee solicitor than their forebears. They should, perhaps, be more eager to attack the work itself, having been energized by the experience of the course, rather than broken by it. They should be more ready to take on the tasks of legal work and understand the effects of their actions. Only the 'hands-on' work of articles itself can give them the real foundation for the work they will have to perform; but an introduction in a well-taught way to those skills at finals stage should cement good practice into the experience of the real world. It should also, if it works properly, teach them how best to learn from that experience.

They will probably know somewhat less law. There are simply not enough hours in the day to do everything. But rather than know great tracts of law, it is more important that they are equipped with the ability to research the law, to understand their clients' needs, to draft legal documents, to negotiate on behalf of their clients, and to advocate their clients' cases. The law, which is dynamic, needs to be checked rather than assumed by the competent practitioner. As European Community law takes more effect, even the nature of our law will change, and the skills and methodology of the 'civil law' as well as the 'common law' approach will have to be taken into account.

ARTICLES, LICENSING, MONITORING, AND THE PROFESSIONAL SKILLS COURSE

The new legal practice course will be but the foundation for a large number of other changes in the system. Trainee solicitors during their two years of articles training with a solicitors' firm will have to undertake the new professional skills course. This course will last for some four weeks during articles and is likely to be able to be taken in-house in solicitors' firms, and to be undertaken in half-day and one-day sessions rather than all in one go.

The practical skills course will cover professional conduct, ethics, interviewing skills, advocacy, personal management skills, and solicitors' accounts rules. It is intended that this course will build on the skills introduced into the legal practice course at a time when the trainee will be involved in the experience of carrying out the real work itself. In this way, theory should begin to marry with practice.

A major problem with this course, especially for smaller firms, will undoubtedly be the cost of having trainees away from their desks for a whole month, as well as fees for the course. It will be imperative for most firms to arrange, if possible, in-house training on the practical skills course element. Indeed, it is clear that the best training will be that which is relevant to the work which the trainees are carrying out within the firm. Reinforcement for the ideas and procedures taught will best be organized from within the work environment or through teaching which takes this properly into account.

The Law Society also intends to ensure that the more informal 'on the job' training which is supposed to take place in articles is also more closely monitored. Current proposals suggest that firms will be 'licensed' or 'authorized' to take trainee solicitors only if they promise to abide by a code of conduct by which training needs are guaranteed through careful review of check-lists and systematic use of appraisals.

The current system of monitoring has been haphazard and poorly implemented. It is the trainees, rather than the firms, who are questioned by panels of solicitors from other firms in the area. Trainees feel extremely vulnerable in these circumstances, and their clear sense of the occasion is that the individual trainee rather than the firm is under investigation. The new system, which proposes some element of central rather than local monitoring, will be different. It will pay more attention to the organized system of 'on the job' training during articles. It will attempt to ensure that all supervisors of trainee solicitors will themselves have had a proper system of training in how to supervise and train others. The monitoring will also try to ensure that one person in each firm will have special overall responsibility for articles of training within that firm. The appointed person may also have to attend an external course in order to ensure their understanding of their functions under the new regime.

However, the new proposals also carry with them some different problems. The costs of the new professional skills course and the administrative cost of complying with the new licensing procedure will make it increasingly less likely that the smaller firms will be able to, or will want to, take on trainees. The specialization of legal work now makes it much more difficult for solicitors to gain qualification and experience in large firms and then move out to the suburbs and high streets. The work areas are different and the experience in each has limited relevance. This, in turn, may mean that there will in future be fewer lawyers available to carry out high street or legal aid work, and this will cause other problems to other parts of the system. Smaller firms which have relied in the past on trainees (less expensive than qualified solicitors) to do much of the lower level work may not now be able to afford them. This, in turn, will reduce the number of smaller firms. The onward march of real progress in training trainees and monitoring articles must be very carefully tempered by a recognition of the growing problems of smaller firms, to ensure that there will still be solicitors' firms or other legal venues for individuals to go to when they need the assistance of the law. Large firms will not be prepared to train lawyers for the high street. The work of the domestic lawyer is at least as important and complex as the work of the commercial lawyer and must therefore be assisted to continue.

Tomorrow's trainee solicitor will therefore, it seems, be more skilled if not so knowledgeable in law. The trainee will also be more likely to be undertaking articles of training in a large firm than in a small one. The new breed will be more open to be taught the skills of practice and be pleased at the thought of not having 'finished their education' before arriving at the firm.

THE NEW MODEL – TOP-LOADING RATHER THAN FRONT- LOADING

The North American washing machine looks very different from the British variety. The bulk of our washing machines are front- loaders. Everyone knows that it is necessary to put all the clothes in right at the beginning as there is no chance to add anything later.

It may not be a cultural difference, but the North American version is quite different. With larger houses and utility rooms, a washing machine does not have to be beneath a work surface and is more likely to be loaded from the top. Although this may not have been the manufacturer's intention, extra items of washing – which somehow do not appear at the right time – can be added later in the cycle.

The traditional system of legal education in England and Wales conformed entirely to our front-loading washing machine. Everything was put in at the beginning, all the clothes loaded at one go. Undergraduate legal education was followed by Law Society finals and, apart from accounts in articles, education was finished. The new approach conforms much more to the North American model. At each stage of the professional's career, more education can be taken on board when relevant to the young practitioner. When everything is taught at the beginning there is information overload, and some things tend to get forgotten. When elements are added at times of greatest relevance, they are more likely to be learned, understood, and remembered.[4]

BEYOND QUALIFICATION

The top-loading, additive idea is taken further forward beyond articles. Possibly as a means of restricting entry during a previous glut of new lawyers,

168

the Law Society added the necessity for qualified solicitors in their first three years to take sixteen points of continuing legal education per annum as well as a compulsory half-day course each year. Such solicitors were not allowed to practice by themselves during that period.

Subsequently this system was so successful that those practitioners were enjoined to take such courses for the rest of their practising lives. Neither are those wonderful benefits of education to be withheld from more senior members of the profession. By 1998, all solicitors under sixty who have qualified since 1965 will have to undertake twenty continuing education hours each year.

Rather than the somewhat strict regime of the past few years, solicitors will be able to obtain their points through a mixture of approaches including taught courses, reading, television programmes and videos, teaching and training others, and distance-learning systems. There will be more self-policing and monitoring of such courses, and the Law Society's involvement will be minimized to reduce the cost of central monitoring. Such systems have existed for medical practitioners, accountants, and other occupational groups for some years. For lawyers, it will be policed benignly over a rolling three-year period, and a statement concerning continuing legal education points will have to be made each year at the time of application for a practising certificate.

IN-HOUSE TRAINING SYSTEMS AND THE DIRECTORS OF EDUCATION

As large firms saw the new educational road, they began to realize the need to control the training of their own lawyers, and to carry out as much of it as possible within their own offices so as to avoid expensive travel time and less relevant courses. At the same time, universities and polytechnics were hard-pressed financially by the government and academics were increasingly attracted by the enhanced salaries available in law firms. It therefore became possible for larger firms to hire training managers or directors of training to administer in-house training.

The administrative functions include induction of trainees and new lawyers, practical and skills training, as well as organizing 'black-letter law' and transaction training for the areas covered by the firm but not dealt with at undergraduate or Law Society finals level. Beyond articles, all such training could attract Law Society points. Some training directors also provide training for non-legal staff in handling clients properly, explaining the bases of legal work and how to provide stronger back-up for qualified staff.

As directors of training became more settled in firms and more accepted into the firms' function, other forms of training apart from law, procedure, and professional skills assumed importance. Bigger firms meant that problems of management and administration differed in both scale and quality from those

169

associated with managing smaller groups of people, less plant, and smaller buildings. The new breed of lawyer had to be a business person and manager as much as a professional practitioner, and thus needed training in these areas. This training could also qualify for Law Society points and could be organized or handled by the directors of education.

THE SEMINAR IN PRACTICE

A particular type of educational approach could then be seen to emanate from the new world of training in practice. It was now possible to hold a seminar within a law firm directed at highly specific practical work coming out of recent experience in real cases. The practice seminar has been developed in a large number of firms, based either on journal articles or new law reviews, or around a case discussion. In the former case, each member of a practice team would have the responsibility of reviewing relevant law and related journals, and law reports appropriate to that particular practice group. During the periodic seminar, they would point out to other members of the group important information which might otherwise go unnoticed. In some of the better organized seminar systems, a note would be taken of all such contributions which could then go into a periodic practice update for the group, be circulated more widely around the firm, or even put into lay terms and published for clients.

In the case discussion-group,[5] a particular case or line of cases in which practitioners have been involved is introduced to a group of other practitioners, either on a didactic basis or with some participatory element, as a workshop in which papers from the original case are distributed. Direct participation in the problems of current cases can be organized in this manner, and directors of education and training have been found to be very useful in promoting this level of transference of information around the firm.

The educational environment, at its best and most useful, is thereby translated into the practice environment for real support of practical work. This might well be seen as the highest level of practical training available within the context of continuing legal education, and also well used to attract Law Society points.

THE ESCALATOR OF PARTNERSHIP REVISITED

Up to this point, a qualified solicitor's life in a law firm appeared to be split into two parts. Until the decision was made to grant partnership or not, the solicitor would work towards this end, trying desperately to get onto the escalator of partnership. Having once gained the escalator, a new partner could hold tightly to the handrail while standing on the right- hand side, and move slowly up the letter-headed notepaper until reaching the top. Retirement or early demise would allow them to fall off the top of the notepaper – unless they became consultants.

But this system offered no incentives for continuing work beyond the stage of initial partnership. Incentives had to be created for producing more and more clients and billings as the partner moved up the escalator. It also had to be possible for partners to overtake other partners or receive higher earnings if their profits made this possible.

All this meant that there needed to be training in new skills like marketing, bringing in work, managing teams, managing their own time, appraising personnel, selecting the right people, and managing the whole organization.

Managerial training for every step of the way up the escalator, and before arriving on it, will become an essential part of the work of tomorrow's lawyers. Continuing education for more senior staff will undoubtedly assist in supporting the new managerial roles which are emerging from larger law firms, merged cultures, and a substantial majority of employed professionals.

The old generalist all-rounder who could manage a business, head a law firm, and handle clients and cases in any area of law is increasingly a thing of the past. The new specialist or legal technologist will need all the training possible to provide the legal and managerial expertise necessary for reacting to the changes in the law and the outside world. Tomorrow's lawyers will increasingly be open to education and learning and other commercial disciplines.

The Law Society had already begun to recognize the need for this approach in 1989 when it instituted the 'Best Practice Course' which had to be taken by all qualified solicitors in their third year after qualification. This course, lasting a day and paid for by firms of solicitors themselves, was based on a massive, five-section tome prepared by management experts in consultation with the Law Society. As before, the Law Society's universalist approach to problems throughout an increasingly diverging profession fell on stony ground. For most third-year qualified practitioners, many of the themes of law-firm management taught in the best practice course were some way ahead of their own responsibilities. In the larger firm, issues associated with financing the firm, managing other staff, marketing services, and setting out management structures were not likely to affect them for many years.

Many of the ideas arrived too late. The approach of the Law Society materials, suggesting, for example, that third-year qualified solicitors ask for a copy of last year's accounts for their firms, were divorced from reality. In-house practices inside major industries, commercial corporations or local authorities employ an increasing number of solicitors. These solicitors also need some management training but were forced to take the best practice course where management focuses entirely on the partnership firm.

An entirely well-motivated scheme was therefore blown apart by the singularity of the approach as it impacted on such highly diverging needs. A failure like this in a new form of training does not leave the participants neutral. On the contrary, it becomes much more difficult to introduce management ideas to them later in their careers when it is actually relevant to

171

their needs. Such failures which inevitably end up as mere 'window- dressing' rather than effective management training, must be avoided in the future. It is hoped that tomorrow's lawyers will be able to obtain their relevant management training at the escalator level appropriate to the sort of work and firm in which they find themselves, and the sort of responsibility they currently enjoy. The continuing education system will allow for, and encourage, the proper kind of opportunity, provided the Law Society does not once again spoil its good intentions with compulsory window-dressing.

Changes have occurred so fast in the last five years that it has been difficult for the Law Society and practitioners to keep pace. But there needs to be effective consultation across the entire spectrum of the legal industry before major changes, such as the best practice episode, are introduced.

TRAINING FOR LIFE, NOT JUST FOR LAW

In common with other occupational groupings, legal training is therefore changing, tending towards a continuing system of education which involves learning by experience and from experience. In this sense, tomorrow's lawyers will be better trained to deal with life as a lawyer rather than simply being trained in law-book law.

Because their training will be partly in the behavioural skills necessary for handling other people, they are more likely to be saved from degenerating into the classical distant hardness of the more experienced practitioner. Needful appraisal of others, and appraisal of themselves by others, may well ensure a move away from fossilization, and some control over the excesses of professional individualism.

THE UNIVERSITY/PRACTITIONER DIVIDE RECONSIDERED

As a result of many of these changes, a new vision of the links between the academic and the professional worlds begins to appear. Each clearly needs the other. Academics spend all their teaching time attempting to provide practitioners with their new recruits. It would be crass to ignore what practitioners wanted from them. Practitioners need the academics to teach the appropriate material in an appropriate way, and also to have explained to them the meaning and effects of changes in the law and what might be involved in legal, professional, and managerial skills. Academics also need extra help in funding for research and sometimes even for basic facilities. Firms, in good times, do have money to provide. The firms need help with coping with their new environment, advice on how to face the future, and directed training to assist them to do so.

Tomorrow's lawyers will not look down at their academic counterparts with the same level of distrust as previously. The crackpot image will disappear. Academic lawyers will not have to treat their practitioner friends as intellectual pygmies, realizing that the difficulties of law in the real world can produce complexity unseen in the ivory tower.

CONCLUSION

Tomorrow's lawyers will therefore be much more aware of their educational and training needs and much more open to being involved in the learning and teaching process. Continuing education is likely to provide a more reflective practitioner with the opportunity to consider both work and inter-personal problems and to devise more rational solutions and approaches that the rote and vicissitudes of practice life has previously allowed.

There should also be a greater flow of ideas between the generations, with more senior practitioners spending time passing on elements of their experience to more junior members of their firms. The idea of a practitioner being buried with a set of precedents will be long gone. Rather than each new generation being forced to re-invent the wheel to keep its practice going, even the most experienced and senior members of staff are likely to hand on their immediate knowledge to those that follow them.

A new vision therefore emerges, at least as an ideal. Tomorrow's lawyers will not think of themselves as complete or perfect when they march into their firms as new trainees. Nor will they consider themselves complete when they begin work as qualified solicitors. Nor will partnership bring omniscience or omni-competence. Tomorrow's lawyers will be top-loading their knowledge, information, abilities, and skill from the first day of their legal work until the last day of their professional practice. And at each stage they will be handing on their lessons to succeeding generations.

Whether this dream is viable or whether it too will fall foul of commercialism, window-dressing, and poor quality education is the major challenge for both professional and academic lawyers in the next decade.

NOTES AND REFERENCES

1   Domberger and A. Sherr, 'The Impact of Competition on Pricing and Quality of Legal Services' (1989) 9 *International Rev. of Law and Economics* 41–56.
2   See K. Economides and G. Smallcombe, *Preparatory Skills Training for Solicitors* (1991), following on A. Sherr, *Solicitors and their Skills* (1991).
3   Enlightenment may soon shine through here finally, with recent news of possible changes in the course for those intending to practise overseas.
4   Karl Mackie used this particular analogy in a paper at the Institute of Advanced Legal Studies Legal Skills conference in 1989; it was a brief excursus for him, and he cannot be blamed for the excesses to which I have taken the metaphor.
5   See A. Sherr, 'Lip Service under Articles, or Chances Missed' (1982) 132 *New Law J.* 395–9.

Legal Education in the 1990s

MARTIN PARTINGTON*

INTRODUCTION

Predicting the precise shape and structure of legal education by the end of this decade is impossible; there are at present too many uncertainties, the implications of which cannot yet be foreseen. This very lack of certainty does, however, provide a freedom to speculate on what the future might hold. This paper argues that, despite the uncertainties, there are substantial opportunities ahead for professional legal educators. It will, however, be necessary for the leaders of this branch of the legal profession to offer a clear sense of vision as to what the future might be like, if they are to seize the opportunities that could lie ahead.

This paper is divided into two sections. The first attempts to bring together the main factors which are likely to influence the structure of legal education in this country over the next decade; in Part II the implications of the analysis in Part I are drawn together in order to present a summary of the issues likely to shape legal education over the next decade.

Legal Education: A Definition

Before proceeding, however, it is essential to remember that legal education can be provided in two ways: directly by the provision of courses which are delivered directly to students, whether by the students attending at institutions of higher education on a full-time or part-time basis, or by alternative programmes of instruction such as distance learning; and indirectly by the provision of analyses of areas of law which are published in textbooks, monographs, articles or other formats which may not be directly utilized as teaching material but nevertheless provide instruction, to those who read what has been published, and which is the product of the research and scholarship of the legal academic. Any consideration of the structure of legal education must include *both* taught courses – in a variety of forms and at a variety of levels – *and* published research output.

* *Faculty of Law, University of Bristol, Bristol BS8 IRJ, England*

I. FACTORS LIKELY TO SHAPE THE PROVISION OF LEGAL EDUCATION OVER THE NEXT DECADE

If we are to think about the structure of legal education a decade from now, it is first necessary to identify the variables likely to influence the shaping of that structure. At least four categories of issue need to be taken into consideration:

government policy in relation to higher education;

the responses of institutions of higher education;

professional factors;

developments in the legal environment.

1. *Government Policy in Relation to Higher Education*

No consideration of legal education can take place without taking into account wider questions of government policy on higher education. During the late 1960s and 1970s, thinking on higher education policy was dominated by the report of the Robbins Committee[1] which set in motion an expansion of the higher education sector, but which implied a substantially increased investment of public funds in higher education. During the 1970s, it became clear that the cost of the Robbins model, particularly as it related to the universities, was not one that government would sustain. In addition, during the 1970s, the polytechnic sector expanded substantially, providing increasing numbers of undergraduate places at a reduced unit of resource.

The essential difference between the two sectors was that staff in the polytechnics were not provided with significant funding for research. At the same time, it is clear that the polytechnics did begin to address a number of matters such as access to higher education, and innovation in teaching methods more directly than many of their university counterparts.

When the Thatcher government first came to power in 1979, the policy makers imposed a severe cut in levels of state funding available for higher education, underpinned by official predictions of a substantial drop in demand for places in higher education, based on the demographic trend of the fall in the number of 18 year olds. This policy assumption was vigorously attacked by leaders of the higher education sector who predicted that demand for places would increase. The 'market' for higher education would expand to include not only a higher percentage of 18 year-olds, but also other categories such as mature students, access students or students seeking re-training.

The government's response to this pressure, and other arguments pointing to the comparatively low levels of participation in higher education in Britain, compared with that in other advanced countries, led to a clear shift of policy. By 1987 it was accepted that numbers should expand.[2] However, it was made equally clear that, while some extra money would be made available through the fees paid by government on behalf of students, expansion of student numbers was to be achieved primarily by 'greater efficiency' – government-speak for a reduction in the unit of resource available for teaching.

175

Although there was some public outcry at what the government was doing to higher education, political protest was neither loud nor sustained. Indeed, by 1991, it has to be concluded that the legacy of the last decade in relation to policy on higher education is that there is now no significant difference of approach at the party political level. While the precise contours of government policy may change a little with any change in political complexion after an election, the basic approach to questions such as student numbers and their funding is, so far as one can judge from the statements of education spokespersons and party policy documents, essentially an uncontroversial and bi-partisan one.[3]

Having said this, and despite the publication in 1991 of a White Paper and a Bill on higher education, it is not totally easy to discern the full policy agenda in relation to higher education. Some elements are clear and public; others are considerably less so. The most significant items which have been made public are:

(i)   the merger of the universities and polytechnics;
(ii) the expansion of student numbers;
(iii) the funding of students' maintenance: grants and loans;
(iv) the funding of research;
(v)   increased quality audit and quality assurance.

The matters on which there is less clarity – the hidden agenda – are:

(i)   policy in relation to student fees;
(ii) the possible creation of a 'tiered' university system;
(iii) the development of locally negotiated terms and conditions of employment, or the development of discipline – related terms and conditions (to reflect competition for talent in the job market);
(iv) the extent to which there should be, in effect, a privatization of the higher education system.

A number of these matters from both the public and hidden agendas are considered further in the paragraphs that follow.

(a) The Plan For Expansion

The Major government announced that it wished to:

(i)   increase the 'age participation' rate;
(ii) maintain high quality teaching and research;
(iii) introduce quality control of teaching and assessment standards.[4]

While each of these objectives may be more or less desirable individually, taken together they are not wholly consistent. The increase in student numbers is to be driven by 'cost effective expansion',[5] code for the reduction in the unit of resource available from the government for teaching and research. In addition, there is to be 'greater competition',[6] implying *some* increase in resource for those who teach *substantially* greater numbers of students. At some point, the quality of teaching is bound to suffer, and it is quite clear that

176

not all those teaching the increased numbers will be able to maintain a high-quality research output.

A key element in the achievement of this objective is the abolition of the binary line between universities and polytechnics, (with the related merger of the universities and polytechnics and colleges funding councils into a single Higher Education Funding Council.) While many in the polytechnic sector hope that merger would result in a levelling up of these resources to those available in the universities, it seems much more likely that the pressure will be the other way; abolition of the binary line will reinforce pressures to bring down the level of resource available to universities so that it becomes closer to that of the polytechnics. The government's vision of expanded numbers is not matched by substantially expanded resources.

(b) Funding of Students

Significant changes to the ways in which students are funded for their courses have already occurred. First, there has been a move towards making the tuition fee relate more closely to the actual cost of the teaching provided. All United Kingdom students recruited into institutions of higher education for full-time degree courses have this fee paid for them by the government, through local education authorities. Many teaching institutions have taken the view that it is better to have not inconsiderable numbers of 'fees-only' students to boost their income. However this has the inevitable consequence of actually reducing the effective 'funded' unit of resource for teaching each student, since – in all subjects – the fee element which is paid is less than the fully-funded unit of resource.

There has been considerable argument that the fee element should be increased still further, to reflect the full cost of the teaching provided. But whereas a number of university vice-chancellors have taken the view that a move to full-cost fees would be desirable as a mechanism for bringing more money into the higher education system, the government has not yet moved to introduce this and no university or polytechnic has risked the publicity damage that would undoubtedly follow, by unilaterally putting up fee levels for undergraduate courses beyond that which the government will pay.

The second aspect of student funding on which decisions have been taken, is the move away from an exclusively grant-based system for the maintenance of students, to a mixed system of grants and loans.[7] Although starting slowly, the shift in balance between grants and loans will become very marked indeed during the decade.[8] The implications of this are very profound but have not yet been sufficiently understood. If students are going to finish their days at university in substantial debt – which they will be required to pay off – it seems very likely that this will not only affect the choice of subjects that students take – they will wish to become as 'marketable' as possible in the job market – but is also likely to affect modes of teaching. Courses that enhance job prospects will

177

be more likely to attract students – who will have an increasingly personal financial interest in what they are being offered at university – than those which do not. This does not necessarily mean that all students will take vocational courses; much will depend on the signals which potential employers send to the students. But what it does mean is that the structure of higher education may be driven less by what the academics think ought to be taught; there will also be a clearly defined and increasingly articulate consumer voice.

(c) The Funding of Research

Important changes to the structures for the funding of research have already been determined. More of the core funding for research is, from 1992, being handed to the Research Councils with the Universities Funding Council (later the Higher Education Funding Council) distributing additional money for research on the basis of judgment and evaluation. It seems inevitable that one consequence of the new funding framework will be an increasingly differentiated higher education sector; only a limited number of universities will have the resources to carry out basic research; others will have a reduced research objective; and some may be categorized as 'teaching' universities only. It is to be anticipated that this policy will be likely to affect the high-cost science departments more than the lower-cost library-based research departments; but the higher education system as a whole – including law – will be affected by this policy.

(d) Pay and Conditions

The government White Paper, *Higher Education, A New Framework*[9] has a short chapter on pay and conditions of service. Here, rather little has been announced, save the suggestion that the negotiation of terms and conditions of service will continue much as before. However, increasingly overt hints have come from government that they would like to see greater flexibility on the pay-bargaining structure. For the last three years, universities have been obliged to use 1 per cent of each salary settlement on a flexible/reward basis, rather than by simple across-the-board pay rises.

One of the problems that has confronted teaching institutions has been the challenge of attracting and/or retaining high-quality staff when the rewards in other sectors of the economy are very high, and when the quality of life in the institutions themselves has been under intense pressure. It may well be that more locally determined wage agreements will be reached by institutions seeking to attract good quality staff; or there might be a shift to discipline-based wage negotiations, as already exists with the doctors. Either of these steps could have a particular effect in the area of legal education.

(e) Central Direction versus Local Autonomy

The White Paper clearly implies that it wishes to have more control over the ways in which the resources provided by the state are utilized by the teaching institutions. It wants more flexible patterns of teaching and learning, the use of credit accumulation and transfer, more intensive courses, making more effective use of existing buildings and equipment. Such arguments are, of course, superficially attractive; we all like to see better 'value for money'. But what effect will pressure for more intensive teaching have on the quality of what the students learn? How will subject areas (such as law) that are rapidly expanding be able to cope if the government 'sees no case for an increase in the average length of courses'?[10] To what extent will the freedom of individual academic institutions to determine their own course structures and course objectives in practice be steered by the demands placed on them externally by government? These are all questions currently confronting the higher education sector.

(f) Privatization

Although the White Paper asserts that the government 'accepts that public funds will remain the main source of income for funding the projected expansion of student numbers',[11] it also states that institutions of higher education must look for yet higher levels of resource from private individuals, companies, benefactors, and alumni. 'Such private income can enhance considerably the independence of individual institutions.'[12] This implies that only institutions that can attract substantial sources of non-governmental funding will be fully independent. Of course, much private money comes with strings attached. Thus, the extent to which such money will, in fact, encourage independence may be in doubt. But it has become equally clear that money from the state also comes with strings attached. Institutions may therefore need to choose which set of strings they should be attached to. There seems little doubt that institutions that wish to flourish financially will have to attract higher levels of private finance.

(g) Europe

The influence of Europe is likely to increase during the next decade, both in the European Community, and by individual states. Clearly, through initiatives such as the ERASMUS programme, exchanges of staff and students are already being encouraged. There is a very substantial European dimension to the funding of research, where funding levels are more realistic. Many universities and polytechnics now run collaborative teaching and research programmes. There must be a possibility of the development of yet further Community policy initiatives in this area, as moves towards political and economic union intensify. This could be particularly significant in the context of legal education. Similarly, the development of specific policies in particular

179

countries in relation to legal education will be of potentially great importance in the United Kingdom.

2. *The Responses of the Institutions of Higher Education*

The majority of institutions of higher education are not only fully aware of the agenda that government is setting for them, but they are also trying to anticipate new directions for these policies. In many respects, the responses of the universities and polytechnics have been both vigorous and competitive, and considerably more extensive than is usually reported in the public media and understood by the public at large.

It is difficult to summarize briefly all the developments that have occurred in recent years, but they include: the development of new courses; the creation of more flexible programmes; the encouragement of access; permitting work done in one institution to be credited alongside work done in other institutions. Part-time degrees, distance-learning degrees, modular programmes, semesters and trimesters, mixed degrees, degrees with periods of study abroad (particularly in other parts of Europe), have been introduced in many institutions. There is also much greater provision of postgraduate programmes – particularly taught programmes, often linked to the development of specialist expertise and other forms of professional development. Higher education institutions have also moved increasingly into the short course/continuing education market. One can anticipate that many more moves in these directions will occur in the next ten years.

For all the willingness of institutions to be creative and to provide new opportunities, it cannot be said that they have been wholly successful in demonstrating to government the value of what they have achieved and there is a real danger that, if the institutions do not think carefully about what they are doing, short-term efforts to curry favour with government and the funding bodies may lead to long-term fundamental problems which will not go away, and which, if not tackled, will become very expensive to deal with.

Five such problems can already be perceived which, if not carefully addressed, may well affect higher education in general, and legal education in particular:

(a) There are clear pressures on institutions seeking greater 'cost-effectiveness' to move away from three-year programme as the 'normal' course length. Managerial pressures to reduce course length clearly conflict with opposing academic pressures to expand course length in order to provide an adequate introduction to ever expanding disciplines; this is a problem that particularly affects legal education.

(b) Pressures to reduce course length, combined with other factors such as modularization and the increasing availability of mixed and joint degrees throw up equally difficult questions about the nature of a discipline and the extent to which that discipline can be said to have a central 'core'. In the context of law, it will be necessary to retain the principle that there really is an irreducible minimum syllabus to which anyone purporting to call themselves 'lawyer' should be directed.

(c) More specific attention must be given to modes of teaching and, in particular, the ways in which new technologies may assist in the development of new forms of teaching programme. This will require not only investment in hardware and software[13] but, of equal importance, investment in sufficient time to train staff to use and develop that investment in educationally valuable ways.

(d) Much more consideration will have to be given to the debate about the extent to which there is a distinction between 'academic' education and 'practical' training. Many of the current problems of higher education derive from an assumption that those involved in higher education are interested only in the former and not at all in the latter. While there is no point in wasting expensive academic time on simple office skills (which is what many assume 'practical training' to involve), it is important to recognize that higher education does not just involve reading books and writing essays; it must go further, to enable students to apply what they have learned to problems and develop the skills needed to solve those problems and have the confidence to move from areas of law that they have studied into new areas.

(e) Most fundamental of all, the institutions of higher education must address more directly the problems of the attraction and retention of really able staff in the context of a highly competitive job market. To some extent, this may be achieved at the individual level, for example, by providing increased opportunities for flexible career patterns, with staff moving between teaching posts, practice posts, and research posts. More fundamental questions about the level of resource for teaching must, however, continue to be pressed if the very purpose of higher education – to provide an intelligent and well-grounded body of graduates equipped to work in a fast-changing world – is not to be destroyed by lack of investment. It is in this respect that the response of the institutions to government policies will be most crucial.

3. *Professional Factors*

While government policies and the responses of the institutions to these policies is clearly a complex part of the context within which legal education will develop over the next decade, legal education is also particularly affected by two further sets of issues: professional factors, to be discussed here; and the general legal environment, to be considered below.

(a) The Structure of Professional Legal Education

Certain important changes have taken place. Supreme among them is the fact that both practising branches of the profession now agree that legal education

181

is not just something that occurs at the onset of a career in the law. They have accepted that the structure for professional legal education should involve the initial 'academic' stage; a 'practice skills' stage; a 'professional development' stage; and an on-going 'continuing education' stage.[14]

The importance of these developments for legal educators cannot be overemphasized. It means that there now exists a framework for a much broader approach to the education of lawyers and the acquisition of knowledge of the law. While the early stages of a legal education career can focus on basic questions of understanding how the law and the legal system operate, later on, as people mature and become more involved in legal practice, they can be given more advanced instruction in new specialized areas of law and its practice. The university law schools should have, as their mission, the *formation* of professional personalities, able to make a full contribution to society, whether as practising lawyers or working in other sectors of the economy.

(b) Review of the Academic Stage

At the time of writing, the Law Society has embarked upon a review of the academic stage of legal education. There is no doubt that the rapid expansion of law departments during the 1970s and 1980s has been broadly welcomed by the legal profession. Indeed there is some frustration that the expansion was not substantial enough, given the numbers now entering the legal profession via the common professional examination (CPE) route – the one-year conversion course taken by non-law graduates.

There are, in this context, two important areas of debate. The first relates to the question whether the present concept of the academic stage, with its focus on six 'core' subjects,[15] is necessarily the best. Although there is widespread agreement that there does have to be a 'core' of instruction in the discipline of the law if anyone is, sensibly, to describe himself or herself as a lawyer, the present subject-based structure was devised at a time when it was assumed that the only effective legal education lawyers would receive was at the beginning of their careers. The new structure (noted above) based on the need for the continuance of legal education throughout professional life, can allow for a quite different approach to the academic stage.

There are specific criticisms that the present structure does not give a sufficient introduction to certain important areas of law, particularly European Community law. (Although most law schools do now introduce the institutional structure of the European Community, students are not necessarily introduced to the rather different methodologies of case law and statutory interpretation used by the European Court of Justice.)[16] There are also concerns that the focus on 'core' subjects encourages tunnel-vision and discourages students from thinking about a wider range of questions: how law is made, why it is made, what impact on society does it have. There is a lack of understanding of the social, political, and economic context of the law which produces, it is suggested, rather too narrow-minded practitioners. Finally,

182

there are complaints that insufficient attention is given to the methods of enabling students to 'break into' new areas of law.

A second, more specific concern that is being increasingly aired relates to the adequacy of the common professional examination as an initial training in the law. Although very cost-effective, it does seem, on the face of it, extraordinary that graduates in subjects other than law should only be required to do one year of, admittedly rather intensive, study before going into finals examinations. Although no one could doubt the value of encouraging graduates in non-law subjects to come into the legal profession, it is highly arguable whether the current one year programme provides a sufficient grounding. The brevity of this programme is in stark contrast to the longer programmes found elsewhere, in North America and other parts of Europe.

The outcome of these two newly developing areas of debate is, at this point, by no means certain. But there is a good chance that the ground rules for the academic stage may change. It will be necessary to think very clearly about what the purposes of this stage of legal education are, and then go on to structure courses so that they achieve those purposes. This will require rather different modes of thinking from those which currently exist.

One specific point must be stressed: if one of the reasons why the legal profession likes CPE recruits is because they come into the profession with a rather broader educational background, the legal profession should be very careful not to so constrain the law schools that they are themselves prevented from offering as rounded a programme of instruction as possible.

(c) The Emphasis on Skills

Within this new framework there has emerged a new professional interest in providing education in the skills of lawyering, as well as in the arts and techniques of handling legal material. The new Bar final course, introduced in 1990, and the new Law Society legal practice course, to be started in 1993 imply a shift away from a concentration on learning more and more 'black-letter' law, to courses which introduce students to the skills that will enable them to practise the law: specifically, legal research and problem-solving, drafting, advocacy, and interviewing and negotiating.

The impact of these new professional interests is likely to be substantial in the higher education institutions. First, whereas the old Law Society Final was offered only by the College of Law and certain polytechnics, at least some universities will enter the field and will offer newly devised postgraduate diplomas in legal practice. Second, certain skills issues will be incorporated more widely into the undergraduate curriculum. A logical extension of these two trends is likely to mean, certainly by the end of the decade, that many law schools will offer 'integrated' courses, involving a blending of the now distinct 'academic' and 'professional' stages of legal education. Whatever position individual law teachers may take on the question of the relevance of skills training in an academic course, consumer pressure from students themselves will tend to push law schools in this direction.

These developments will in turn open up new areas of legal scholarship as the nature of legal skills is analysed[17] and greater theoretical attention is given to the educational issues that they imply.[18]

(d) A Common Professional Education?

A third development that could well emerge from the last two noted above is the creation of a common professional final examination. Given the recent history of competition between the Bar and the Law Society, this might not seem likely at present. But while the public stance of both sides of the profession is to maintain their independence, increasingly powerful voices on both sides are being heard that such a development would be both logical and desirable. It would give students greater freedom before committing themselves to one branch or other of the profession. And the very real difficulties the Bar currently faces about the level of recruitment it needs could be (more or less) solved at a stroke if the Bar moved to concentrate exclusively on the advanced advocacy skills-training that potential barristers will still need. It may well be that the newly created Lord Chancellor's advisory committee on legal education and conduct (see below) will be influential in pushing thinking further in this direction.

(e) Specialization

Another notable current trend in legal practice is the move to greater specialization. More and more practising lawyers are spending more of their time practising within narrower areas of expertise. This development too has implications for legal educators. They should be providing opportunities for those who wish to break into new specialisms to do so by the provision of advanced courses of study. Those practitioners who wish to advertise the fact that they have acquired expertise in a particular area may need to be able to demonstrate this by obtaining specialist degree/diploma qualifications from law schools able to offer appropriate forms of instruction.

(f) Career Flexibility

An equally important factor arises at times of economic down-turn – such as the present. Practitioners have, perhaps, been too willing to respond to the effects of economic recession by cutting staff costs and making skilled practitioners redundant. A more constructive approach would be for practitioners to combine with the legal educators to devise new programmes for retraining or redirecting practitioners with experience, but whose specialist area of expertise is not, for the present, needed in the firm.

Such a development also implies an increased awareness on the part of practitioners of new areas of practice opportunity. They need to think more broadly about new market areas which could be opened up for legal practice. Comparison with, for example, the accountancy profession is instructive. The accountants have been both aggressive and successful in colonizing many areas of expertise (not just in the area of tax law, but more broadly in the area of management consultancy and the provision of advice on the commercial opportunities created by new legislation) which could equally be the province of the legal profession. There would certainly be scope for collaboration between practice development partners and academics in creating the bases for expansion into such new areas.

(g) Expansion of the Legal Profession

Another factor in this review of the relationship between developments in the legal profession and the law schools is the extent to which the legal profession itself will continue to expand – and thus be able to take the graduates of the law schools.

As a result of the Courts and Legal Services Act 1990, the Bar will certainly not cease to exist, as some predicted during the passage of the Bill through Parliament. But expansion of the rights of audience is likely to mean that the Bar will contract in size over the next decade. It is also likely that, with the increase in jurisdiction of the county courts, there will be yet further decentralization of the Bar from London to the provinces.[19] On the solicitors' side, a period of very rapid expansion, accompanied by alarm at the 'recruitment crisis' in the late 1980s, has been replaced by a period of contraction, with staff being laid off and, in some cases, firms ceasing to exist. Such violent changes of gear are bad for the profession and solicitors should be encouraged to make appropriate financial provision in the good times to ensure less volatility in the bad times. But, when the economic up-turn comes, it is not clear to what extent solicitors' firms will be wishing to expand.

At the same time, as noted earlier, the universities (newly merged) will be expanding substantially: a 50 per cent increase in size over the decade is predicted. Law schools will clearly be part of this expansion. At present, many law graduates go into careers other than the legal profession. If the profession itself is not expanding, this trend will be exacerbated. This may therefore result in the academic branch of the legal profession having to rethink, at least to some degree, its relationship with the practising branch.

(h) In-house Trainers and Private Sector Trainers

The new emphasis on continuing legal education has, itself, resulted in the substantial development of two new groups of legal training: those providing in-house programmes; and the private sector companies providing short, or in some cases, not-so-short courses of professional legal education. At present, there has been no serious challenge to the universities and polytechnics as being the sole providers of degrees in law. But one could certainly anticipate some developments, on the model of the London University external LL B degree programme, with non-university institutions providing the tuition for syllabuses and examinations determined by the particular teaching institutions. One could also imagine groups of in-house trainers and/or private sector trainers beginning to seek accreditation of their programmes from university law schools.

(i) The Lord Chancellor's Advisory Committee on Legal Education and Conduct

The impact that the newly created Lord Chancellor's Advisory Committee, under the chairmanship of Lord Griffiths, will make on legal education is, as yet, wholly unclear, for the very practical reason that their initial programme of work is being dominated by applications for rights of audience. However, the new committee does have statutory responsibility for ensuring that standards of legal education are appropriate for those who intend to practice law. It is therefore likely that the committee will have a considerable influence in the shaping of legal education during the latter part of this decade. The newly created Standing Conference on Legal Education will have an important role to play in ensuring that this influence is both benign and constructive.

4. *Developments in the Legal Environment*

The final set of factors, that will inevitably influence the structure of legal education in the 1990s, must be developments in the legal environment itself. Despite claims that the 1980s would be an era in which the 'boundaries of the state would be rolled back', it turned out to be a period of unparalleled legal development. Whole new areas of the regulation of industry and commerce emerged in the context of the privatization programmes and the reforms in the City and financial services. A shift from the public provision of welfare to the private provision of welfare has brought its own new areas of regulatory law. The growing influence of the European Community has had an increasing impact on British law. The internationalization of business enterprise has resulted in the expansion of the legal environment in which we live. New concerns with the fundamental problems of our physical environment and corporate responsibility have already begun to generate new law and will do so increasingly. One can already envisage, at the more private level, new provisions in relation to the regulation of the family. The impact of the European Social Charter will be increasingly felt. If the 'Citizen's Charter' ever develops into anything more than a set of political slogans, this too will influence the structure and content of our law.

Although many commentators have pointed to the dangers, evils even, of 'juridification'[20] and the 'explosion' of litigation[21] – and the implications this may have for the operation of our society in general – there is no sign of any diminution in the flow of new law which must be taken into account by those who live in this 'legalized society'.

The significance of all those developments is that they all open up new areas for teaching and research. Even without the pressures for expansion cited earlier in this article, there would be an academically justifiable case for expansion driven by the scope for creating new areas of legal scholarship. The boundaries of that scholarship are also likely to expand. For many years, 'black-letter' legal scholarship has been complemented by a more inter-disciplinary 'socio-legal' scholarship, supplemented now by a more theoretical 'critical' legal scholarship. It is to be anticipated that all three schools of legal scholarship will develop during the next decade, with the 'socio-legal' school developing particularly strongly in discussion and analysis of the relationship between the role of law and the impact of a variety of social and economic policies.

II. LEGAL EDUCATION IN THE 1990s

The analysis in the first part of this paper of the range of factors likely to influence the shape of legal education over the next ten years may seem daunting. Indeed there is a real danger that those who wish to develop the appropriate models and structures for legal education will end up simply responding to pressures imposed upon them. This would be a profound mistake. Although legal educators do face challenges, they must develop their own vision, or mission, about what it is they wish to achieve. Despite all the constraints law teachers currently face, this is a time both to claim credit for past success and to look forward, with some confidence, to a challenging future. What might the structure of legal education look like in ten years time?

1. *A Merged System*

The most fundamental change that will occur over the next decade is the merger of the universities and the polytechnics. It does seem likely that this will result in important changes in the academic culture. It is highly likely that many of the more flexible approaches to, for example, recruitment of students, and course structure, which have been pioneered in the polytechnics, will be increasingly embraced by the former universities. The rather sharp division, apparent in some university circles, between the 'academic' and the 'practical' will largely disappear. No longer will the 'practical' stage be monopolized by the College of Law and a number of polytechnics. Many institutions on both sides of the current binary line will offer 'integrated' degrees, combining the academic and the practical stages of legal education.

While the changes noted in the last paragraph will reflect the influence of the polytechnics on the universities, there will be equally significant influences operating in the other direction. The emphasis in the universities on the importance of engaging in research in order to produce good teaching will increasingly influence those working in the ex-polytechnics. Many polytechnic teachers already undertake research; but one can anticipate the numbers increasing substantially. As advanced study spreads, so too will the variety of postgraduate taught law courses. There will be a further expansion of LL M courses, taught in a variety of formats, designed to provide more specialist education for practitioners.

The effects of the newly merged system will be seen not only at the individual institutional level but also at the representative level. The present, rather fragmented, representation of law teachers' scholarly and other interests through the Society of Public Teachers of Law, the Association of Law Teachers, the Committee of Heads of University Law Schools, and the Committee of Heads of Polytechnic Law Schools will be replaced. Discussions as to the shape of this new structure have already begun. What would seem sensible would be two bodies (or perhaps a single body with a powerful sub-committee) which brings the collective interests of law teachers together.

This will not necessarily be an easy task for if the newly merged university structure becomes 'tiered', with divisions between research and teaching universities, it will not inevitably be the case that all law schools will share a sufficiently common set of interests to enable a single body to provide effective representation. Nonetheless, during the next decade it is inevitable that there will be moves in this direction.

2. *An Expanded System*

Although the universities and polytechnics will merge, of itself creating a new context for legal education in higher education, there is not likely to be any substantial increase in the total number of law schools. Capital costs will effectively prevent this. However, nearly all law schools will have more students, frequently substantially more. At the same time, staff-student ratios will worsen, so that while total numbers of law teachers will increase, this will not be at the same rate as the student expansion, unless new resources can be found.

The components of the student body are also likely to change. For example, there will be increased pressure on students to study at their local institutions, and not leave home; there will be more access students, more mature students. Each will generate specific teaching demands.

3. *Teaching Structures*

As already noted, there are likely to be major changes in the organization of teaching. In my view, moves towards semesterization will, on balance, be of considerable benefit to law schools, enabling them to construct more 'staged' programmes of instruction. The rush to modularization, however, must be carefully watched if the core discipline is not to be destroyed. It seems very likely that there will be some move away from the full-time degree as the predominant form of instruction; more institutions will offer part-time and distance learning programmes. Credit transfer systems are likely to increase student choice and flexibility.

4. *Undergraduate Programmes*

Given the likelihood that the rate of expansion of the profession is likely to be less marked than that occurring in the teaching institutions, I anticipate at the undergraduate level, the emergence of a 'twin-track' approach: law degrees, probably increasingly integrated with the legal practice course and/or Bar final, for those intending to practice, alongside law degrees not linked to professional qualifications for those looking for prestigious and demanding courses providing an entry into careers other than the law.

There is likely to be a redefinition of the 'core' curriculum that will have significant implications for the content and structure of undergraduate programmes. At the same time, the reassertion that the academic discipline of the law does have a 'core' may slow the expansion of mixed and joint degrees, particularly for those seeking to complete the 'professional' track.

For those who take the 'non-practice' track, new types of conversion course will be needed for those who change their minds. On both tracks there will be a rapid expansion in the availability of language options – particularly European languages, but perhaps also others such as Japanese or certain Chinese languages. It is likely also that there will be more instruction in the substantive law of the countries either through teachers from abroad working in Britain, or through students taking part of their course in other universities overseas. Given appropriate investment, there should be a rapid development in educational technology, providing new methods of instruction in the law.

5. Conversion Programmes

The attractiveness of conversion courses for non-law graduates will depend very much on the recruitment needs of the profession itself. In the short-term, I anticipate some levelling off (or even fall) in demand. The format of the CPE will come under increasingly critical scrutiny, particularly if the core academic training is fundamentally rethought, and may be replaced by new postgraduate diplomas in law. Two-year conversion programmes are likely to increase in number.

6. Legal Practice Courses

The range of institutions offering legal practice courses will expand, as already noted, with at least some institutions offering integrated degrees. However the total number of legal practice course places may not expand substantially, given the very staff-intensive nature of such courses.

7. Postgraduate Programmes

These will increase in number, reflecting not only research expertise in particular law schools but the market for continuing professional development. It is clear that the Universities' Funding Council is not planning to increase the numbers of funded places on such courses; it is therefore unlikely that the Higher Education Funding Council will either. Funding will therefore need to come increasingly from private or commercial sources.

8. *Quality*

In all areas of teaching, there will be increased monitoring of teaching performance and assessment of the quality of the education provided. This will seem – at least initially – very threatening to many teachers. However, it is likely that the market for students will become increasingly competitive and appropriate evaluation of teaching performance is likely to become an indicator of attractiveness to potential students. Teaching staff themselves should benefit if such assessments are properly linked to questions of pay and promotion.

9. *Research and Scholarship*

I have focused mainly on the teaching side of legal education. As noted at the outset, however, research must also be considered. Although the expansion of student numbers is seen by government simply in terms of increase numbers of graduates, the academic community must seize the opportunity that increases in staff will bring to ensure an expansion of legal research and scholarship. After all, it is through our published work that academics seek not only to expand the law but to assist in its development.

At present, there are too many – particularly, perhaps, in newly developed areas of commercial law practice – areas of law where the 'cutting-edge' work is being done in the offices of legal practitioners, not in the universities. Not all universities will want, or be able, to cover all areas of law. But it must be the boast of the universities to be at the cutting edge of legal research. Scholars must endeavour to forge new links with practitioners to enable them to gain access to areas of law in practice that could be the foundation for valuable and influential legal scholarship. Such involvement will then also feed back into the development of new monographs, textbooks, and new courses.

If adequate core funding for research is not to be made available to all law schools (because of judgements made in the research evaluations), greater efforts will be needed to devise research programmes that will attract alternative sources of funding. This will not be easy, but the recent establishment of the Socio-Legal Studies Association has been designed, in part, to support those scholars who wish to develop research proposals in the socio-legal field. The Society of Public Teachers of Law is committing itself to a more dynamic role in the support of other categories of legal scholarship and research. Were a new Humanities Research Council to be created, or even the Economic and Social Research Council to expand its remit to include the humanities, new sources of funds for legal scholarship could be created of which advantage should be taken.

10. *Pay and Conditions*

The problem of the gap between levels of pay in legal practice and legal academia has now reached the point at which urgent consideration must be given as to whether law, as an important university discipline, can be adequately sustained if pay levels continue to be determined nationally and on a par with every other university discipline (save medicine). It is obvious that any steps taken to propose special treatment for academic lawyers will be resisted not only by external bodies such as the Higher Education Funding Council, but also internally by colleagues in other disciplines and by the academic trade unions. Indeed, were legal academics to take such a step, other disciplines might well move in the same direction. But I do not think this is an issue that can be wholly avoided over the next decade. An alternative idea, which might be less controversial, would be to improve career prospects by moving more to the North American model of academic status (as increasingly adopted in other countries), whereby existing senior grades (senior lecturer, reader) are replaced by new categories of professor. This, too, should be explored over the next decade.

11. *Funding*

Underlying the whole future of law schools is the question of funding. Present indications are that the expansion of the university system is to be achieved in the view of the government, by modest increases in income from fees, set against continuing 'efficiency gains'. If the government will not be persuaded to change this policy, law schools will have to increase their income from other sources.

In recent years they have been very successful, particularly by the recruitment of overseas students; this is, however, a finite market which may be reaching its limits. The recent survey on sponsorship[22] also demonstrates the success at least some law schools have had in attracting new sources of funds from private practice. But welcome though these are, they are, in fact, relatively modest and are not equally available throughout the higher education system. Appeals to alumni will, inevitably, be more successful for the older, longer established universities than the newer ones whose graduates are both fewer in number and not so well off. The widely publicized fund-raising successes of Oxford and Cambridge Universities will not, necessarily, be reflected in other institutions.

Notwithstanding the difficulties, however, it seems inevitable that another development over the next decade will be an increasing private sponsorship of teaching posts, equipment and books, and buildings.

12. *The Status of the Academic Lawyer*

Recent pressures have, in many institutions, left colleagues feeling not a little beleaguered and confused. Pressures will undoubtedly continue over the next decade. At the same time, however, the place of the academic lawyer in the wider community has changed. The academic must look beyond his or her department and seek both to understand and to influence the wider legal world beyond. The changing relationship between the legal academic and the legal practitioner has been the subject of discussion in *The Journal of Law and Society*.[23] The influence of academic work on the practice of the law is beginning to be better understood.[24] During the next decade, legal academics must continue this trend to begin to have the influence that jurists in North America, the rest of Europe, and other countries have long had. Through the quality of our published research, and of the teaching we provide, we must assert in a responsible fashion the importance of the role we play in the development of law in this country. Such an assertion must not be overstated. The day-to-day administration of the law rests with practitioners; they are responsible for many significant developments in the law. But neither must we understate our case. Particularly in England and Wales, legal academics for too long – and with notable and honourable exceptions – failed to demonstrate to the full their ability to give leadership to the development of the discipline of the law. This position has changed and is still changing rapidly. During the 1990s, those in legal education must consolidate the gains they have begun to make, and enhance the contribution that we make to the development of the law, the legal system, and the legal services provided by practitioners.

NOTES AND REFERENCES

1 Committee on Higher Education, *Higher Education* (1963; Cmnd. 2154).
2 *Higher Education: Meeting the Challenge* (1987; Cm. 114).
3 Some staff still seem to think that, with a change of government, policy would be altered in favour of the institutions; I see no evidence for this view and regard it as futile to contemplate the future on that basis.
4 *Higher Education: a New Framework* (1991; Cm. 1541).
5 id.
6 id.
7 This has been accompanied by a sharp reduction in the availability of social security benefits and housing benefits.
8 There seems to be a chance that an alternative government might amend this policy and introduce instead some form of graduate taxation, as has been urged by Nicholas Barr at the London School of Economics.
9 op. cit., n. 4.
10 id., para. 16.
11 id., para. 14.
12 id.
13 BILETA, *Report of the BILETA Inquiry into the Provision of Information Technology in UK Law Schools* (1991).
14 Broadly, the model proposed by the Ormrod Committee on Legal Education, *Legal Education* (1971; Cmnd. 4594).
15 Criminal law, constitutional law, land law, trusts, contract law, and tort.
16 See the report by the College of Law, *European Community Law Research Project* (1991).
17 See, for example, K. Economides and J. Smallcombe, *Preparatory Skills Training for Trainee Solicitors* (1991); A. Sherr, *Solicitors and their Skills* (1991).
18 See, for example, J. Macfarlane, 'Look before you leap: theory to support the development of skills education in the law school' (Forthcoming, 1992).
19 M. Partington, 'Change or no-change? Reflections on the Courts and Legal Services Act 1990' (1991) 54 *Modern Law Rev.* 702–12.

20 G. Teubner (ed.), *Juridification of the Social Spheres* (1987).

21 M. Galanter, 'Law Abounding: Legislation around the North Atlantic' (1992) 55 *Modern Law Rev.* 1–24.

22 S. Bright and M. Sunkin, *Commercial Sponsorship of Legal Education* (1991).

23 M. Partington, 'Academic Lawyers and "Legal Practice" in Britain' (1988) 15 *J. of Law and Society* 374–91; P. McAuslan, 'The Coming Crisis in Legal Education' (1989) 16 *J. of Law and Society* 310–18.

24 R. Goff, 'The Search for Principle' (1983) 69 *Proceedings of the Royal Academy* 169–88.